THE ROUGH GUIDE

GERMAN PHRASEBOOK

Compiled by
LEXUS

www.roughguides.com

Credits

German Phrasebook	Rough Guides Reference
Compiled by Lexus with Horst Koplek Lexus series editor: Sally Davies Layout: Ankur Guha Picture research: Nicole Newman	Director: Andrew Lockett Editors: Kate Berens, Tom Cabot, Tracy Hopkins, Matthew Milton, Joe Staines

Publishing information

First edition published in 1995.
This updated edition published August 2011 by
Rough Guides Ltd, 80 Strand, London, WC2R 0RL
Email: mail@roughguides.com

Distributed by the Penguin Group:
Penguin Books Ltd, 80 Strand, London, WC2R 0RL
Penguin Group (USA), 375 Hudson Street, NY 10014, USA
Penguin Group (Australia), 250 Camberwell Road, Camberwell, Victoria 3124,
Australia, Penguin Group (New Zealand), Cnr Rosedale and Airborne Roads,
Albany, Auckland, New Zealand

Rough Guides is represented in Canada by Tourmaline Editions Inc., 662 King
Street West, Suite 304, Toronto, Ontario, M5V 1M7

Printed in Singapore by Toppan Security Printing Pte. Ltd.

264 pages

A catalogue record for this book is available from the British Library.

978-1-84836-738-8

3   5   7   9   8   6   4   2   1

CONTENTS

How to use this book

The **Rough Guide German Phrasebook** is a highly practical introduction to the contemporary language. It gets straight to the point in every situation you might encounter: in bars and shops, on trains and buses, in hotels and banks, on holiday or on business. Laid out in clear A–Z style with easy-to-find, colour-coded sections, it uses key words to take you directly to the phrase you need – so if you want some help booking a room, just look up "room" in the dictionary section.

The phrasebook starts off with **Basics**, where we list some essential phrases, including words for numbers, dates and telling the time, and give guidance on pronunciation, along with a short section on the different regional accents you might come across. Then, to get you started in two-way communication, the Scenarios section offers dialogues in key situations such as renting a car, asking directions or booking a taxi, and includes words and phrases for when something goes wrong, from getting a flat tyre or asking to move apartments to more serious emergencies. You can listen to these and download them for free from www.roughguides.com/phrasebooks for use on your computer, MP3 player or smartphone.

Forming the main part of the guide is a double dictionary, first English–German, which gives you the essential words you'll need plus easy-to-use phonetic transliterations wherever pronunciation might be a problem. Then, in the German–English dictionary, we've given not just the phrases you'll be likely to hear (starting with a selection of slang and colloquialisms) but also many of the signs, labels and instructions you'll come across in print

or in public places. Scattered throughout the sections are travel tips direct from the authors of the Rough Guides guidebook series.

Finally, there's an extensive **Menu reader**. Consisting of separate food and drink sections, each starting with a list of essential terms, it's indispensable whether you're eating out, stopping for a quick drink or looking around a local food market.

Gute Reise!
Have a good trip!

BASICS

Pronunciation

In this phrasebook, the German has been written in a system of imitated pronunciation so that it can be read as though it were English. Bear in mind the notes on pronunciation given below:

ay	as in may
e	as in get
g	always hard as in goat
ī	as the 'i' sound in might
J	like the 's' sound in pleasure
KH	as in the Scottish way of saying loch
oo	as in book
oo	as in monsoon
∞	like the 'ew' in few but without any 'y' sound
ow	as in cow
uh	like the 'e' in butter
ur	as in fur but without any 'r' sound

The common German sound 'ei', as in Einstein, is written either with a 'y' or as 'ine'/'ite'/'ile' etc, as in fine/kite/while, or as ī.

Abbreviations

adj	adjective		*n*	neuter (the = das)
f	feminine (the = die)		*pl*	plural
m	masculine (the = der)		*sing*	singular

Notes

In the English-German section, when two forms of the verb are given in phrases such as **'can you...?'** 'kannst du/können Sie...?', the first is the familiar form and the second the polite form.

Basic phrases

yes ja yah

no nein nine

OK okay

hello hallo

good morning guten Morgen
gooten

good evening guten Abend
gooten ahbent

good night gute Nacht
goot-uh naκHt

goodbye auf Wiedersehen
owf-veederzayn

please bitte bitt-uh

yes please ja bitte yah

thanks, thank you danke
dank-uh

no thanks nein danke nine

thank you very much
vielen Dank feelen

don't mention it bitte bitt-uh

how do you do? guten Tag!
gooten tahk

how are you? wie geht es dir/
Ihnen? vee gayt ess deer/**ee**nen

fine, thanks danke, gut
dank-uh goot

nice to meet you freut mich
froyt mish

excuse me entschuldigen Sie!
ent-sh**oo**ldigen zee

(to get attention) Entschuldigung!
ent-sh**oo**ldigoong

sorry: (I'm) sorry tut mir Leid
toot meer lite

sorry? (didn't understand)
wie bitte? vee bitt-uh

I see/I understand ich verstehe
ish fairsht**ay**-uh

I don't understand das verstehe
ich nicht nisht

do you speak English?
sprechen Sie Englisch?
shpreshen zee eng-lish

I don't speak German
ich spreche kein Deutsch
ish shpresh-uh kine doytch

could you say it slowly?
könnten Sie das etwas langsamer
sagen? k**u**rnten zee dass etvass
langzahmer z**ah**gen

could you repeat that?
können Sie das noch einmal
wiederholen? k**u**rnen zee dass
noκH **ine**-mahl veederh**oh**len

could you write it down?
könnten Sie es aufschreiben?
k**u**rnten zee ess **owf**-shryben

I'd like a... ich möchte gern
ein... m**u**rsht-uh gairn

I'd like to... ich würde gern...
v**oo**rd-uh

can I have a...? kann ich ein...
haben? kan ish ine... h**ah**ben

how much is it? was kostet das?
vass

cheers! (toast) Prost! prohst

it is... es ist...

where is it? wo ist es? vo

is it far from here? ist es weit von hier? vite fon heer

how long will it/does it take? wie lange dauert es? vee lang-uh dowert ess

Dates

Dates are expressed with ordinal numbers (see p.12):

the first of July der erste Juli dair airst-uh yoolee

on the first of July am ersten Juli am airsten yoolee

the twentieth of March der zwanzigste März dair tsvantsishst-uh mairts

on the twentieth of March am zwanzigsten März am tsvantsishsten mairts

At the beginning of letters, the following form should be used:

Frankfurt, March 20 Frankfurt, den 20. März

Days

Monday Montag mohntakh

Tuesday Dienstag deenstahk

Wednesday Mittwoch mittvoкн

Thursday Donnerstag donnerstahk

Friday Freitag frytahk

Saturday Samstag zamstahk

Sunday Sonntag zonntahk

Months

January Januar yanooar

February Februar faybrooar

March März mairts

April April a-prill

May Mai my

June Juni yoonee

July Juli yoolee

August August owgoost

September September zeptember

October Oktober

November November

December Dezember daytsember

Time

what time is it? wie spät ist es? vee shpayt ist ess

one o'clock ein Uhr ine oor

two o'clock zwei Uhr tsvy oor

it's one o'clock es ist ein Uhr ess ist ine oor

it's two o'clock es ist zwei Uhr ess ist tsvy oor

it's ten o'clock es ist zehn Uhr ess ist tsayn oor

five past one fünf nach eins
fOOnf naKH ine-ss

ten past two zehn nach zwei
tsayn nahKH tsvy

quarter past one Viertel nach
eins feertel nahKH ine-ss

quarter past two Viertel nach
zwei feertel naKH tsvy

*half past ten halb elf halp elf

twenty to ten zwanzig vor zehn
tsvantsish for tsayn

quarter to two Viertel vor zwei
feertel for tsvy

at half past four um halb fünf
oom halp fOOnf

at eight o'clock um acht Uhr
oom aKHt OOr

14.00 14 Uhr feertsayn OOr

17.30 siebzehn Uhr dreißig
zeeptsayn OOr dryssish

2 a.m. 2 Uhr morgens
tsvy OOr morgens

2 p.m. 2 Uhr nachmittags
tsvy OOr nahKHmittahks

10 a.m. 10 Uhr vormittags
tsayn OOr formittahks

10 p.m. 10 Uhr abends
tsayn OOr ahbents

noon Mittag mittahk

midnight Mitternacht mitternaKHt

an hour eine Stunde
ine-uh shtoond-uh

a/one minute eine Minute
ine-uh minOOt-uh

two minutes zwei Minuten
tsvy minOOten

a second eine Sekunde
ine-uh zekoond-uh

a quarter of an hour eine
Viertelstunde ine-uh feertel-
shtoond-uh

half an hour eine halbe Stunde
ine-uh halb-uh shtoond-uh

three quarters of an hour
eine Dreiviertelstunde ine-uh
dryfeertel-shtoond-uh

*Note the difference here. German
for 'half past ten/three/five' etc is,
literally, 'half eleven/four/six' etc.

Numbers

0 null nooll

1 eins ine-ss

2 zwei tsvy

3 drei dry

4 vier feer

5 fünf fOOnf

6 sechs zeks

7 sieben zeeben

8 acht aKHt

9 neun noyn

10 zehn tsayn

11 elf elf

12 zwölf tsvurlf

13 dreizehn dry-tsayn

14 vierzehn feer-tsayn

15 fünfzehn fOOnf-tsayn

16 sechzehn zesh-tsayn

17 siebzehn zeep-tsayn

18 achtzehn aKH-tsayn

19 neunzehn noyn-tsayn

20 zwanzig tsvantsish

21 einundzwanzig ine-oont-tsvantsish

22 zweiundzwanzig tsvy-oont-tsvantsish

23 dreiundzwanzig dry-oont-tsvantsish

30 dreißig dryssish

31 einunddreißig ine-oont-dryssish

40 vierzig feertsish

50 fünfzig fOOnftsish

60 sechzig zeshtsish

70 siebzig zeeptsish

80 achtzig aKHtsish

90 neunzig noyntsish

100 hundert hoondert

110 hundertzehn hoondert-tsayn

200 zweihundert tsvy-hoondert

300 dreihundert dry-hoondert

1,000 tausend towzent

2,000 zweitausend tsvy-towzent

10,000 zehntausend tsayn-towzent

50,000 fünfzigtausend fOOnftsish-towzent

100,000 hunderttausend hoondert-towzent

1,000,000 eine Million ine-uh mill-yohn

Ordinals

Ordinal numbers are formed by adding -te or -ste if the number ends in -ig. For example, fünfte fOOnft-uh (fifth), zwanzigste tsvantsishst-uh (twentieth).

1st erste airst-uh

2nd zweite tsvite-uh

3rd dritte dritt-uh

4th vierte feert-uh

5th fünfte fOOnft-uh

6th sechste zekst-uh

7th siebte zeept-uh

8th achte aKHt-uh

9th neunte noynt-uh

10th zehnte tsaynt-uh

Regional accents

The spoken German you will hear on your travels will vary hugely in accent. However, the pronunciation given in this book will stand you in good stead wherever you are in Germany (or Austria or German-speaking Switzerland).

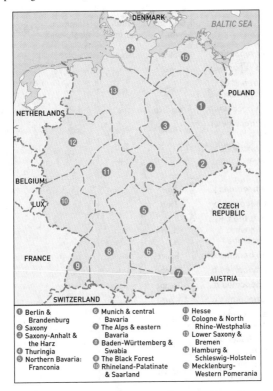

❶ Berlin & Brandenburg
❷ Saxony
❸ Saxony-Anhalt & the Harz
❹ Thuringia
❺ Northern Bavaria: Franconia
❻ Munich & central Bavaria
❼ The Alps & eastern Bavaria
❽ Baden-Württemberg & Swabia
❾ The Black Forest
❿ Rhineland-Palatinate & Saarland
⓫ Hesse
⓬ Cologne & North Rhine-Westphalia
⓭ Lower Saxony & Bremen
⓮ Hamburg & Schleswig-Holstein
⓯ Mecklenburg-Western Pomerania

In the very south of the German-speaking world there is Swiss German and in the far north, Friesian. Both of these can be considered separate languages, although speakers will also be able to speak and understand what is known as Hochdeutsch or High German – the standard. The region where the local accent is closest

	German word	High German	Hamburg, Westphalia	Berlin
st separated	Stein	shtine	stine	shtine
sp separated	spät	shpayt	spayt	shpayt
s at end of word becomes t	was	vass	vat	vat
ch becomes k	machen	maкнen	mahken	maкнen
pf becomes p or b	Apfel	apfel	appel	appel
a becomes e or o	das	dass	dat	det
g becomes j	gut	goot	goot	joot
f becomes p	Dorf	dorf	dorp	dorf
b at the end of a word becomes f	lieb	leep	leef	leep
au becomes uu	Bauer	bower	boo-er	bower
p becomes b	Mappe	mapp-uh	mapp-uh	mapp-uh
t becomes d	Treppe	trepp-uh	trepp-uh	trepp-uh
k becomes g	Kappe	kapp-uh	kapp-uh	kapp-uh
ei becomes ee or oa	Bein	bine	bine	bine
ein becomes een	ein	ine	ayn	ayn
e often not sounded	haben	hahben	hahm	hahben

to High German is Lower Saxony. It is said that in Hanover even the tramps speak High German.

The following chart gives examples of some of the accent differences. There are, of course, quite a number of regional overlaps.

the Rhine, Cologne	Southeast, Saxony, Franconia, Thuringia	Bavaria, Swabia, most of the south, Austria, Switzerland
shtayn	shtayn	shtayn
shpayt	shpayt	shpayt
vat	vass	voss
maкнen	maкнen	maкн-uh
appel	abbel	apfel, opfel
dat	dess	doss
joot	goot	gOOt
dorp	dorf	dorf
leef	leep	leep
bOO-er	bower	bower
mapp-uh	mabb-uh	mapp-uh
trepp-uh	drebb-uh	trepp-uh
kapp-uh	gabb-uh	kapp-uh
bayn	bayn	boh-an
ayn	ayn	oh-an, ahn
hahn	hahben	hahm

SCENARIOS

Download these scenarios as MP3s from
www.roughguides.com/phrasebooks

1. Accommodation

▶ Is there an inexpensive hotel you can recommend?
Können Sie mir ein günstiges Hotel empfehlen?
kurnen zee meer ine goonstigess hotel empfaylen

>> I'm sorry, they all seem to be fully booked.
Tut mir Leid, aber es scheint alles ausgebucht zu sein.
toot meer lite ahber ess shynt al-ess owss-gebookHt tso zine

▶ Can you give me the name of a good middle-range hotel?
Können Sie mir ein gutes Mittelklasse-Hotel nennen?
kurnen zee meer ine gootess mittel-klassuh-hotel nennen

>> Let me have a look; do you want to be in the centre?
Mal sehen, möchten Sie im Zentrum sein?
mal zay-en murshten zee im tsentroom zine

▶ If possible.
Wenn möglich.
venn murglish

>> Do you mind being a little way out of town?
Macht es Ihnen etwas aus, etwas außerhalb der
Stadt zu sein?
makHt ess eenen etvass owss etvass owsserhalp dair shtatt tsoo zine

▶ Not too far out.
Nicht zu weit außerhalb.
nisht tsoo vite owsserhalp

▶ Where is it on the map?
Wo ist es auf dem Stadtplan?
vo ist ess owf daym shtattplahn

▶ Can you write the name and address down?
Können Sie mir Namen und Adresse aufschreiben?
kurnen zee meer nahmen oont adress-uh owf-shryben

▶ I'm looking for a room in a private house.
Ich suche ein Zimmer in einem Privathaus.
ish zooKH-uh ine tsimmer in ine-em privaht-howss

2. Banks

bank account	das Bankkonto	bank-konto
to change money	Geld wechseln	gelt **vek**seln
cheque	der Scheck	shek
to deposit	einzahlen	**ine**-tsahlen
euro	der Euro	**oy**-ro
pin number	die PIN-Nummer	pin-**noo**mer
pound	das Pfund	pfoont
to withdraw	abheben	**ap**-hayben

▶ Can you change this into euros?
Würden Sie das bitte in Euro umtauschen?
v**oo**rden zee dass b**i**ttuh in **oy**-ro **oo**m-towshen

> ▶▶ How would you like the money?
> **Wie möchten Sie Ihr Geld?**
> vee m**ur**shten zee eer gelt

▶ Small notes.   ▶ Big notes.
Kleine Scheine.   **Große Scheine.**
kl**ine**-uh sh**ine**-uh   gr**oh**ss-uh sh**ine**-uh

▶ Do you have information in English about opening an account?
Haben Sie Information auf Englisch, wie man ein Konto eröffnet?
h**ah**ben zee informats-**yoh**n owf **e**ng-lish vee man ine **k**onto air-**ur**fnet

> ▶▶ Yes, what sort of account do you want?
> **Ja, was für ein Konto möchten Sie?**
> yah vass f**oo**r ine **k**onto m**ur**shten zee

▶ I'd like a current account.
Ich möchte ein Girokonto eröffnen.
ish m**ur**shtuh ine J**ee**ro-konto air-**ur**fnen

> ▶▶ Your passport, please.
> **Ihren Pass, bitte.**
> **ee**ren pas b**i**tt-uh

▶ Can I use this card to draw some cash?
Kann ich mit dieser Karte Geld abheben?
kann ish mit d**ee**zer k**a**rt-uh gelt **ap**-hayben

> ▶▶ You have to go to the cashier's desk.
> **Sie müssen zum Schalter gehen.**
> zee m**oo**ssen tsoom sh**a**lter g**ay**-en

▶ I want to transfer this to my account at the Dresdner Bank.
Ich möchte das auf mein Konto bei der Dresdner Bank überweisen.
ish m**ur**sht-uh dass owf mine **k**onto by dair dr**ay**zdner bank **oo**ber-v**y**-zen

▶▶ OK, but we'll have to charge you for the phonecall.
OK, aber wir müssen Ihnen dieses Gespräch berechnen.
OK **ah**ber veer m**oo**ssen **ee**nen d**ee**zess geshpr**ay**sh ber**e**shnen

3. Booking a room

shower	die Dusche	d**oo**sh-uh
telephone in the room	das Zimmertelefon	ts**i**mmer-telefohn
payphone in the lobby	der Münzfernsprecher in der Eingangshalle	m**oo**nts-fairn-shpresher in dair **ine**-gangs-hal-uh

▶ Do you have any rooms?
Haben Sie Zimmer frei?
h**ah**ben zee ts**i**mmer fry

▶▶ For how many people?
Für wie viele Personen?
f**oo**r vee **fee**l-uh pairz**oh**nen

▶ For one/for two.
Für eine Person/für zwei Personen.
f**oo**r **ine**-uh pairz**oh**n/f**oo**r tsvy pairz**oh**nen

▶▶ Yes, we have rooms free.
ja, wir haben Zimmer frei.
ja veer h**ah**ben ts**i**mmer fry

▶▶ For how many nights?
Für wie lange?
f**oo**r vee l**a**ng-uh

▶ Just for one night.
Nur für eine Nacht.
n**oo**r f**oo**r **ine**-uh naκHt

▶ How much is it?
Was kostet es?
vass k**o**stet ess

▶▶ Ninety euros with bathroom and seventy euros without bathroom.
Neunzig Euro mit Bad und siebzig Euro ohne Bad.
n**oy**ntsish **oy**-ro mit baht oont z**ee**ptsish **oy**-ro **oh**n-uh baht

▶ Does that include breakfast?
Ist das inklusive Frühstück?
ist dass inkl00zeev-uh fr00sht00ck

▶ Can I see a room with bathroom?
Kann ich ein Zimmer mit Bad sehen?
kann ish ine tsimmer mit baht zay-en

▶ OK, I'll take it.
Gut, ich nehme es.
g00t ish naym-uh ess

▶ When do I have to check out?
Wann muss ich das Zimmer räumen?
vann mooss ish dass tsimmer roymen

▶ Is there anywhere I can leave luggage?
Kann ich irgendwo mein Gepäck unterstellen?
kann ish eergentvo mine gepeck oonter-shtellen

4. Car hire

automatic	der Automatikwagen	owtomahtik-vahgen
full tank	ein voller Tank	foller tank
manual	ein Auto mit	owto mit
	Gangschaltung	gang-shaltoong
rented car	das Mietauto	meet-owto

▶ I'd like to rent a car.
Ich möchte ein Auto mieten.
ish mursht-uh ine owto meeten

> ▶▶ For how long?
> Für wie lange?
> foor vee lang-uh

▶ Two days.　　　　▶ I'll take the...
Zwei Tage.　　　　Ich nehme den...
tsvy tahg-uh　　　ish naym-uh dayn

▶ Is that with unlimited mileage?
Ist das ohne Kilometerbeschränkung?
ist dass ohn-uh keelo-mayter-beshrenkoong

> ▶▶ It is.
> Ja.
> yah

> ▶▶ Can I see your driving licence, please?
> Kann ich bitte Ihren Führerschein sehen?
> kann ish bitt-uh eeren foorershine zay-en

> ▶▶ And your passport.
> Und Ihren Pass.
> oont eeren pas

▶ Is insurance included?
Ist Versicherung inbegriffen?
ist fairzisheroong inbegriffen

> ▶▶ Yes, but you have to pay the first 100 euros.
> Ja, aber die ersten hundert Euro müssen Sie selbst
> bezahlen.
> yah ahber dee airsten hoondert oy-ro moossen zee zelpst betsahlen

> ▶▶ Can you leave a deposit of 100 euros?
> Könnten Sie eine Anzahlung von hundert Euro leisten?
> kurnten zee ine-uh an-tsahloong fon hoondert oy-ro lysten

▶ And if this office is closed, where do I leave the keys?
Und wo gebe ich die Schlüssel ab, wenn dieses Büro
geschlossen hat?
oont vo gayb-uh ish dee shloossel ap venn deeezess booro geshlossen hat

> ▶▶ You drop them in that box.
> Werfen Sie sie in den Kasten dort.
> vairfen zee zee in dayn kasten dort

5. Car problems

brakes	die Bremse	bremzuh
to break down	eine Panne haben	pann-uh hahben
clutch	die Kupplung	kooploong
diesel	Diesel	deezel
flat battery	eine leere Batterie	lair-uh batteree
flat tyre	ein platter Reifen	platter ryfen
petrol	das Benzin	bentseen

▶ Excuse me, where is the nearest petrol station?
Entschuldigung, wo finde ich die nächste Tankstelle?
entshooldigoong vo find-uh ish dee naykst-uh tank-shtell-uh

    ▶▶ In the next town, about five kilometres away.
    Im nächsten Ort, etwa fünf Kilometer von hier.
    im nayksten ort etva foonf keelo-mayter fon heer

▶ The car has broken down.
Ich habe eine Autopanne.
ish hahb-uh ine-uh owto-pann-uh

    ▶▶ Can you tell me what happened?
    Können Sie mir sagen, was passiert ist?
    kurnen zee meer zahgen vass passeert ist

▶ I've got a flat tyre.
Ich habe einen platten Reifen.
ish hahb-uh ine-en platten ryfen

▶ I think the battery is flat.
Ich glaube, die Batterie ist leer.
ish glowb-uh dee batteree ist lair

    ▶▶ Can you tell me exactly where you are?
    Wo genau befinden Sie sich?
    vo genow befinden zee zish

▶ I'm about two kilometres outside of Hanover on the A7.
Ich befinde mich ungefähr zwei Kilometer vor Hannover auf der A7.
ish befind-uh mish oon-gefair tsvy keelo-mayter for hanover owf dair ah-zeeben

    ▶▶ What type of car? What colour?
    Was für ein Auto ist es? Welche Farbe hat es?
    vass foor ine owto ist ess, velsh-uh farb-uh hat ess

▶ Can you send a tow truck?
Können Sie einen Abschleppwagen schicken?
kurnen zee ine-en ap-shlepp-vahgen shicken

6. Children

baby	das Baby	**bay**bee
baby food	die Babynahrung	**bay**bee-nahroong
boy	der Junge	y**oo**ng-uh
child	das Kind	kint
children	die Kinder	**kin**-der
cot	das Kinderbett	**kin**-der-bett
girl	das Mädchen	**may**tshen
highchair	der Hochstuhl	**hohKH**-shtool
nappies (diapers)	die Windeln	**vin**deln

▶ We need a babysitter for tomorrow evening.
Wir brauchen einen Babysitter für morgen Abend.
veer bro**wKH**en **ine**-en **bay**bee-sitter for morgen **ah**bent

    ▶▶ For what time?
    Von wann bis wann?
    fon van biss van

▶ From 7.30 to 11.00.
Von neunzehn Uhr dreißig bis dreiundzwanzig Uhr.
fon n**oy**n-tsayn oor dr**y**ssish biss dr**y**-oont-tsvantsish oor

    ▶▶ How many children? How old are they?
    Wie viele Kinder? Wie alt sind sie?
    vee f**ee**l-uh **kin**-der, vee alt zint zee

▶ Two children, aged four and eighteen months.
Zwei Kinder, eines vier Jahre, das andere achtzehn Monate.
tsvy **kin**-der **ine**-ess feer **yah**r-uh das **an**der-uh **ah**KH-tsayn m**oh**naht-uh

---

▶ Where can I change the baby?
Wo kann ich das Baby wickeln?
vo kann ish dass **bay**bee **vi**ckeln

▶ Could you please warm this bottle for me?
Könnten Sie bitte diese Flasche für mich warm machen?
kurnten zee **bit**t-uh d**ee**z-uh fl**a**sh-uh for mish varm ma**KH**en

▶ Can you give us a child's portion?
Könnten Sie uns bitte einen Kinderteller geben?
kurnten zee oonss **bit**t-uh **ine**-en **kin**-der-teller g**ay**ben

▶ We need two child seats.
Wir brauchen zwei Kindersitze.
veer bro**wKH**en tsvy **kin**-der-zits-uh

▶ Is there a discount for children?
Gibt es eine Ermäßigung für Kinder?
geept ess **ine**-uh airm**ayss**-igoong foor **kin**-der

7. Communications: Internet

@	at	et
at sign	der Klammeraffe	kl**a**mmer-aff-uh
computer	der Computer	computer
email	die E-Mail	e-mail
Internet	das Internet	internet
keyboard	die Tastatur	tastat**oo**r
mouse	die Maus	mowss

▶ Is there somewhere I can check my emails?
Kann ich hier irgendwo meine E-Mails abrufen?
kann ish heer **ee**rgent-vo m**ine**-uh e-mails **a**p-roofen

▶ Do you have Wi-Fi?
Haben Sie WLAN-Zugang?
h**ah**ben zee v**ay**-lahn-ts**oo**gang

▶ Is there an Internet café around here?
Gibt es hier in der Gegend ein Internetcafé?
geept ess heer in dair g**ay**gent ine **i**nternetkafay

▶▶ Yes, there's one in the shopping centre.
Ja, es gibt eins im Einkaufszentrum.
ya ess geept ine-ss im **ine**-kowfs-tsentroom

▶▶ Do you want fifteen minutes, thirty minutes or one hour?
Möchten Sie fünfzehn, dreißig oder sechzig Minuten?
m**u**rshten zee f**oo**nf-tsayn dr**y**ssish **oh**der z**e**shtsish min**00**ten

▶ Thirty minutes please. Can you help me log on?
Dreißig Minuten, bitte. Können Sie mir beim Einloggen helfen?
dr**y**ssish min**00**ten b**i**tt-uh, k**u**rnen zee meer bime **ine**-loggen h**e**lfen

▶▶ OK, here's your password.
Ja, hier ist Ihr Passwort.
yah heer ist eer p**a**ss-vort

▶ Can you change this to an English keyboard?
Können Sie das auf eine englische Tastatur umstellen?
k**u**rnen zee dass owf **ine**-uh **e**ng-lish-uh tastat**00**r **oo**m-shtellen

▶ I'll take another quarter of an hour.
Ich möchte noch eine weitere Viertelstunde.
ish **mur**sht-uh noKH **ine**-uh **vy**ter-uh **fee**rtel-shtoond-uh

▶ Is there a printer I can use?
Haben Sie einen Drucker, den ich benutzen kann?
ha**h**ben zee **ine**-en dr**oo**cker dayn ish ben**oo**tsen kann

8. Communications: phones

mobile phone (cell phone)	das Handy	**hen**di
payphone	ein öffentliches Telefon	**ur**fentlishess telef**oh**n
phone call	der Anruf	**an**-roof
phone card	eine Telefonkarte	telef**oh**nkartuh
phone charger	ein Handy-Ladegerät	hendi-**lah**d-uh-gerayt
SIM card	eine SIM-Karte	z**i**m-kart-uh

▶ Can I call abroad from here?
Kann ich von hier ins Ausland telefonieren?
kann ish fon heer inss **ow**sslant telefon**ee**ren

▶ How do I get an outside line?
Wie kann ich nach draußen telefonieren?
vee kann ish naKH dr**ow**ssen telefon**ee**ren

▶ What's the code to call the UK/US from here?
Welche Vorwahl hat Großbritannien/haben die USA?
v**e**lsh-uh **f**orvahl hat grohss-brit**a**nnee-en, ha**h**ben dee oo-ess-**ah**

▶ Hello, can I speak to Michael Kaufmann?
Hallo, könnte ich bitte mit Michael Kaufmann sprechen?
hallo k**ur**nt-uh ish b**i**tt-uh mit m**i**sh-ah-el k**ow**fmann shpr**e**shen

▶▶ Yes, that's me speaking.
Ja, am Apparat.
yah am appar**ah**t

zero	null	nool
one	eins	**ine**-ss
two	zwei	tsvy
three	drei	dry
four	vier	feer
five	fünf	f**oo**nf
six	sechs	zeks
seven	sieben	**zee**ben
eight	acht	aKHt
nine	neun	noyn

▶ Do you have a charger for this?
Haben Sie ein Ladegerät hierfür?
hah*ben zee ine la*hd-uh-gerayt heerfoor

▶ Can I buy a SIM card for this phone?
Haben Sie eine SIM-Karte für dieses Handy?
hah*ben zee ine-uh zim-kart-uh foor dee*zess hendi

9. Directions

turn off	abbiegen	ap-beegen
past the...	an dem... vorbei	an daym... forby
over there	dort drüben	dort drooben
opposite	gegenüber	gaygenoober
straight ahead	geradeaus	gerahduh-owss
just after	gleich nach	glysh naKH
on the left	links	
next	nächste	naykst-uh
near	neben	nayben
on the right	rechts	reshts
street	Straße	shtrahss-uh
in front of	vor	for
further	weiter	vyter
back	zurück	tsooroock

▶ Hi, I'm looking for Ortlerstraße.
Hallo, ich suche die Ortlerstraße.
hallo ish zooKH-uh dee ortler-shtrahss-uh

> ▶▶ Sorry, never heard of it.
> **Tut mir Leid, nie gehört.**
> toot meer lite nee gehurt

▶ Can you tell me where Ortlerstraße is?
Können Sie mir sagen, wo die Ortlerstraße ist?
kurnen zee meer zahgen vo dee ortler-shtrahss-uh ist

> ▶▶ I'm a stranger here too.
> **Ich bin auch fremd hier.**
> ish bin owKH fremt heer

▶ Hi, Ortlerstraße, do you know where it is?
Hallo, wo ist bitte die Ortlerstraße?
hallo vo ist bittuh dee ortler-shtrahss-uh

► Where?
Wo?
vo

► Which direction?
Welche Richtung?
velshuh rishtoong

▶▶ Around the corner.
Um die Ecke.
oom dee eck-uh

▶▶ Left at the second traffic lights.
Bei der zweiten Ampel links.
by dair tsvyten ampel links

▶▶ Then it's the first street on the right.
Es ist dann die erste Straße rechts.
ess ist dann dee airst-uh shtrahss-uh reshts

10. Emergencies

accident	der Unfall	oonfal
ambulance	der Krankenwagen	kranken-vahgen
consul	der Konsul	konzool
embassy	die Botschaft	bohtshafft
fire brigade	die Feuerwehr	foy-er-vair
police	die Polizei	politsy

► Help!
Hilfe!
hilf-uh

► Can you help me?
Können Sie mir helfen?
kurnen zee meer helfen

► Please come with me! It's really very urgent.
Kommen Sie bitte mit mir! Es ist wirklich sehr dringend.
kommen zee bitt-uh mit meer, ess ist veerklish zair dringent

► I've lost my keys.
Ich habe meine Schlüssel verloren.
ish hahb-uh mine-uh shloossel fairloren

► My car is not working.
Mein Auto ist nicht in Ordnung.
mein Auto ist nisht in ordnoong

▶ My purse has been stolen.
Mein Portmonee ist gestohlen worden.
mine port-monnay ist geshtohlen vorden

▶ I've been mugged.
Ich bin überfallen worden.
ish bin ooberfal-en vorden

>> What's your name?
Wie heißen Sie?
vee hice-en zee

>> I need to see your passport.
Können Sie mir bitte Ihren Pass zeigen?
kurnen zee meer bitt-uh eeren pas tsygen

▶ I'm sorry, all my papers have been stolen.
Tut mir Leid, aber alle meine Ausweispapiere sind gestohlen worden.
toot meer lite ahber al-uh mine-uh owss-vice-papeer-uh zint geshtohlen vorden

11. Friends

▶ Hi, how're you doing?
Hallo, wie gehts?
hallo vee gayts

>> OK, and you?
OK, und dir?
OK oont deer

▶ Yeah, fine.   ▶ Not bad.
Ja, ganz gut.   Nicht schlecht.
yah gants goot   nisht shlesht

▶ D'you know Mark?
Kennst du Mark?
kennst doo mark

▶ And this is Hannah.
Und das ist Hannah.
oont dass ist hannah

>> Yeah, we know each other.
Ja, wir kennen uns.
yah veer kennen oonss

▶ Where do you know each other from?
Woher kennt ihr euch?
vohair kennt eer oysh

▶▶ We met at Daniel's place.
Wir haben uns bei Daniel kennen gelernt.
veer hahben oonss by daniel kennen gelairnt

▶ That was some party, eh?
Das war vielleicht eine Party, oder?
dass var feelysht ine-uh party ohder

▶▶ The best!
Einmalig!
ine-mahlish

▶ Are you guys coming for a beer?
Kommt ihr mit auf ein Bier?
kommt eer mit owf ine beer

▶▶ Cool, let's go.
Cool, gehen wir.
kool gay-en veer

▶▶ No, I'm meeting Sarah.
Nein, ich treffe Sarah.
nine ish tref-uh sarah

▶ See you at Daniel's place tonight.
Dann bis heute Abend bei Daniel.
dann biss hoyt-uh ahbent by daniel

▶▶ See you!
Bis dann!
biss dann

12. Health

antibiotics	die Antibiotika	antibiotika
antiseptic ointment	eine antiseptische Salbe	antizeptish-uh zalb-uh
cystitis	eine Blasenentzündung	blahzen-ent-tsoondoong
dentist	der Zahnarzt	tsahnartst
diarrhoea	der Durchfall	doorshfal
doctor	der Arzt	artst
hospital	das Krankenhaus	kranken-howss
ill	krank	
medicine	das Medikament	medikament
painkillers	die Schmerztabletten	shmairts-tabletten
pharmacy	die Apotheke	apotayk-uh
to prescribe	verschreiben	fair-shryben
thrush	eine Pilzinfektion	pilts-infeks-yohn

▶ I'm not feeling very well.
Es geht mir nicht gut.
ess gayt meer nisht goot

▶ Can you get a doctor?
Können Sie einen Arzt holen?
ku**r**nen zee **ine**-en artst ho**h**len

▶▶ Where does it hurt?
Wo tut es weh?
vo toot ess vay

▶ It hurts here.
Es tut hier weh.
ess toot heer vay

▶▶ Is the pain constant?
Tut es ständig weh?
toot ess sht**e**ndish vay

▶ It's not a constant pain.
Es tut nicht ständig weh.
ess toot nisht sht**e**ndish vay

▶ Can I make an appointment?
Kann ich einen Termin machen?
kann ish **ine**-en tairm**ee**n ma**kH**en

▶ Can you give me something for…?
Können Sie mir etwas für… geben?
ku**r**nen zee meer **e**tvass f**oo**r… g**ay**ben

▶ Yes, I have insurance.
Ja, ich bin versichert.
yah ish bin fairz**i**shert

13. Hotels

maid	das Zimmermädchen	ts**i**mmer-m**ay**tshen
manager	der Manager/die Managerin	m**e**nager/m**e**nagerin
room service	der Zimmerservice	ts**i**mmer-surv**i**ss

▶ Hello, we've booked a double room in the name of Cameron.
Guten Tag, wir haben ein Doppelzimmer auf den Namen Cameron gebucht.
g**oo**ten tahk veer h**ah**ben ine d**o**ppel-tsimmer owf dayn n**ah**men cameron geb**oo**KHt

> ▶▶ That was for four nights, wasn't it?
> Das war für vier Nächte, richtig?
> dass var f**oo**r feer n**e**sht-uh r**i**shtish

▶ Yes, we're leaving on Saturday.
Ja, wir fahren am Samstag wieder ab.
yah veer f**ah**ren am z**a**mstakH v**ee**der ap

> ▶▶ Can I see your passport please?
> Könnte ich bitte Ihren Reisepass sehen?
> k**u**rnt-uh ish b**i**tt-uh **ee**r-uh r**i**ze-uh-pas z**ay**-en

> ▶▶ There you are: room 321 on the third floor.
> Hier, bitte sehr: Zimmer dreihunderteinundzwanzig im dritten Stock.
> heer b**i**tt-uh zair ts**i**mmer dr**y**-hoondert-ine-oont-tsvantsish im dr**i**tten shtock

▶ I can't get this keycard to work.
Diese Schlüsselkarte funktioniert nicht.
d**ee**z-uh shl**oo**ssel-kart-uh foonkts-yohn**ee**rt nisht

▶▶ Sorry, I need to reactivate it.
Ach Entschuldigung, ich muss sie reaktivieren.
aKH entsh**oo**ldigoong ish mooss zee ray-aktiv**ee**ren

▶ What time is breakfast?
Wann gibt es Frühstück?
van geept ess fr**oo**sht**oo**ck

▶ There aren't any towels in my room.
Ich habe keine Handtücher in meinem Zimmer.
ish h**ah**b-uh k**i**ne-uh hant-t**oo**sher in m**i**ne-em ts**i**mmer

▶ My flight isn't until this evening, can I keep the room a bit longer?
Mein Flug geht erst heute Abend. Kann ich das Zimmer noch etwas länger behalten?
mine fl**oo**k gayt airst h**oy**t-uh **ah**bent, kann ish dass ts**i**mmer noKH **e**tvass l**e**ng-er beh**a**lten

▶ Can I settle up? Is this card ok?
Kann ich bitte zahlen? Akzeptieren Sie diese Karte?
kann ish b**i**tt-uh ts**ah**len, aktsept**ee**ren zee d**ee**z-uh k**a**rt-uh

14. Language difficulties

a few words	ein paar Wörter	ine pahr v**u**rter
interpreter	der Dolmetscher	d**o**lmetsher
to translate	übersetzen	**oo**berz**e**tsen

▶▶ Your credit card has been refused.
Ihre Kreditkarte wurde abgelehnt.
eer-uh krayd**ee**t-kart-uh v**oo**rd-uh **a**p-gelaynt

▶ What, I don't understand; do you speak English?
Wie bitte, das verstehe ich nicht; sprechen Sie Englisch?
vee b**i**tt-uh dass fairsht**ay**-uh ish nisht, shpr**e**shen zee **e**ng-lish

▶▶ This isn't valid.
Die ist nicht gültig.
dee ist nisht g**oo**ltish

▶ Could you say that again?
Können Sie das wiederholen?
k**u**rnen zee dass veeder-h**oh**len

▶ Slowly.
Langsam.
l**a**ngzahm

▶ I understand very little German.
Ich verstehe nur sehr wenig Deutsch.
ish fairsht**ay**-uh n**oo**r zair **vay**-nish doytch

▶ I speak German very badly.
Ich spreche sehr schlechtes Deutsch.
ish shpr**e**sh-hu zair shl**e**sht-ess doytch

▶▶ You can't use this card to pay.
Sie können mit dieser Karte nicht bezahlen.
zee k**u**rnen mit d**ee**zer k**a**rt-uh nisht bets**ah**len

▶▶ Do you understand?
Verstehen Sie?
fairsht**ay**-en zee

▶ Sorry, no.
Nein, tut mir Leid.
nine t**oo**t meer lite

▶ Is there someone who speaks English?
Spricht hier jemand Englisch?
shprisht heer y**ay**mant **e**ng-lish

▶ Oh, now I understand.
Ach so, jetzt verstehe ich.
ach zo yetst fairsht**ay**-uh ish

▶ Is that OK now?
Ist das jetzt in Ordnung?
ist dass yetst in **o**rdnoong

15. Meeting people

▶ Hello.
Hallo.
hallo

▶▶ Hello, my name's Claudia.
Hallo, ich heiße Claudia.
hallo ish h**i**ce-uh kl**ow**d-ya

▶ Graham, from England, Thirsk.
Ich bin Graham; ich komme aus Thirsk in England.
ish bin graham ish k**o**mm-uh owss thirsk in **e**ng-lant

▶▶ Don't know that, where is it?
Kenne ich nicht, wo ist das?
k**e**nn-uh ish nisht vo ist dass

▶ Not far from York, in the North; and you?
Nicht weit von York entfernt, im Norden, und Sie?
nisht vite fon york ent-fairnt im norden oont zee

>> ▶▶ I'm from Berlin; here by yourself?
>> **Ich komme aus Berlin; sind Sie alleine hier?**
>> ish komm-uh owss bairleen zint zee al-ine-uh heer

▶ No, I'm with my wife and two kids.
Nein, meine Frau und meine zwei Kinder sind dabei.
nine mine-uh frow oont mine-uh tsvy kinder zint da-by

▶ What do you do?
Was machen Sie beruflich?
vass maKHen zee berooflish

>> ▶▶ I'm in computers.
>> **Ich arbeite im Computerbereich.**
>> ish arbyt-uh im computer-berysh

▶ Me too.
Ich auch.
ish owKH

▶ Here's my wife now.
Hier kommt meine Frau.
heer kommt mine-uh frow

>> ▶▶ Nice to meet you.
>> **Freut mich, Sie kennen zu lernen.**
>> froyt mish zee kennen tsoo lairnen

16. Nightlife

▶ What's a good place for music? I'm into...
Wo kann man hier gute Musik hören? Ich stehe auf...
vo kann man heer goot-uh moozeek hur-ren, ish shtay-uh owf

heavy metal	Heavy Metal	heavy metal
folk	Folk	folk
jazz	Jazz	jezz
hip-hop	Hip-Hop	hip-hop
electro	Electro	elektro
rock	Rock	rock

▶▶ There's going to be a great gig at the Capitol tomorrow night.
Morgen Abend findet ein toller Gig im Capitol statt.
morgen **ah**bent **f**indet ine toller gig im **k**apitol shtatt

▶ Where can I hear some local music?
Wo kann ich mir lokale Bands anhören?
vo kann ish meer lok**ah**l-uh bends **a**n-hur-ren

▶ What's a good place for dancing?
Wo kann man hier gut tanzen gehen?
vo kann man heer g**oo**t **t**antsen g**ay**-en

▶ Can you write down the names of the best bars around here?
Können Sie mir die Namen der besten Bars in der Gegend
aufschreiben?
kurnen zee meer dee **nah**men dair b**e**sten bars in dair g**ay**gent **o**wf-shryben

▶▶ That depends what you're looking for.
Das hängt davon ab, was Ihnen gefällt.
dass hengt d**a**fon ap vass **ee**nen gef**e**lt

▶ The place where the locals go.
Dort, wo Einheimische hingehen.
dort vo **ine**-hymish-uh h**i**n-gay-en

▶ A place for a quiet drink.
Dort, wo man in Ruhe etwas trinken kann.
dort vo man in r**oo**-uh **e**tvass tr**i**nken kann

▶▶ The casino across the river is very good.
Das Kasino am anderen Flussufer ist sehr gut.
dass kazeeno am anderen floos-oofer ist zair goot

▶ I suppose they have a dress code.
Ich nehme an, dort herrscht eine Kleiderordnung.
ish naym-uh an dort hairsht ine-uh klyder-ordnoong

▶▶ You can wear what you like.
Sie können anziehen, was Sie möchten.
zee kurnen antsee-en vass zee murshten

▶ What time does it close?
Wann schließt es?
van shleest ess

17. Post offices

airmail	Luftpost	looft-posst
post card	die Postkarte	posst-kart-uh
post office	die Post	posst
stamp	die Briefmarke	breef-mark-uh

▶ What time does the post office close?
Wann schließt die Post?
van shleest dee posst

▶▶ Five o'clock weekdays.
Um siebzehn Uhr Montag bis Freitag.
oom zeep-tsayn oor mohntahk biss frytahk

▶ Is the post office open on Saturdays?
Ist die Post samstags geöffnet?
ist dee posst zamstahks guh-urfnet

▶▶ Until midday.
Bis Mittag.
biss mittahk

▶ I'd like to send this registered to England.
ich möchte dies per Einschreiben nach England senden.
ish mursht-uh deess pair ine-shryben naкн eng-lant zenden

▶▶ Certainly, that will cost 10 euros.
Gut, das macht zehn Euro.
goot dass maкнt tsayn oy-ro

▶ And also two stamps
for England, please.
**Und auch zwei Briefmarken
nach England, bitte.**
oont owкн tsvy breef-marken
naкн eng-lant bitt-uh

AUSLANDS...	international
BRIEFE	letters
INLANDS...	domestic
PAKETE	parcels
POSTLAGERND	poste restante

▶ Do you have some airmail
stickers?
Hätten Sie ein paar Luftpost-Aufkleber?
hetten zee ine pahr looft-posst-owf-klayber

▶ Do you have any mail for me?
Ist Post für mich gekommen?
ist posst foor mish gekommen

18. Restaurants

bill	die Rechnung	reshnoong
menu	die Speisekarte	shpyz-uh-kart-uh
table	der Tisch	tish

▶ Can we have a non-smoking table?
Können wir bitte einen Nichtrauchertisch haben?
kurnen veer bittuh ine-en nisht-rowкнer-tish hahben

▶ There are two of us.
Wir sind zu zweit.
veer zint tsoo tsvite

▶ There are four of us.
Wir sind zu viert.
veer zint tsoo feert

▶ What's this?
Was ist das?
vass ist dass

▶▶ It's a type of fish.
Es ist eine Fischsorte.
ess ist ine-uh fish-zort-uh

▶▶ It's a local speciality.
Es ist eine regionale Spezialität.
ess ist ine-uh rayg-yohnahl-uh shpetsi-alitayt

▶▶ Come inside and I'll show you.
Kommen Sie herein, ich zeige es Ihnen.
kommen zee hair-ine ish tsyg-uh ess eenen

▶ We would like two of these, one of these, and one of those.
Wir hätten gern zwei von diesen, eins von diesen und eins von
denen dort.
veer hetten gairn tsvy fon deezen ine-ss fon deezen oont ine-ss fon daynen dort

▶▶ And to drink?
Und zu trinken?
oont tsoo trinken

▶ Red wine.   ▶ White wine.
Rotwein.   Weißwein.
roht-vine   vice-vine

▶ A beer and two orange juices.
Ein Bier und zwei Orangensaft.
ine beer oont tsvy oronJen-zaft

▶ Some more bread please.
Noch etwas Brot bitte.
noKH etvass broht bitt-uh

▶▶ How was your meal?
Wie hat es Ihnen geschmeckt?
vee hat ess eenen geshmeckt

▶ Excellent, very nice!
Wunderbar!, sehr schön!
voonderbar zair shurn

▶▶ Anything else?
Noch etwas?
noKH etvass

▶ Just the bill thanks.
Nur die Rechnung, danke.
noor dee reshnoong dank-uh

19. Self-catering accommodation

air-conditioning	die Klimaanlage	kleema-anlahg-uh
apartment	das Apartment	apartment
cooker	der Herd	hairt
fridge	der Kühlschrank	koolshrank
heating	die Heizung	hytsoong
hot water	heißes Wasser	hice-ess vasser
lightbulb	eine Glühbirne	gloobeern-uh
toilet	die Toilette	twalett-uh

▶ The toilet's broken, can you get someone to fix it?
Die Toilette ist kaputt. Können Sie jemanden schicken,
der sie repariert?
dee twalett-uh ist kapoot, kurnen zee yaymanden shicken dair zee repareert

▶ There's no hot water.
Wir haben kein heißes Wasser.
veer hahben kine hice-ess vasser

▶ Can you show me how the air-conditioning works?
Können Sie mir zeigen, wie die Klimaanlage funktioniert?
kurnen zee meer tsygen vee dee kleema-anlahg-uh foonkts-yohneert

▶▶ OK, what apartment are you in?
Okay, in welchem Apartment wohnen Sie?
okay in velshem apartment vohnen zee

▶ We're in number five.
Wir wohnen in Nummer fünf.
veer vohnen in noommer foonf

▶ Can you move us to a quieter apartment?
Können wir in ein ruhigeres Apartment wechseln?
kurnen veer in ine roo-igeress apartment vekseln

▶ Is there a supermarket nearby?
Gibt es einen Supermarkt in der Nähe?
geept ess ine-en zoopermarkt in dair nay-uh

▶▶ Have you enjoyed your stay?
Hatten Sie einen schönen Aufenthalt?
hatten zee ine-en shurnen owf-ent-hallt

▶ Brilliant holiday, thanks!
Der Urlaub war fantastisch, danke!
dair oorlowp vahr fantastish dank-uh

20. Shopping

▶▶ Can I help you?
Kann ich Ihnen behilflich sein?
kann ish eenen behilflish zine

▶ Can I just have a look around?
Kann ich mich kurz umschauen?
kann ish mish koorts oom-show-en

▶ Yes, I'm looking for…
Ja, ich suche…
yah ish zOOkH-uh…

DER AUSVERKAUF	sale
GEÖFFNET	open
GESCHLOSSEN	closed
DIE KASSE	cash desk
UMTAUSCHEN	to exchange

▶ How much is this?
Wie viel kostet dies?
vee feel kostet deess

▶▶ Thirty-two euros.
Zweiunddreißig Euro.
tsvy-oont-dryssish oy-ro

▶ OK, I think I'll have to leave it; it's a little too expensive for me.
Ich glaube, ich muss es lassen, es ist mir ein bisschen zu teuer.
ish glowbuh ish mooss ess lassen ess ist meer ine biss-shen tsOO toy-er

▶▶ How about this?
Wie ist es hiermit?
vee ist ess heermit

▶ Can I pay by credit card?
Kann ich mit Kreditkarte bezahlen?
kann ish mit kraydeet-kart-uh betsahlen

▶ It's too big.   ▶ It's too small.
Es ist zu groß.   Es ist zu klein.
ess ist tsOO grohss   ess ist tsOO kline

▶ It's for my son – he's about this high.
Es ist für meinen Sohn – er ist etwa so groß.
ess ist fOOr mine-en zohn – air ist etvah zo grohss

▶▶ Will there be anything else?
Darf es sonst noch etwas sein?
darf ess zonst nokH etvass zine

▶ That's all thanks.
Nein danke, das ist alles.
nine dank-uh dass ist al-ess

▶ Make it twenty euros and I'll take it.
Für zwanzig Euro nehme ich es.
fOOr tsvantsish oy-ro naym-uh ish ess

▶ Fine, I'll take it.
Gut, ich nehme es.
gOOt ish naym-uh ess

21. Shopping for clothes

to alter	ändern lassen	endern lassen
bigger	größer	grursser
just right	genau richtig	genow rishtish
smaller	kleiner	kline-er
to try on	anprobieren	an-probeeren

▶▶ Can I help you?
Kann ich Ihnen behilflich sein?
kann ish **ee**nen beh**i**lflish zine

▶ No thanks, I'm just looking.
Nein danke, ich schaue mich nur um.
nine d**a**nk-uh ish sh**ow**-uh mish n**oo**r oom

▶▶ Do you want to try that on?
Möchten Sie das anprobieren?
m**u**rshten zee dass **a**n-probeeren

▶ Yes, and I'll try this one too.
Ja, und das hier möchte ich auch anprobieren.
yah oont dass heer m**u**rsht-uh ish owкн **a**n-probeeren

▶ Do you have it in a bigger size?
Haben Sie das eine Nummer größer?
hahben zee dass ine-uh noommer grursser

▶ Do you have it in a different colour?
Haben Sie das in einer anderen Farbe?
hahben zee dass in ine-er anderen farb-uh

> ▶▶ That looks good on you.
> **Das steht Ihnen gut.**
> dass shtayt eenen goot

▶ Can you shorten this?
Können Sie es kürzen?
kurnen zee ess koortsen

> ▶▶ Sure, it'll be ready on Friday, after 12.00.
> **Sicher, Sie können ihn Freitag nach zwölf Uhr abholen.**
> zisher zee kurnen een frytahk naKH tsvurlf oor ap-hohlen

22. Sightseeing

art gallery	die Kunstgalerie	koonst-gal-leree
bus tour	eine Stadtrundfahrt	shtatt-roont-fahrt
city centre	das Stadtzentrum	shtatt-tsentroom
closed	geschlossen	geshlossen
guide	der Führer	foorer
museum	das Museum	moozay-oom
open	geöffnet	guh-urfnet

▶ I'm interested in seeing the old town.
Ich würde gerne die Altstadt sehen.
ish voord-uh gairn-uh dee alt-shtatt zay-en

▶ Are there guided tours of the town?
Gibt es eine Stadtführung?
geept ess ine-uh shtatt-fooroong

> ▶▶ I'm sorry, it's fully booked.
> **Tut mir Leid, es ist voll ausgebucht.**
> toot meer lite ess ist foll owssgebooKHt

▶ How much would you charge to drive us around for four hours?
Wie viel würde es kosten, wenn Sie uns vier Stunden lang herumfahren?
vee feel voord-uh ess kosten venn zee oonss feer shtoonden lang hairoom-fahren

▶ Can we book tickets for the concert here?
Können wir die Konzertkarten hier buchen?
kurnen veer dee kontsairt-karten heer booKHen

> ▶▶ Yes, in what name?
> Ja, auf welchen Namen?
> yah owf velshen nahmen

> ▶▶ Which credit card?
> Was für eine Kreditkarte?
> vass foor ine-uh kraydeet-kart-uh

▶ Where do we get the tickets?
Wo bekommen wir die Karten?
vo bekommen veer dee karten

> ▶▶ Just pick them up at the entrance.
> Holen Sie sie einfach am Eingang ab.
> hohlen zee zee ine-faKH am ine-gang ap

▶ Is it open on Sundays?
Ist es sonntags geöffnet?
ist ess zonntahks guh-urfnet

▶ How much is it to get in?
Wie viel kostet der Eintritt?
vee feel kostet dair **ine**-tritt

▶ Are there reductions for groups of six?
Gibt es Ermäßigungen für Gruppen von sechs Personen?
geept ess air-**may**ssigoongen foor groopen fon zeks pairz**oh**nen

▶ That was really impressive!
Das war wirklich beeindruckend!
dass vahr **vee**rklish buh-**ine**-droockent

23. Taxis

▶ Can you get us a taxi?
Können Sie uns ein Taxi rufen?
ku**r**nen zee oonss ine taxi r**oo**fen

▶▶ For now? Where are you going?
Für jetzt gleich? Wo möchten Sie hin?
foor yetst glysh, vo m**ur**shten zee hin

▶ To the town centre.
Ins Stadtzentrum.
inss shtatt-ts**e**ntroom

▶ I'd like to book a taxi to the airport for tomorrow.
Ich möchte für morgen ein Taxi zum Flughafen bestellen.
ish m**ur**sht-uh foor m**o**rgen ine taxi tsoom fl**oo**khhahfen best**e**llen

▶▶ Sure, at what time? How many people?
Gerne. Für wann? Und für wie viele Personen?
ga**i**rn-uh, foor van, oont foor vee feel-uh pairz**oh**nen

▶ How much is it to Fechenheim?
Wie viel kostet es nach Fechenheim?
vee feel kostet ess nakH f**e**shen-hime

▶ Right here is fine, thanks.
Sie können mich hier rauslassen.
zee ku**r**nen mish heer r**ow**ss-lassen

▶ Can you wait here and take us back?
Können Sie hier warten und uns wieder zurückfahren?
ku**r**nen zee heer v**a**rten oont oonss v**ee**der tsoor**oo**ck-fahren

▶▶ How long are you going to be?
Wie lange werden Sie brauchen?
vee l**a**ng-uh v**a**irden zee br**ow**kHen

24. Trains

to change trains	umsteigen	**oo**m-shtygen
platform	der Bahnsteig	**bah**nshtike
return	die Rückfahrkarte	r**oo**ck-fahrkart-uh
single	einfach	**ine**-faKH
station	der Bahnhof	b**ah**nhohf
stop	die Haltestelle	h**a**llt-uh-shtell-uh
ticket	die Fahrkarte	**fah**rkart-uh

▶ How much is...?
Wie viel kostet...?
vee feel k**o**stet...

▶ A single, second class to...
Einfach zweiter Klasse nach...
ine-faKH tsv**y**ter kl**a**ss-uh naKH...

▶ Two returns, second class to...
Zwei Rückfahrkarten zweiter Klasse nach...
tsvy r**oo**ck-fahrkarten tsv**y**ter kl**a**ss-uh naKH...

▶ For today.   ▶ For tomorrow.   ▶ For next Tuesday.
Für heute.   **Für morgen.**   **Für nächsten Dienstag.**
f**oo**r h**oy**t-uh   f**oo**r m**o**rgen   f**oo**r n**ay**ksten d**ee**nstahk

▶▶ There's a supplement for the Intercity.
Sie brauchen einen Zuschlag für den Intercity.
zee browKHen **ine**-en ts**00**shlahk f00r dayn inter**ci**ty

▶▶ Do you want to make a seat reservation?
Möchten Sie einen Platz reservieren?
mu**r**shten zee **ine**-en plats rezairv**ee**ren

▶▶ You have to change at Frankfurt.
Sie müssen in Frankfurt umsteigen.
zee m**00**ssen in frankfoort **oo**m-shtygen

▶ Is this seat free?
Ist dieser Platz frei?
ist d**ee**zer plats fry

▶ Excuse me, which station are we at?
Entschuldigung, welcher Bahnhof ist das hier?
ent-sh**oo**ldigoong ve**l**sher b**ah**nhohf ist dass heer

▶ Is this where I change for Heidelberg?
Muss ich hier nach Heidelberg umsteigen?
mooss ish heer naKH heidelberg **oo**m-shtygen

ENGLISH
→ GERMAN

A

a, an ein ine
  (*nouns with die*) eine ine-uh
  10 euros a bottle 10 Euro
  pro Flasche
about: about twenty etwa
  zwanzig etvah
  at about 5 o'clock gegen
  fünf Uhr gaygen
  a film about Germany ein
  Film über Deutschland oober
above über oober
abroad im Ausland owsslant
  to go abroad ins Ausland gehen
absolutely (I agree) genau genow
accelerator das Gaspedal
  gahss-pedahl
accept akzeptieren aktsepteeren
accident der Unfall oonfal
  there's been an accident
  es hat einen Unfall gegeben
  gegayben
accommodation die Unterkunft
  oonter-koonft
accurate genau genow
ache der Schmerz shmairts
  my back aches mein Rücken
  tut weh toot vay
across: across the road über
  die Straße oober
adapter der Adapter
address die Adresse adress-uh
  what's your address? was ist
  Ihre Adresse? eer-uh
address book das Adressbuch
  adressbookH

admission charge der Eintritt
  ine-tritt
adult der Erwachsene
  airvaksen-uh
advance: in advance im voraus
  forowss
aeroplane das Flugzeug
  flooktsoyk
after nach nakH
  after you nach Ihnen eenen
afternoon der Nachmittag
  nakHmit-tahk
  in the afternoon am
  Nachmittag
  this afternoon heute
  Nachmittag hoyt-uh
aftershave das After-shave
aftersun cream die
  Après-Lotion
  apray-lohts-yohn
afterwards danach danakH
again wieder veeder
against gegen gaygen
age das Alter al-ter
ago: a week ago vor einer
  Woche for ine-er
  an hour ago vor einer Stunde
agree: I agree ich bin
  einverstanden ine-fair-shtanden
AIDS Aids
air die Luft looft
  by air mit dem Flugzeug
  flooktsoyk
air-conditioning die
  Klimaanlage kleema-anlahg-uh
airmail: by airmail per Luftpost
  pair looftpost

airmail envelope der Luftpost-Briefumschlag l**oo**ftposst br**ee**f-oomshlahk

airport der Flughafen fl**oo**k-hahfen

to the airport, please zum Flughafen bitte tsoom

airport bus der Flughafenbus fl**oo**k-hafenbooss

aisle seat der Sitz am Gang

alarm clock der Wecker v**e**cker

alcohol der Alkohol

alcoholic alkoholisch alko-h**oh**lish

all: all the boys alle Jungen **a**l-uh

all the girls alle Mädchen

all of it alles **a**l-ess

all of them alle

that's all, thanks das ist alles, danke

allergic: I'm allergic to... ich bin allergisch gegen... ish bin all**ai**rgish g**ay**gen

allowed: is it allowed? ist es erlaubt? airl**ow**pt

all right ok**ay**

I'm all right ich bin okay

are you all right? bist du/sind Sie okay?

almond die Mandel

almost fast fasst

alone allein al-**ine**

alphabet das Alphabet alfa-b**ay**t

a	ah	**f**	eff	**k**	kah
b	bay	**g**	gay	**l**	el
c	tsay	**h**	hah	**m**	em
d	day	**i**	ee	**n**	en
e	ay	**j**	yot	**o**	oh

p	pay	**t**	tay	**x**	eeks
q	k00	**u**	00	**y**	**00**psilon
r	air	**v**	fow	**z**	tset
s	ess	**w**	vay	**ß**	ess-tset

Alps die **A**lpen

already schon shohn

also auch owKH

although obwohl opv**oh**l

altogether insges**a**mt

aluminium foil die Alufolie ahl00-f**oh**l-yuh

always **i**mmer

am: I am ich bin ish

a.m.: at seven a.m. um sieben Uhr m**o**rgens oom – **oo**r

amazing (surprising) erstaunlich airsht**ow**nlish

(very good) fant**a**stisch

ambulance der Krankenwagen kranken-vahgen

call an ambulance! rufen Sie einen Krankenwagen r**oo**fen zee **ine**-en

America Amerika am**ai**reeka

American (adj) amerikanisch amairik**ah**nish

I'm American (male/female) ich bin Amerik**a**ner/Amerik**a**nerin

among unter **oo**nter

amount die Menge m**e**ng-uh

(money) der Betrag bet**ra**hk

amp: a 13 amp fuse eine dreizehn-Ampere-Sicherung amp**ai**r z**i**sheroong

and und oont

angry wütend v**oo**tent

animal das Tier teer

ankle der Knöchel knurshel

anniversary (wedding) der Hochzeitstag hoKH-tsites-tahk

annoy: this man's annoying me dieser Mann belästigt mich belestisht mish

annoying ärgerlich airgerlish

another ein anderer ine anderer

can we have another room? können wir ein anderes Zimmer haben?

another beer, please noch ein Bier, bitte noKH ine

antibiotics die Antibiotika anti-bee-ohteeka

antifreeze das Frostschutzmittel frost-shoots-mittel

antihistamine das Antihistamin

antique: is it an antique? ist es antik? anteek

antique shop das Antiquitätengeschäft antikvitayten-gesheft

antiseptic das Antiseptikum

any: have you got any bread/ tomatoes? haben Sie Brot/ Tomaten? hahben zee

sorry, I don't have any tut mir Leid, ich habe keine toot meer lite, ish hahbuh kine-uh

anybody jemand yaymant

does anybody speak English? spricht jemand Englisch?

there wasn't anybody there es war keiner da kine-er

anything etwas etvass

anything else? sonst noch etwas?

nothing else, thanks sonst nichts, danke nishts, dank-uh

would you like anything to drink? möchten Sie etwas trinken? murshten

I don't want anything, thanks ich möchte nichts, danke nishts

apart from abgesehen von ap-gezay-en fon

apartment die Wohnung vohnoong

apartment block der Wohnblock vohnblock

appendicitis die Blinddarm- entzündung blint-darm-ent- ts00ndoong

aperitif der Aperitif apairee-teef

apology die Entschuldigung ent-shooldigoong

appetizer die Vorspeise for-shpize-uh

apple der Apfel

appointment der Termin tairmeen

good afternoon, how can I help you? guten Tag, kann ich Ihnen behilflich sein? g00ten tahk, kan ish eenen behilflish zine

I'd like to make an appointment ich möchte

einen Termin vereinbaren
fair-**ine**-bahren

what time would you like?
welche Zeit wäre Ihnen
recht? **ve**lsh-uh tsite **vair**-uh
eenen resht

three o'clock drei Uhr **oo**r

I'm afraid that's not possible, is four o'clock all right? tut mir Leid, das
ist nicht möglich, ist vier
Uhr in **O**rdnung? **mur**glish

yes, that will be fine ja, das
ist mir recht meer

the name was...? Ihr Name
war...? eer **nah**m-uh vahr

apricot die Aprikose aprik**oh**z-uh

April der April a-**pri**ll

are: we are wir sind veer zint

you are du bist/Sie sind
d**oo**.../zee

they are sie sind zee

area die Gegend g**ay**gent

area code die Vorwahl **for**vahl

arm der Arm

arrange: will you arrange it for us? k**ö**nnen Sie das für uns
regeln? **ray**geln

arrival die Ankunft **an**koonft

arrive **a**nkommen

when do we arrive?
wann kommen wir an?
van **ko**mmen veer an

has my fax arrived yet? ist mein Fax schon
angekommen?

we arrived today wir sind
heute angekommen

art die Kunst k**oo**nst

art gallery die Kunstgalerie
k**oo**nstgal-leree

artist der Künstler k**oo**nstler

as: as big as so groß wie
zoh grohss vee

as soon as possible so bald
wie möglich **mur**glish

ashtray der Aschenbecher
ashen-besher

ask fragen fr**ah**gen

I didn't ask for this
das habe ich nicht bestellt
dass h**ah**b-uh ish nisht besht**ell**t

could you ask him to...?
könnten Sie ihn bitten...?
kurnten zee een **bi**tten

asleep: she's asleep sie schläft
shl**ay**ft

aspirin das Kopfschmerzmittel
k**o**pf-shmairts-mittel

asthma das Asthma **a**st-mah

astonishing erstaunlich
airsht**ow**nlish

at: at the hotel im Hotel

at the station am B**ah**nhof

at six o'clock um 6 Uhr **oo**m

at Günter's bei Günter by

athletics Leichtathletik
l**y**sht-at-laytik

ATM der Geldautomat
g**e**lt-owtomaht

at sign, @ die Klammeraffe
kl**a**mmer-aff-uh

attractive attraktiv atrakt**ee**f

aubergine die Aubergine ohbair.Jeen-uh

August der August owg**oo**st

Australia Australien owst**rah**lee-en

Australian (*adj*) australisch owst**rah**lish

I'm Australian (*male/female*) ich bin Australier owst**rah**lee-er/ Australierin

Austria Österreich **ur**ster-rysh

Austrian (*male/female*) der Österreicher **ur**ster-rysher/die Österreicherin

(*adj*) österreichisch **ur**ster-rysh-ish

the Austrians die Österreicher

Austrian Alps die österreichischen **A**lpen

Austrian Tirol Tirol tee-r**oh**l

automatic (car) der Automatikwagen owto-m**ah**tik-vahgen

autumn der Herbst hairpst

in the autumn im Herbst

avenue die Allee all**ay**

average (not good) mittelmäßig mittel-maysish

(ordinary) durchschnittlich d**oo**rsh-shnitt-lish

on average im D**u**rchschnitt

awake: is he awake? ist er wach? va**KH**

away: go away! gehen Sie weg! g**ay**-en zee vek

is it far away? ist es weit? vite

awful furchtbar f**oo**rsht-bar

axle die Achse **a**x-uh

B

baby das Baby

baby food die Babynahrung -nahroong

baby's bottle das Fläschchen flesh-shen

baby-sitter der Babysitter

back (of body) der Rücken r**oo**cken

(back part) die Rückseite r**oo**ck-zite-uh

at the back hinten

can I have my money back? kann ich mein Geld zurückbekommen? ts**oo**r**oo**ck-bekommen

to come back zurückkommen

to go back zur**ü**ckgehen -g**ay**-en

backache die Rücken-schmerzen r**oo**cken-shmairtsen

bacon der Speck shpeck

bad schlecht shlesht

a bad headache schlimme Kopfschmerzen shlimm-uh

badly schlecht shlesht

bag die Tasche t**a**sh-uh

(handbag) die Handtasche hant-tash-uh

(plastic) die Tüte t**oo**t-uh

baggage das Gepäck gep**e**ck

baggage check (US) die Gepäckaufbewahrung gep**e**ck-owfbevahroong

baggage reclaim die Gepäckrückgabe gep**e**ck-r**oo**ck-gahb-uh

bakery die Bäckerei beckerr̄

balcony der Balkon bal-**koh**n

  a room with a balcony ein
Zimmer mit Balkon ine tsimmer

bald kahl

ball (large) der Ball bal

  (small) die Kugel k**oo**gel

ballet das Ballett bal-**ett**

ballpoint pen der
Kugelschreiber k**oo**gel-shryber

Baltic Sea die Ostsee **o**st-zay

banana die Banane ban**ah**n-uh

band (musical) die Band bent

bandage der Verband fair**bant**

bank (money) die Bank

bank account das Bankkonto
bank-konto

bar die Bar

bar of chocolate die Tafel
Schokolade t**ah**fel shoko-l**ah**d-uh

barber's der Frisör friz**ur**

basket der Korb korp

  (in shop) der Einkaufskorb
ine-kowfs-korp

bath das Bad baht

  can I have a bath? kann ich
ein Bad nehmen? n**ay**men

bathroom das Bad baht

  with a private bathroom
mit eigenem Bad **ī**-gen-em

bath towel das Badehandtuch
b**ah**duh-hant-t**oo**KH

battery die Batterie batter**ee**

Bavaria Bayern by-ern

Bavarian Alps die Bayrischen
Alpen by-rishen

be sein zine

beach der Strand shtrant

beach mat die Strandmatte
shtrant-mat-uh

beach umbrella der
Sonnenschirm z**o**nnen-sheerm

beans die Bohnen

  runner beans die Stangen-
bohnen shtangen-

  broad beans dicke Bohnen
dick-uh

beard der Bart

beautiful schön shurn

because weil vile

  because of... wegen... v**ay**gen

bed das Bett

  I'm going to bed ich gehe zu
Bett ish g**ay**-uh ts**oo**

bed and breakfast
Übernachtung mit Frühstück
oobernaKHtoong mit fr**oo**sht**oo**ck

bedroom das Schlafzimmer
shl**ah**f-tsimmer

beef das Rindfleisch rint-flysh

beer das Bier beer

  two beers, please zwei Bier,
bitte bitt-uh

beer mug der Bierkrug
beerkr**oo**k

before vorher f**o**rhair

  before that davor daf**o**r

  before me vor mir

begin: when does it begin?
wann fängt es an?
van fengt ess an

beginner (male/female) der
Anfänger **a**nfeng-er/die
Anfängerin

beginning: at the beginning
am **A**nfang

behind h**i**nten

behind me h**i**nter mir

beige beige bayJ

Belgian (adj) belgisch b**e**lgish

Belgium Belgien b**e**l-gee-en

believe glauben gl**ow**ben

below unten **oo**nten

below... unter... **oo**nter

belt der Gürtel g**oo**rtel

bend (in road) die Kurve k**oo**rv-uh

Berlin Wall die (Berliner) Mauer (bairl**ee**ner) m**ow**-er

berth (on ship) die Kabine kab**ee**n-uh

beside: beside the wall neben der Mauer n**ay**ben dair m**ow**er

best beste b**e**st-uh

better b**e**sser

are you feeling better?
geht es dir/Ihnen besser? gayt ess deer/**ee**nen

between zwischen tsv**i**shen

beyond jenseits y**ay**n-zites

bicycle das Fahrrad f**ah**r-raht

big groß grohss

too big zu groß ts**oo**

it's not big enough es ist nicht groß genug nisht – gen**oo**k

bike das Rad raht

(motorbike) das Motorrad mot**oh**r-raht

bikini der Bikini

bill die Rechnung r**e**shnoong

(US: money) der Geldschein g**e**lt-shine

could I have the bill, please?
kann ich bitte bezahlen? kan ish bitt-uh bets**ah**len

bin der Abfalleimer **a**pfal-ime-er

binding (ski) die Bindung b**i**ndoong

bin liners die Mülltüten m**oo**ll-t**oo**ten

bird der Vogel f**oh**gel

biro der Kugelschreiber k**oo**gel-shryber

birthday der Geburtstag geb**oo**rts-tahk

happy birthday! herzlichen Glückwunsch zum Geburtstag! h**ai**rts-lishen gl**oo**ckvoonsh tsoom

biscuit das Plätzchen pl**e**ts-shen

bit: a little bit ein bisschen ine b**i**ss-shen

a big bit ein großes Stück gr**oh**ssess sht**oo**ck

a bit of... ein Stück von...

a bit expensive etwas teuer

bite (by insect) der Stich sht**i**sh

(by dog) der Biss

bitter (taste etc) b**i**tter

black schwarz shvarts

Black Forest der Schwarzwald shvarts-valt

blanket die Decke d**e**ck-uh

bless you! Gesundheit! gez**oo**nt-hite

blind blind blint

blinds die Jalousie Jal**oo**zee

blister die Blase bl**ah**z-uh

blocked (road, sink) verstopft fairsht**o**pft

block of flats der Wohnblock
vohnblock

blond blond blont

blood das Blut bloot

high blood pressure hoher
Blutdruck bloot-droock

blouse die Bluse blooz-uh

blow-dry (*verb*) fönen furnen

I'd like a cut and blow-dry
schneiden und fönen, bitte
shnyden oont

blue blau blow

blusher das Rouge rooJ

boarding house die Pension
pangz-yohn

boarding pass die Bordkarte
bortkart-uh

boat das Boot boht

(for passengers) das Schiff shiff

body der Körper kurper

boil (water, potatoes) kochen koкнen

boiled egg ein gekochtes Ei
gekoкнtess ī

bone der Knochen k-noкнen

bonnet (of car) die Haube howb-uh

book das Buch booкн

to book buchen booкнen,
bestellen beshtellen

can I book a seat? kann ich
einen Platz reservieren lassen?
rezair-veeren

DIALOGUE

**I'd like to book a table for
two** ich möchte einen Tisch
für zwei Personen bestellen
ish mursht-uh ine-en tish foor
tsvy pairzohnen

**what time would you like
it booked for?** für wann
ist die Reservierung?
rezair-veeroong

half past seven halb acht

that's fine das geht in
Ordnung gayt in ordnoong

and your name? Ihr Name,
bitte? nahm-uh

bookshop die Buchhandlung
booкн-hantloong

bookstore die Buchhandlung

boot (footwear) der Stiefel
shteefel

(of car) der Kofferraum
koffer-rowm

border (of country) die Grenze
grents-uh

bored: I'm bored ich habe
langeweile ish hahb-uh
lang-uh-vile-uh

boring langweilig langvile-ish

**born: I was born in
Manchester** ich bin in
Manchester geboren gebohren

I was born in 1960 ich bin
neunzehnhundertsechzig
geboren

borrow leihen ly-en

may I borrow...? kann ich...
leihen?

both beide by-duh

**bother: sorry to bother you
with this** es tut mir Leid,
Sie damit zu belästigen ess
toot meer lite zee dahmit tsoo
belestigen

bottle die Flasche flash-uh

  a bottle of dry white wine eine Flasche trockenen Weißwein

bottle-opener der Flaschen-öffner flashen-urfner

bottom (of person) der Hintern

  at the bottom of the hill am Fuß des Berges fooss

box die Schachtel shaKHtel

  (larger) der Karton

box office die Kasse kass-uh

boy der Junge yoong-uh

boyfriend der Freund froynt

bra der BH bay-hah

bracelet das Armband armbant

brake die Bremse bremz-uh

brandy der Weinbrand vine-brant

bread das Brot broht

  some more bread, please noch etwas Brot, bitte etvass

  white bread das Weißbrot vice-broht

  brown bread das Graubrot grow-broht

  wholemeal bread das Vollkornbrot follkorn-broht

break (verb) brechen breshen

  I've broken... mir ist… kaputtgegangen meer – kapoot-gegangen

  I think I've broken my wrist ich glaube, ich habe mir das Handgelenk gebrochen gebroKHen

breakdown die Panne pann-uh

breakdown service die Pannenhilfe pannen-hilf-uh

break down (in car) eine Panne haben ine-uh pann-uh hahben

  I've broken down ich habe eine Panne

breakfast das Frühstück frooshtoock

  English/full breakfast ein englisches Frühstück eng-lish-ess

break-in: I've had a break-in bei mir ist eingebrochen worden by meer ist ine-gebroKHen vorden

breast die Brust broost

breathe atmen a**h**tmen

breeze die Brise breez-uh

brewery die Brauerei browerī

bridge (over river) die Brücke br**oo**ck-uh

brief kurz koorts

briefcase die Aktentasche akten-tash-uh

bright (light etc) hell

bright red hellrot hell-ro**h**t

brilliant (idea) glänzend gl**e**ntsent

(person) großartig gr**oh**ss-artish

bring br**i**ngen

I'll bring it back later ich bringe es später zurück bring-uh ess shp**ay**ter tsoor**oo**ck

Britain Großbritannien grohss-brit**a**nnee-en

British britisch br**ee**tish

brochure die Broschüre brosh**oo**r-uh

broken kap**u**tt

bronchitis die Bronchitis bron-sh**ee**tis

brooch die Brosche brosh-uh

broom der Besen b**a**yzen

brother der Bruder br**oo**der

brother-in-law der Schwager shv**ah**ger

brown braun brown

bruise der blaue Fleck bl**ow**-uh

brush die Bürste b**oo**rst-uh

(artist's) der Pinsel p**i**nzel

Brussels Brüssel br**oo**ssel

bucket der Eimer **i**me-er

buffet car der Speisewagen shp**ize**-uh-vahgen

buggy (for child) der Sportwagen shp**o**rt-vahgen

building das Gebäude geb**oyd**-uh

bulb (light bulb) die Birne b**ee**rn-uh

bumper die Stoßstange sht**oh**ss-shtang-uh

bunk das Bett

bureau de change die Wechselstube v**e**ksel-sht00b-uh

burglary der Einbruch **i**ne-brooKH

burn die Verbrennung fair-br**e**nnoong

(*verb*) br**e**nnen

burnt: this is burnt das ist angebrannt **a**n-gebrannt

burst: a burst pipe ein geplatztes Rohr

bus der Bus booss

what number bus is it to…? welcher Bus fährt nach…? v**e**lsher booss fairt naKH

when is the next bus to…? wann fährt der nächste Bus nach…? n**ay**kst-uh

what time is the last bus? wann fährt der letzte Bus? l**e**tst-uh

could you let me know when we get there? können Sie mir Bescheid sagen, wenn wir da sind? k**u**rnen zee meer besh**i**te z**ah**gen

does this bus go to...?
fährt dieser Bus nach…?
fairt

no, you need a number...
nein, Sie müssen mit der…
fahren

where does it leave from?
wo fährt er ab? vo

business das Geschäft gesheft

bus station der Busbahnhof
booss-bahnhohf

bus stop die Bushaltestelle
booss-halt-uh-shtell-uh

bust der Büsen boozen

busy (restaurant etc) voll foll

(telephone) besetzt bezetst

I'm busy tomorrow
morgen bin ich beschäftigt
beshef-tisht

but aber ahber

butcher's der Metzger metsger

butter die Butter bootter

button der Knopf k-nopf

buy kaufen kowfen

where can I buy...? wo kann
ich… bekommen? vo

by: by bus/car mit dem Bus/
Auto daym

written by... geschrieben von

by the window am Fenster

by the sea am Meer

by Thursday bis Donnerstag

bye auf Wiedersehen
owf-veederzayn

C

cabbage der Kohl

cable car die Drahtseilbahn
drahtzile-bahn

café das Café kaffay

cagoule das Windhemd
vint-hemt

cake der Kuchen kooкнen

cake shop die Konditorei
kondeetorī

call (verb) rufen roofen

(to phone) anrufen anroofen

what's it called? wie heißt
das? vee hyst dass

he/she is called... er/sie
heißt…

please call a doctor bitte
rufen Sie einen Arzt

**please give me a call
at 7.30 a.m. tomorrow
morning** könnten Sie mich
morgen früh um sieben
Uhr dreißig wecken?
kurnten zee mish morgen
froo – vecken

please ask him to call me
sagen Sie ihm bitte, er möchte
mich anrufen mursht-uh

call back: I'll call back later
ich komme später noch einmal
wieder ish komm-uh shpayter
nокн ine-mahl veeder

(phone back) ich rufe später
noch einmal an roof-uh

**call round: I'll call round
tomorrow** ich komme morgen
vorbei komm-uh – for-by

camcorder der Camcorder

camera die Kamera

camera shop der Fotoladen foto-lahden

camp (*verb*) zelten tselten

camping gas das Campinggas kemping-gahss

campsite der Campingplatz kempingplats

can (tin) die Dose dohz-uh

 a can of beer eine Dose Bier

can: can you...? kannst du/können Sie...? doo/kurnen zee

 can I have...? kann ich... haben? hahben

 I can't... ich kann nicht... nisht

Canada Kanada

Canadian (*adj*) kanadisch kanahdish

 I'm Canadian (*male/female*) ich bin Kanadier kanahdee-er/Kanadierin

canal der Kanal kanahl

cancel (reservation) rückgängig machen rook-geng-ish maKHen

candle die Kerze kairts-uh

candy die Süßigkeiten zoossish-kyten

canoe das Kanu kahnoo

canoeing das Kanufahren kahnoo-fahren

can-opener der Dosenöffner dohzen-urfner

cap (hat) eine Mütze moots-uh
 (of bottle) der Deckel

car das Auto owto

by car mit dem Auto

carafe die Karaffe karaff-uh

 a carafe of house white, please eine Karaffe weißen Tafelwein, bitte

caravan der Wohnwagen vohnvahgen

caravan site der Wohnwagenplatz vohnvahgen-plats

carburettor der Vergaser fair-gahzer

card (birthday etc) die Karte kart-uh

 here's my (business) card hier ist meine Karte

cardigan die Strickjacke shtrick-yack-uh

cardphone das Kartentelefon

careful vorsichtig for-zishtish

 be careful! seien Sie vorsichtig! zy-en zee

caretaker der Hausmeister howss-myster

car ferry die Autofähre owto-fair-uh

car hire die Autovermietung owto-fairmeetoong

carnival der Karneval karn-uh-val

car park der Parkplatz parkplats

carpet der Teppich teppish

carriage (of train) der Wagen vahgen

carrier bag die Tragetasche trahg-uh-tash-uh

carrot die Möhre mur-uh

carry tragen trahgen

carry-cot die Säuglingstragetasche zoyglings-trahg-uh-tash-uh

carton (of orange juice etc) die Packung packoong

carwash (place) die Autowaschanlage owto-vash-anlahg-uh

case (suitcase) der Koffer

cash das Bargeld bahrgelt

(*verb*) einlösen ine-lurzen

will you cash this for me? können Sie das für mich einlösen? kurnen

cash desk die Kasse kass-uh

cash dispenser der Geldautomat gelt-owtomaht

cassette die Kassette kassett-uh

cassette recorder der Kassettenrecorder

castle das Schloss shloss

casualty department die Unfallstation oonfal-shtats-yohn

cat die Katze kats-uh

catch fangen

where do we catch the bus to...? wo können wir den Bus nach… bekommen?

cathedral der Dom dohm

Catholic (*adj*) katholisch katohlish

cauliflower der Blumenkohl bloomenkohl

cave die Höhle hurl-uh

CD die CD tsay-day

ceiling die Decke deck-uh

celery der Sellerie zelleree

cellar (for wine) der Weinkeller vine-keller

cell phone das Handy hendi

cemetery der Friedhof freet-hohf

Centigrade Celsius tselzee-oos

centimetre der Zentimeter tsentimayter

central zentral tsentrahl

central heating die Zentralheizung tsentrahl-hytsoong

centre das Zentrum tsentroom

how do we get to the city centre? wie kommt man zum Stadtzentrum? tsoom shtatt-tsentroom

cereal die Zerealien tsairay-ahlee-en

certainly sicher zisher

certainly not ganz bestimmt nicht gants beshtimmt nisht

chair der Stuhl shtool

chairlift der Sessellift zessel-lift

champagne der Champagner shampan-yer

change (*noun: money*) das Wechselgeld veksel-gelt

to change (money) wechseln wekseln

to change a reservation umbuchen oombookHen

can I change this for...? kann ich das gegen… umtauschen? gaygen… oom-towshen

I don't have any change ich habe kein Kleingeld hahb-uh kine kline-gelt

can you give me change for a 50 euro note? können Sie einen 50-Euro-Schein

wechseln? **ku**rnen zee **ine**-en –
oyro-shine

**do we have to change
(trains/buses)?** müssen
wir umsteigen? m**oo**ssen veer
oom-shtygen

yes, change at Düsseldorf
ja, Sie müssen in Düsseldorf
umsteigen

no, it's direct nein, das ist
eine Direktverbindung

changed: to get changed sich
umziehen zish **oo**m-tsee-en

chapel die Kapelle kap**e**ll-uh

charge der Preis price

charge (*verb*) verlangen fair**l**angen

charge card die Kreditkarte
krayd**ee**t-kart-uh

cheap billig b**i**llish

**do you have anything
cheaper?** haben Sie
etwas billigeres? h**ah**ben zee
etvass b**i**lligeress

check (*verb*) überprüfen
oober-pr**oo**fen

**could you check the…
please?** könnten Sie die…
überprüfen, bitte? k**u**rnten
(US) der Scheck sheck
(in restaurant etc) die Rechnung
r**e**shnoong

check-in der Check-in

check in (at hotel) sich anmelden
zish
(at airport) einchecken
ine-checken

**where do we have to
check in?** wo müssen wir
einchecken?

cheek (of face) die Backe
b**a**ck-uh

cheerio! (bye-bye) tschüs! ch**oo**ss

cheers! (toast) Prost! prohst
(thanks) danke d**a**nkuh

cheese der Käse k**a**yz-uh

chemist's die Apotheke
apot**ay**k-uh

cheque der Scheck sheck

do you take cheques?
nehmen Sie Schecks?
n**ay**men zee shecks

cheque book das Scheckheft
sh**e**ck-heft

cheque card die Scheckkarte
sh**e**ck-kart-uh

cherry die Kirsche k**ee**rsh-uh

chess Schach shaкн

chest (body) die Brust broost

chewing gum der Kaugummi
k**ow**-goommee

chicken (as food) das Hähnchen
h**ay**nshen

chickenpox die Windpocken
v**i**ntpocken

child das Kind kint

children die Kinder

child minder die Tagesmutter
t**ah**gess-mootter

children's pool das
Kinderschwimmbecken
k**i**nder-shvimmbecken

children's portion der
Kinderteller k**i**nder-teller

chin das Kinn

china (*noun*) das Porzellan portsell**ah**n

Chinese (*adj*) chinesisch shin**ay**zish

chips die Pommes frites pom frit (US) die Chips

chocolate die Schokolade shokol**ah**d-uh

milk chocolate die Milchschokolade m**i**lsh-

plain chocolate die Bitterschokolade

chocolates die Pralinen pral**ee**nen

hot chocolate der Kakao kak**ow**

choose wählen v**ay**len

Christian name der Vorname f**o**rnahm-uh

Christmas Weihnachten v**y**naкнten

Christmas Eve der Heiligabend hylish-**ah**bent

merry Christmas! frohe Weihnachten fr**oh**-uh

church die Kirche k**ee**rsh-uh

cider der Apfelwein **a**pfel-vine

cigar die Zigarre tsig**a**rr-uh

cigarette die Zigarette tsig**a**rett-uh

cigarette lighter das Feuerzeug f**oy**er-tsoyk

cinema das Kino k**ee**no

circle der Kreis krice

(in theatre) der Balkon balk**oh**n

city die Stadt shtatt

city centre die Innenstadt **i**nnenshtatt

clean (*adj*) sauber z**ow**ber

can you clean this for me? können Sie dies für mich reinigen? k**ur**nen zee deess f**oo**r mish r**y**nigen

cleaning solution (for contact lenses) die Reinigungslösung r**y**nigoongs-lurzoong

cleansing lotion (cosmetic) die Reinigungscreme r**y**nigoongs-kraym

clear klar

clever klug kl**oo**k

cliff die Klippe kl**i**pp-uh

climbing das Bergsteigen b**ai**rk-shtygen

cling film die Frischhaltefolie fr**i**sh-halt-uh-fohlee-uh

clinic die Klinik kl**ee**nik

cloakroom (for coats) die Garderobe garder**oh**b-uh

clock die Uhr oor

close schließen shl**ee**essen

what time do you close?
wann schließen Sie?

we close at 8 p.m. on weekdays and 6 p.m. on Saturdays wir schließen wochentags um zwanzig Uhr und samstags um achtzehn Uhr voкнen-tahks oom – zams-tahks

do you close for lunch? haben Sie mittags geschlossen? geshlossen

yes, between 1 and 2.30 p.m. ja, von dreizehn Uhr bis vierzehn Uhr dreißig

closed geschlossen geshlossen
cloth (fabric) der Stoff shtoff
(for cleaning etc) der Lappen
clothes die Kleider klyder
clothes line die Wäscheleine vesh-uh-line-uh
clothes peg die Wäscheklammer vesh-uh-klammer
cloud die Wolke volk-uh
cloudy wolkig volkish
clutch (of car) die Kupplung kooploong
coach (bus) der Bus booss
(on train) der Wagen vahgen
coach station der Busbahnhof boossbahnhohf
coach trip die Busreise booss-rize-uh
coast die Küste koost-uh
on the coast an der Küste

coat (long coat) der Mantel
(jacket) die Jacke yack-uh
coathanger der Kleiderbügel klyderboogel
cockroach die Küchenschabe kooshen-shahb-uh
cocoa der Kakao kakow
code (for phoning) die Vorwahl forvahl
what's the (dialling) code for Berlin? was ist die Vorwahl für Berlin?
coffee der Kaffee kaffay
two coffees, please zwei Kaffee bitte
coin die Münze moonts-uh
Coke die Cola kohla
cold (adj) kalt
I'm cold mir ist kalt meer
I have a cold ich bin erkältet ish bin airkeltet
collapse: he's collapsed er ist zusammengebrochen air ist tsoozammengebrokнen
collar der Kragen krahgen
collect sammeln
I've come to collect... ich komme, um... abzuholen ish komm-uh oom... ap-tsoo-hohlen
collect call das R-Gespräch air-geshpraysh
college das College
Cologne Köln kurln
colour die Farbe farb-uh
do you have this in other colours? haben Sie dies noch

in anderen Farben? ha**h**ben zee deess no**KH** in **a**nder-en f**a**rben

comb (*noun*) der Kamm

come k**o**mmen

where do you come from? woher kommen Sie? voh**ai**r

I come from Edinburgh ich komme aus Edinburgh ish k**o**mm-uh owss

come back zurückkommen ts**oo**r**oo**ck-kommen

I'll come back tomorrow ich komme morgen zurück k**o**mm-uh m**o**rgen zur**oo**ck

come in hereinkommen hair-**ine**-kommen

comfortable (hotel etc) komfortabel komfort**ah**bel

compact disc die Compact-Disc

company (business) die Firma f**ee**rma

compartment (on train) das Abteil apt**ile**

compass der Kompass k**o**mpass

complain sich beschweren zish beshv**ai**ren

complaint die Beschwerde beshv**ai**rd-uh

I have a complaint ich möchte mich beschweren m**u**rsht-uh mish beshv**ai**ren

completely völlig f**u**rlish

computer der Computer

concert das Konzert konts**ai**rt

concussion die Gehirn-erschütterung geh**ee**rn-airsh**oo**tteroong

conditioner (for hair) der Festiger

condom das Kondom kond**oh**m

conference die Konferenz konfair**e**nts

confirm bestätigen besht**ay**tigen

congratulations! herzlichen Glückwunsch! h**ai**rtslishen gl**oo**ckvoonsh

connecting flight der Anschlussflug **a**nshlooss-flook

connection (in travelling) die Verbindung fairb**i**ndoong

conscious (medically) bei Bewusstsein by bev**oo**st-zine

constipation die Verstopfung fair-sht**o**pfoong

consulate das Konsulat konzool**ah**t

contact: where can I contact

him? wo kann ich ihn
erreichen? vo – een air-ryshen

contact lenses die
Kontaktlinsen kontakt-linzen

contraceptive das
Verhütungsmittel
fairhootoongs-mittel

convenient (time, location)
günstig goonstish

that's not convenient das ist
nicht sehr günstig nisht zair

cook kochen koKHen

not cooked (underdone) nicht
gar nisht gahr

cooker der Herd hairt

cookie (US) das Plätzchen
plets-shen

cooking utensils die
Küchengeräte kooshen-gerayt-uh

cool kühl kool

cork der Korken

corkscrew der Korkenzieher
korken-tsee-er

corner: on the corner an der
Ecke eck-uh

in the corner in der Ecke

cornflakes die Corn-flakes

correct (right) richtig rishtish

corridor der Gang

cosmetics die Kosmetika
kosmaytika

cost (verb) kosten

how much does it cost? was
kostet das? vass kostet dass

cot (for baby) das Kinderbett

cotton die Baumwolle
bowmvoll-uh

cotton wool die Watte vat-uh

couch (sofa) die Couch

couchette der Liegewagen
leeg-uh-vahgen

cough (noun) der Husten hoosten

cough medicine das
Hustenmittel hoosten-mittel

could: could you…? könnten
Sie…? kurnten zee

could I have…? könnte ich…
haben? kurnt-uh ish… hahben

I couldn't… (wasn't able to) ich
konnte nicht…
ish konnt-uh nisht

country das Land lant

countryside die Landschaft
lant-shafft

couple (man and woman)
das Paar pahr

a couple of… ein paar…
ine pahr

courier der Reiseleiter rize-
uh-lyter

course (of meal) der Gang

of course natürlich natoorlish

of course not natürlich nicht
nisht

cousin (male) der Vetter fetter
(female) die Kusine koozeen-uh

cow die Kuh koo

crab die Krebs krayps

cracker (biscuit) der Kräcker
krecker

craft shop der Handwerksladen
hantvairks-lahden

crash (noun) der Zusammenstoß
tsoo-zammen-shtohss

I've had a crash ich hatte

einen Unfall ish hatt-uh **ine**-en **oo**nfal

crazy verrückt fair-r**oo**ckt

cream (on milk, in cake) die Sahne **zah**n-uh

(lotion) die Creme kraym

(colour) cremefarben kra**y**m-farben

creche (for babies) die Kinderkrippe **k**inderkripp-uh

credit card die Kreditkarte kred**ee**t-kart-uh

can I pay by credit card? kann ich mit Kreditkarte bezahlen? bets**ah**len

which card do you want to use? mit welcher Karte möchten Sie bezahlen? **v**elsher

what's the number? was ist die Nummer? n**oo**mmer

and the expiry date? und das Ablaufdatum? a**p**l**ow**f-dahtoom

credit crunch die Kreditkrise kra**y**d**ee**t-kreez-uh

crisps die Chips chips

crockery das Geschirr gesh**ee**r

crossing (by sea) die Überfahrt **oo**berfahrt

crossroads die Kreuzung kr**oy**tsoong

crowd die Menge m**e**ng-uh

crowded (streets, bars) voll foll

crown (on tooth) die Krone kr**oh**n-uh

cruise (by ship) die Kreuzfahrt

kr**oy**ts-fahrt

crutches die Krücken kr**oo**ck-en

cry weinen v**y**nen

cucumber die Gurke g**oo**rk-uh

cup die Tasse t**a**ss-uh

a cup of... please eine Tasse..., bitte **ine**-uh

cupboard der Schrank shrank

curly (hair) kraus kr**o**wss

current (electrical, in water) der Strom shtrohm

(in sea) die Strömung sht**r**u**r**moong

curtains die Vorhänge f**o**rheng-uh

cushion das Kissen k**i**ssen

custom der Brauch br**o**wкн

Customs der Zoll tsoll

cut der Schnitt shnitt

cut (*verb*) schneiden shn**y**den

I've cut myself ich habe mich geschnitten ish h**a**hb-uh mish gesh**ni**tten

cutlery das Besteck besht**e**ck

cycling das Radfahren r**a**htfahren

cyclist (*male/female*) der Radfahrer r**a**htfahrer/die Radfahrerin

Czech (*adj*) tschechisch ch**e**shish

(language) Tschechisch

Czech Republic die Tschechische Republik ch**e**shish-uh rep**oo**-bl**ee**k

D

dad der Vater f**a**hter

daily täglich t**a**yglish

damage (*verb*) beschädigen
besh**ay**digen

I'm sorry, I've damaged
this tut mir Leid, ich habe es
beschädigt t00t meer lite

damaged beschädigt
beshaydisht

damn! verdammt! fairdamt

damp feucht foysht

dance (*noun*) der Tanz tants

dance (*verb*) tanzen tantsen

would you like to dance?
möchtest du/möchten
Sie tanzen? murshtest d00/
murshten zee

dangerous gefährlich gef**air**lish

Danish dänisch daynish

Danube die Donau dohnow

dark dunkel doonkel

it's getting dark es wird
dunkel veert

date: what's the date today?
der Wievielte ist heute?
dair veef**ee**lt-uh ist h**oy**t-uh

let's make a date for next
Monday wir sollten einen
Termin für nächsten Montag
vereinbaren **ine**-en tairmeen f00r
– fair-**ine**-bahren

dates (fruit) die Datteln

daughter die Tochter toKHter

daughter-in-law die
Schwiegertochter
shv**ee**ger-toKHter

dawn das Morgengrauen
m**o**rgen-growen

at dawn bei Tagesanbruch by
t**ah**gess-anbr00KH

day der Tag tahk

the day after am Tag danach
danaKH

the day after tomorrow
übermorgen **00**bermorgen

the day before am Tag zuvor
ts00f**o**r

the day before yesterday
vorgestern f**o**rgestern

every day jeden Tag **yay**den

all day den ganzen Tag dayn
g**a**ntsen

in two days' time in zwei
Tagen t**ah**gen

have a nice day schönen Tag
noch sh**u**rnen – noKH

day trip der Tagesausflug
t**ah**gess-owssfl00k

dead tot toht

deaf taub towp

deal (business) das Geschäft
gesh**e**ft

it's a deal abgemacht
ap-gemaKHt

death der Tod toht

decaffeinated coffee
koffeinfreier Kaffee koffay-**ee**n-
fry-er k**a**ffay

December der Dezember
dayts**e**mber

decide entscheiden ent-sh**y**den

we haven't decided yet
wir haben uns noch nicht
entschieden veer h**a**hben oonss
noKH nisht ent-sh**ee**den

decision die Entscheidung
ent-sh**y**doong

deck (on ship) das Deck

deckchair der Liegestuhl
leeg-uh-shtool

deduct abziehen ap-tsee-en

deep tief teef

definitely bestimmt beshtimmt

definitely not ganz bestimmt
nicht gants

degree (qualification) der
Abschluss apshlooss

delay die Verzögerung
fair-tsurgeroong

deliberately absichtlich
apzishtlish

delicatessen der Feinkostladen
fine-kost-lahden

delicious köstlich kurstlish

deliver liefern leefern

delivery (of mail) die Zustellung
tsoo-shtelloong

Denmark Dänemark dayn-uh-mark

dental floss die Zahnseide
tsahnzide-uh

dentist der Zahnarzt tsahn-artst

DIALOGUE

it's this one here es ist
dieser hier deezer heer
this one? dieser?
no that one nein, dieser nine
here? hier? heer
yes ja yah

dentures das Gebiss

deodorant das Deodorant

department die Abteilung
ap-tyloong

department store das Kaufhaus
kowfhowss

departure die Abreise ap-rize-uh

(of plane) der Abflug apflook

departure lounge die
Abflughalle apflook-hal-uh

depend: it depends es kommt
darauf an ess kommt darowf an

it depends on... es hängt
von... ab hengt fon... ap

deposit (as security) die Kaution
kowts-yohn

(as part payment) die Anzahlung
antsahloong

description die Beschreibung
beshryboong

dessert der Nachtisch naкнtish

destination das Reiseziel
rize-uh-tseel

develop entwickeln entvickeln

diabetic (*male/female*) der
Diabetiker dee-abaytiker/die
Diabetikerin

diabetic foods diabetische Kost
dee-abaytish-uh

dial (*verb*) wählen vaylen

dialling code die Vorwahl
forvahl

diamond der Diamant
dee-amant

diaper die Windel vindel

diarrhoea der Durchfall doorshfal

diary (business etc) der
Terminkalender
tairmeen-kalender

(for personal experiences) das
Tagebuch tahg-uh-booкн

dictionary das Wörterbuch
vurterbooкн

didn't

see **not**

die sterben sht**ai**rben

diesel der D**ie**sel

diet die Diät dee-**ay**t

  I'm on a diet ich mache eine Diät ish ma**KH**-uh **i**ne-uh

  I have to follow a special diet ich muss nach einer Diät leben mooss na**KH** **i**ne-er – l**ay**ben

difference der Unterschied **oo**ntersheet

  what's the difference? was ist der Unterschied?

different verschieden fair-sh**ee**den

  this one is different d**ie**ses ist **a**nders

  a different table ein **a**nderer Tisch

difficult schwer shv**ai**r

difficulty die Schwierigkeit shv**ee**rish-kite

dinghy (rubber) das Schlauchboot shl**ow**KHboht

  (sailing) das Dingi d**i**ng-gee

dining room das Speisezimmer shp**i**ze-uh-tsimmer

dinner (evening meal) das Abendessen **ah**bentessen

  to have dinner zu **A**bend **e**ssen ts**oo**

direct (*adj*) direkt deer**e**kt

  is there a direct train? gibt es eine direkte Zugverbindung? ts**oo**k-fairbindoong

direction die Richtung r**i**shtoong

  which direction is it? in welcher Richtung ist es? v**e**lsher

  is it in this direction? ist es in dieser Richtung? d**ee**zer

directory enquiries die Auskunft **ow**sskoonft

dirt der Schmutz shmoots

dirty schmutzig shm**oo**tsish

disabled behindert

  is there access for the disabled? gibt es Zugang für Behinderte? geept ess ts**oo**gang f**oo**r behindert-uh

disappear verschwinden fairshv**i**nden

  it's disappeared es ist verschwunden fairshv**oo**nden

disappointed enttäuscht ent-t**oy**sht

disappointing enttäuschend ent-t**oy**shent

disaster die Katastrophe katastr**oh**f-uh

disco die Diskothek diskot**ay**k

discount der Rabatt rabb**a**t

  is there a discount? gibt es einen Rabatt? geept ess **i**ne-en

disease die Krankheit kr**a**nk-hite

disgusting widerlich v**ee**derlish

dish (meal) das Gericht ger**i**sht

  (bowl) der T**e**ller

dishcloth das Spültuch shp**oo**ltooKH

disinfectant das Desinfektionsmittel dezinfekts-y**oh**ns-mittel

disk (for computer) die Diskette disk**e**tt-uh

disposable nappies/diapers
die Papierwindeln *papeer-vindeln*

distance die Entfernung *ent-fairnoong*

in the distance weit weg *vite vek*

distilled water destilliertes Wasser *destilleertess vasser*

district das Gebiet *gebeet*

disturb stören *shtur-ren*

diversion (detour) die Umleitung *oom-lytoong*

diving board das Sprungbrett *shproongbrett*

divorced geschieden *gesheeden*

dizzy: I feel dizzy mir ist schwindlig *meer ist shvintlish*

do tun *toon*

what shall we do? was sollen wir tun? *vass zollen veer toon*

how do you do it? wie machen Sie das? *vee makhen zee*

will you do it for me? können Sie das für mich tun? *kurnen Sie das für mich tun*

what are you doing this evening? was machst du/machen Sie heute abend? *makhst doo/makhen zee hoyt-uh ahbent*

we're going out for a drink, do you want to join us? wir gehen einen trinken, möchtest du/möchten Sie mitkommen? *murshtest doo/murshten zee*

do you want cream? möchtest du/möchten Sie Sahne?

I do, but she doesn't ich ja, aber sie nicht *yah*

doctor der Arzt *artst*

we need a doctor wir brauchen einen Arzt *veer browkhen ine-en*

please call a doctor bitte rufen Sie einen Arzt *bitt-uh roofen zee*

document das Dokument
dok00ment

dog der Hund hoont

doll die Puppe poop-uh

domestic flight der Inlandflug
inlant-fl00k

don't *see* **not**

don't do that! tu das/tun
Sie das nicht! t00 dass/t00n
zee dass nisht

door die Tür t00r

doorman der Portier portyay

double doppelt

double bed das Doppelbett

double room das
Doppelzimmer doppel-tsimmer

doughnut der Berliner
bairleener

down: down here hier unten
heer oonten

put it down over there
setzen Sie es hier ab
zetsen zee ess heer ap

it's down there on the right
es ist hier unten rechts

it's further down the road
es ist weiter die Straße entlang
vyter dee shtrahss-uh entlang

downhill skiing der Abfahrtslauf
apfahrts-lowf

download (*verb*) herunterladen
hair00nter-lahden

downmarket (restaurant etc)
weniger anspruchsvoll vayniger
anshprookHsfoll

downstairs unten oonten

dozen das Dutzend d00tsent

half a dozen sechs Stück

zeks sht00ck

drain (in sink, street) der Abfluss
ap-flooss

draught beer das Fassbier
fassbeer

draughty: it's draughty es zieht
ess tseet

drawer die Schublade
sh00plahd-uh

drawing die Zeichnung
tsyshnoong

dreadful furchtbar foorshtbar

dream der Traum trowm

dress das Kleid klite

dressed: to get dressed sich
anziehen zish antsee-en

dressing (for cut) der Verband
fairbant

salad dressing die Salatsoße
zalahtzohss-uh

dressing gown der Bademantel
bahd-uh-mantel

drink (alcoholic) der Drink
(non-alcoholic) das Getränk
getrenk
(*verb*) trinken

a cold drink ein kaltes
Getränk

can I get you a drink?
kann ich Ihnen etwas zu
trinken besorgen? etvass ts00
– bezorgen

**what would you like to
drink?** was möchtest du/
möchten Sie zu trinken?
murshtest d00/murshten zee

no thanks, I don't drink
nein danke, ich trinke nicht

trink-uh nisht

**I'll just have a drink of
water** ich möchte nur etwas
Wasser

drinking water das Trinkwasser
trinkvasser

is this drinking water?
ist das Trinkwasser?

drive (*verb*) fahren

we drove here wir sind mit
dem Auto gekommen veer zint
mit daym **ow**to gekommen

I'll drive you home ich fahre
Sie nach Hause ish fahr-uh zee
naKH howz-uh

driver (*male/female*) der Fahrer/
die Fahrerin

driving licence der
Führerschein f**oo**rer-shine

drop: just a drop please
(of drink) nur einen Tropfen
noor **ine**-en

drug (medical) das Medikament

drugs (narcotics) die Drogen
dro**h**gen

drunk (*adj*) betrunken betr**oo**nken

drunken driving Trunkenheit
am Steuer tr**oo**nken-hite
am sht**oy**er

dry (*adj*) trocken

dry-cleaner die chemische
Reinigung sh**ay**mish-uh
r**y**nigoong

duck die Ente **ent**-uh

**due: he was due to arrive
yesterday** er sollte gestern
ankommen air z**o**llt-uh

when is the train due? wann
kommt der Zug an?

dull (pain) dumpf doompf
(weather) trüb tr**oo**p

dummy (baby's) der Schnuller
shn**oo**ller

during während v**ai**rent

dust der Staub shtowp

dusty staubig sht**ow**bish

dustbin die Mülltonne
m**oo**lltonn-uh

Dutch (*adj*) holländisch h**o**llendish
(language) Holländisch

duty-free (goods) zollfreie
Waren ts**o**llfry-uh v**ah**ren

duty-free shop der Duty-
free-Shop

duvet das Federbett f**ay**derbet

DVD die DVD day-vay-d**ay**

E

each (every) jeder y**ay**der

  how much are they each?
was kosten sie pro Stück?
vass k**o**sten zee pro sht**oo**k

ear das Ohr

earache Ohrenschmerzen
ohren-shm**ai**rtsen

early früh fr**oo**

  early in the morning
früh am M**o**rgen

  I called by earlier
ich war schon einmal hier
sh**oh**n **ine**-mahl heer

earring der **O**hrring

east der **O**sten

  in the east im Osten

Easter Ostern **oh**stern

easy leicht l**y**sht

eat **e**ssen

  **we've already eaten,
thanks** d**a**nke, wir haben
schon gegessen h**ah**ben sh**oh**n

eau de toilette das Eau de
toilette

EC die EG ay-g**ay**

economy class die Touristen-
klasse t**oo**risten-klass-uh

egg das Ei **ī**

Eire Irland **ee**rlant

either: either… or… entweder…
oder… **e**ntvayder… **oh**der

  either, I don't mind egal
welcher ayg**ah**l v**e**lsher

elastic der Gummi g**oo**mmee

elastic band das Gummiband
g**oo**mmeebant

elbow der **E**llbogen

electric elektrisch ayl**e**ktrish

electric fire das elektrische
Heizgerät ayl**e**ktrish-uh
h**ī**tes-gerayt

electrician der Elektriker
ayl**e**ktriker

electricity der Strom shtr**oh**m

elevator der Aufzug
owf-ts**oo**k

else: something else etwas
anderes **e**tvass **a**nderess

  somewhere else w**o**anders
vo-**a**nders

  **would you like anything
else?** möchten Sie noch
etwas? m**u**rshten

  no, nothing else, thanks
d**a**nke, das ist alles d**a**nk-uh
dass ist **a**l-ess

e-mail die E-Mail
(*verb*) mailen m**ay**len

embassy die Botschaft
b**oh**t-shafft

emergency der Notfall n**oh**t-fal

  this is an emergency! dies
ist ein Notfall! deess ist ine

emergency exit der Notausgang
n**oh**t-owssgang

empty leer lair

end das Ende **e**nd-uh

  at the end of the street am
Ende der Straße

end (*verb*) enden

when does it end?
wann ist es zu Ende?
vann ist ess ts00 end-uh

engaged (toilet, telephone) besetzt
bezetst

(to be married) verlobt fairlohpt

engine der Motor mohtohr

England England eng-lant

English englisch eng-lish

I'm English (*male/female*)
ich bin Engländer eng-lender/
Engländerin

do you speak English?
sprichst du/sprechen Sie
Englisch? shprisht d00/
shpreshen zee

enjoy: to enjoy oneself sich
amüsieren zish am00zeeren

DIALOGUE

how did you like the film?
wie hat dir/Ihnen der Film
gefallen? vee hat deer/eenen
dair

**I enjoyed it very much –
did you?** er hat mir sehr
gut gefallen – dir/Ihnen
auch? meer zair g00t – deer/
eenen owKH

enjoyable unterhaltsam
oonter-halt-zahm

(meal) angenehm an-genaym

enlargement (of photo) die
Vergrößerung fairgrursseroong

enormous enorm aynorm

enough genug gen00k

there's not enough... es ist
nicht genug... da ess ist nisht

it's not big enough es ist
nicht groß genug

that's enough das genügt dass
gen00kt

entrance der Eingang ine-gang

envelope der Umschlag
oomshlahk

epileptic (*male/female*) der
Epileptiker/die Epileptikerin

equipment (for climbing etc) die
Ausrüstung owss-r00stoong

error der Fehler fayler

especially besonders bezonders

essential wesentlich vayzentlish

it is essential that... es ist
unbedingt notwendig,
dass... oonbedingt nohtvendish

Estonia Estland estlant

EU die EU ay-00

euro der Euro oyro

Eurocheque der Euroscheck
oyro-sheck

Eurocheque card die
Euroscheckkarte oyro-sheck-
kart-uh

Europe Europa oyrohpa

European europäisch
oyrohpayish

even sogar zogahr, selbst zelpst

even if... selbst wenn... ven

evening der Abend ahbent

this evening heute abend
hoyt-uh

in the evening am Abend

evening meal das Abendessen
ahbent-essen

eventually schließlich shl**ee**sslish

ever jemals **yay**mahls

have you ever been to Heidelberg? waren Sie schon einmal in Heidelberg? v**ah**ren zee shohn **ine**-mahl

yes, I was there two years ago ja, ich war vor zwei Jahren da for – y**ah**ren

every jeder y**ay**der

every day jeden Tag y**ay**den tahk

everyone jeder y**ay**der

everything alles **al**-ess

everywhere überall **oo**ber-al

exactly! genau! gen**ow**

exam die Prüfung pr**oo**foong

example das Beispiel b**y**shpeel

for example zum Beispiel tsoom

excellent hervorragend hairf**or**-rahgent

excellent ausgezeichnet owss-gets**y**shnet

except außer **ow**sser

excess baggage das Übergewicht **oo**bergevisht

exchange rate der Wechselkurs v**e**ckselkoorss

exciting (day, holiday) aufregend **ow**f-raygent

(film) spannend sh**pa**nnent

excuse me (to get past) entschuldigen Sie! ent-sh**oo**ldigen zee

(to get attention) Entschuldigung! ent-sh**oo**ldigoong

(to say sorry) Verzeihung fair-ts**y**-oong

exhaust (pipe) der Auspuff **ow**sspooff

exhausted erschöpft airsh**ur**pft

exhibition die Ausstellung **ow**ss-shtelloong

exit der Ausgang **ow**ssgang

where's the nearest exit? wo ist der nächste Ausgang? dair n**ay**kst-uh

expect erwarten airv**ar**ten

expensive teuer t**oy**er

experienced erfahren airf**ah**ren

explain erklären airkl**ai**ren

can you explain that? könnten Sie mir das erklären? k**ur**nten zee meer

express (mail) per Express pair

(train) der Schnellzug shn**e**llts00k

extension (telephone) der Anschluss **a**nshlooss

extension 21, please Anschluss einundzwanzig bitte b**i**tt-uh

extension lead die Verlängerungsschnur fairl**e**ngeroongs-shn00r

extra: can we have an extra one? können wir noch eins haben? k**ur**nen veer noKH **ine**-ss h**ah**ben

do you charge extra for that? k**o**stet das extra?

extraordinary außergewöhnlich **ow**sser-gev**ur**nlish

extremely äußerst **oy**sserst

eye das Auge **ow**g-uh

    will you keep an eye on my suitcase for me? könnten Sie auf meinen Koffer aufpassen? **ku**rnten zee – **ow**fpassen

eyebrow pencil der Augenbrauenstift **ow**genbrowen-shtift

eye drops die Augentropfen **ow**gen-tropfen

eyeglasses die Brille br**i**ll-uh

eyeliner der Eyeliner

eye make-up remover der Augen-Make-up-Entferner **ow**gen-make-up-entf**ai**rner

eye shadow der Lidschatten l**ee**t-shatten

F

face das Gesicht gez**i**sht

factory die Fabrik fabr**ee**k

Fahrenheit Fahrenheit

faint (*verb*) ohnmächtig werden **oh**nmeshtish v**ai**rden

    she's fainted sie ist ohnmächtig geworden zee ist – gev**o**rden

    I feel faint mir ist ganz schwach meer ist gants shvakH

fair (*funfair*) der Jahrmarkt y**ah**rmarkt

    (*trade*) die Messe m**e**ss-uh

fair (*adj*) fair

fairly ziemlich ts**ee**mlish

fake die Fälschung f**e**lshoong

fall (*verb*) fallen f**a**l-en

    she's had a fall sie ist hingefallen zee ist hin-gefal-en

    (US: *autumn*) der Herbst hairpst

false falsch falsh

family die Familie fam**ee**lee-uh

famous berühmt ber**oo**mt

fan (*electrical*) der Ventilator ventilah-tor

    (*hand held*) der Fächer f**e**sher

    (*sports*) der Fan fen

fan belt der Keilriemen k**i**le-reemen

fantastic fant**a**stisch

far weit vite

DIALOGUE

is it far from here? ist es weit von hier? fon heer

no, not very far nein, nicht sehr weit nisht zair

well how far? wie weit denn? vee

it's about 10 kilometres es sind etwa zehn Kilometer **e**tvah

---

fare der Fahrpreis f**a**hrprice

farm der Bauernhof b**ow**ernhohf

fashionable modisch m**oh**dish

fast schnell

fat (*person*) dick

    (*on meat*) das Fett

father der Vater f**a**hter

father-in-law der Schwiegervater shv**ee**ger-fahter

faucet der Wasserhahn v**a**sserhahn

fault der Fehler f**ay**ler

  sorry, it was my fault tut mir Leid, es war mein F**e**hler mine

  it's not my fault es ist nicht meine Schuld nisht m**i**ne-uh shoolt

faulty defekt day**fe**kt

favourite Lieblings- l**ee**plings

fax das Fax faks

fax (*verb*) (person) per Fax benachrichtigen pair faks ben**a**kH-rishtigen

  (document) f**a**xen

February der Februar f**ay**br00ar

feel fühlen f**00**len

  I feel hot mir ist heiß meer ist h**i**ce

  I feel unwell mir ist nicht gut nisht g**00**t

  I feel like going for a walk mir ist nach einem Spaz**ie**rgang n**a**KH

  how are you feeling? wie fühlen Sie sich? vee f**00**len zee zish

  I'm feeling better es geht mir b**e**sser ess gayt meer

felt-tip (pen) der Filzstift f**i**lts-shtift

fence der Zaun tsown

fender (US) die Stoßstange sht**oh**ss-shtang-uh

ferry die Fähre f**ai**r-uh

festival das Festival f**e**stivahl

fetch holen h**oh**len

  I'll fetch him ich hole ihn h**oh**l-uh

will you come and fetch me later? können Sie mich später abholen? k**ur**nen zee mish shp**ay**ter **a**p-hohlen

feverish: she's still feverish sie hat noch immer Fieber zee hat noKH immer f**ee**ber

few: a few ein paar ine pahr

  a few days ein paar T**a**ge

fiancé: my fiancé mein Verlobter mine fairl**oh**pter

fiancée: my fiancée meine Verlobte m**i**ne-uh fairl**oh**pt-uh

field das Feld felt

fight der Kampf

file die Datei da-t**y**

fill füllen f**00**llen

fill in ausfüllen **ow**ssf00llen

  do I have to fill this in? muss ich das ausfüllen? m**oo**ss

fill up voll machen foll m**a**KHen

  fill it up, please volltanken bitte f**o**lltanken b**i**tt-uh

filling (in sandwich) der Belag bel**ah**k

  (in cake, tooth) die Füllung f**00**lloong

film der Film

filter coffee der Filterkaffee f**i**lter-kaffay

filter papers das Filterpapier f**i**lter-papeer

filthy dreckig dr**e**ckish

find finden f**i**nden

  I can't find it ich kann es nicht finden ish kann ess nisht

I've found it ich habe es gefunden ge**foo**nden

find out herausfinden her**ow**ss-finden

could you find out for me? könnten Sie das für mich herausfinden? **kur**nten zee dass f**oo**r mish

fine (weather) schön shurn

(punishment) die Geldstrafe gelt-shtrahf-uh

how are you? wie geht's? vee gayts

I'm fine thanks danke, gut g**oo**t

is that OK? ist das ok**ay**?

that's fine thanks in Ordnung, danke **o**rdnoong

finger der Finger **fi**ng-er

finish (verb) beenden buh-**e**nden

I haven't finished yet ich bin noch nicht fertig ish bin noKH nisht f**ai**rtish

when does it finish? wann ist es zu Ende? van ist ess ts**oo** **e**nd-uh

fire das Feuer f**oy**-er

can we light a fire here? können wir hier ein Feuer machen? **ku**rnen veer heer – ma**KH**en

it's on fire es brennt

fire alarm der Feueralarm f**oy**-er-alarm

fire brigade die Feuerwehr f**oy**-er-vair

fire escape die Feuertreppe f**oy**-er-trepp-uh, die Feuerleiter f**oy**-er-lyter

fire extinguisher der Feuerlöscher f**oy**-er-lursher

first erster **ai**rster

I was first (male/female) ich war der/die erste dair/dee **ai**rst-uh

at first zuerst ts**oo**-**ai**rst

the first time das erste Mal

first on the left die erste Straße links

first aid die Erste Hilfe **ai**rst-uh h**i**lf-uh

first aid kit die Erste-Hilfe-Ausrüstung **ai**rst-uh h**i**lf-uh **ow**ssr**oo**stoong

first class erster Klasse **ai**rster kl**a**ss-uh

first floor der erste Stock **ai**rst-uh shtock

(US) das Erdgeschoss **ai**rt-geshoss

first name der Vorname f**o**rnahm-uh

fish der Fisch fish

fishmonger's der Fischhändler fish-hentler

fit (attack) der Anfall **a**n-fal

it doesn't fit me es passt mir nicht meer nisht

fitting room der Anproberaum anprohb-uh-rowm

fix (arrange, sort out) regeln r**ay**geln

can you fix this? (repair)

können Sie das reparieren?
kurnen zee dass repar**ee**ren

fizzy sprudelnd shpr**oo**delnt

flag die Fahne **fahn**-uh

flannel der Waschlappen
vashlappen

flash (for camera) der Blitz

flat (apartment) die Wohnung
vohnoong

(adj) flach flak**H**

I've got a flat tyre ich habe
einen Platten ish h**ah**b-uh **ine**-en

flavour der Geschmack geshmack

flea der Floh

flight der Flug fl**oo**k

flight number die Flugnummer
fl**oo**k-noommer

flippers die Schwimmflossen
shv**i**mflossen

flood die Flut fl**oo**t

floor (of room) der Fußboden
f**oo**ssbohden

(storey) das Stockwerk
sht**o**ckvairk

on the floor auf dem Boden
owf daym **boh**den

on the third floor im dritten
Stock

florist der Blumenhändler
bl**oo**men-hentler

flour das Mehl mayl

flower die Blume bl**oo**m-uh

flu die Grippe gr**i**pp-uh

**fluent: he speaks fluent
German** er spricht fließend
Deutsch air shprisht fl**ee**ssent
doytch

fly (insect) die Fliege fl**ee**g-uh

fly (verb) fliegen fl**ee**gen

fly in einfliegen **ine**-fleegen

fly out abfliegen **a**pfleegen

fog der Nebel n**ay**bel

foggy: it's foggy es ist neblig
n**ay**blish

folk dancing der Volkstanz
f**o**llks-tants

folk music die Volksmusik
f**o**llks-m**oo**zeek

follow folgen

follow me folgen Sie mir zee
meer

food das Essen

food poisoning die
Lebensmittelvergiftung
l**ay**bensmittel-fairg**i**ftoong

food shop/store das
Lebensmittelgeschäft
l**ay**bensmittel-gesheft

foot der Fuß f**oo**ss

on foot zu Fuß ts**oo**

football der Fußball f**oo**ssbal

football match das Fußballspiel
f**oo**ssbal-shpeel

for für f**oo**r

**do you have something
for...?** (headaches/diarrhoea
etc) haben Sie etwas gegen...?
h**ah**ben zee **e**tvass g**ay**gen

who's the bratwurst for?
für wen ist die Bratwurst?
vayn

that's for me das ist für
mich mish

DIALOGUE

and this one? und das hier?

that's for her das ist für
sie zee

**where do I get the bus for
Stuttgart?** wo fährt der
Bus nach Stuttgart ab? vo
fairt – naKH

**the bus for Stuttgart
leaves from
Schillerstraße** der Bus
nach Stuttgart fährt von der
Schillerstraße

**how long have you been
here for?** wie lange sind
Sie schon hier? vee lang-uh
zint zee shohn heer

**I've been here for two
days, how about you?**
ich bin seit zwei Tagen hier,
und Sie? zite

I've been here for a week
ich bin seit einer Woche
hier

forehead die Stirn shteern

foreign ausländisch **ow**sslendish

foreigner (*male/female*) der
Ausländer **ow**sslender/die
Ausländerin

forest der Wald vallt

forget vergessen fair**ge**ssen

I forget, I've forgotten ich
habe es vergessen ish ha**h**b-uh ess

fork (for eating) die Gabel ga**h**bel

(in road) die Abzweigung
ap-tsvygoong

form (document) das Formular
form**OO**la**hr**

formal (dress) form**ell**

fortnight zwei Wochen
tsvy v**o**KHen

fortress die Festung f**e**stoong

fortunately glücklicherweise
gl**OO**ck-lisher-vize-uh

**forward: could you forward
my mail?** könnten Sie meine
Post nachsenden? **k**ur**n**ten zee
m**i**ne-uh posst na**KH**-zenden

forwarding address die
Nachsendeadresse
na**KH**zend-uh-adress-uh

foundation cream die
Grundierungscreme
groond**ee**roongs-kraym

fountain der Brunnen br**oo**nnen

foyer das Foyer foy-y**ay**

fracture der Bruch br**oo**KH

France Frankreich fr**a**nk-rysh

free frei fry

(no charge) kostenlos
k**o**stenlohss, gratis gr**ah**tiss

is it free (of charge)?
ist es gratis?

freeway die Autobahn **ow**tobahn

freezer die Gefriertruhe
gefr**ee**rtr**OO**-uh

French (*adj*) französisch
frants**u**rzish

(language) Französisch

French fries die Pommes frites
pom frit

frequent häufig h**oy**fish

**how frequent is the bus
to Kiel?** wie oft fährt der Bus

nach Kiel? vee oft fairt

fresh frisch frish

fresh orange juice der
natürliche Orangensaft
nat**oo**rlish-uh or**o**nJenzaft

Friday Freitag fr**y**tahk

fridge der Kühlschrank
k**oo**lshrank

fried gebraten gebr**ah**ten

fried egg das Spiegelei shp**ee**gel-ī

friend (*male/female*) der Freund
fr**oy**nt/die Freundin fr**oy**ndin

friendly freundlich fr**oy**ntlish

from von fon

>   **when does the next train
>   from Bremen arrive?** wann
>   kommt der nächste Zug aus
>   Br**e**men an? der n**a**ykst-uh
>   ts**oo**k owss

>   **from Monday to Friday** von
>   Montag bis Fr**ei**tag

>   **from next Thursday**
>   ab nächsten D**o**nnerstag

DIALOGUE

>   **where are you from?**
>   woher kommst du/
>   kommen Sie? voh**ai**r kommst
>   d**oo**/k**o**mmen zee

>   **I'm from Slough** ich bin aus
>   Slough ish bin owss

front die Vorderseite
f**o**rderzite-uh

>   **in front** vorn

>   **in front of the hotel** vor dem
>   Hotel for

>   **at the front** vorn forn

frost der Frost

frozen gefroren

frozen food die Tiefkühlkost
teefk**oo**lkost

fruit das Obst ohpst

fruit juice der Fruchtsaft
frooKHtzaft

fry braten bra**h**ten

frying pan die Bratpfanne
bra**h**t-pfan-uh

full voll foll

  it's full of… es ist v**o**ller…

  I'm full ich bin satt ish bin zatt

full board die Vollpension
follpangz-yohn

fun: it was fun es hat Spaß
gemacht ess hat shpahss
gema**KH**t

funfair das Volksfest follks-fest

funicular railway die Seilbahn
z**i**le-bahn

funny (strange) seltsam z**e**ltzahm

  (amusing) komisch k**oh**mish

furniture die Möbel m**u**rbel

further weiter v**y**ter

  it's further down the road
es ist weiter die Straße entlang

DIALOGUE

  **how much further is it to
the castle?** wie weit ist es
noch bis zum Schloss? vee
vite ist ess no**KH** bis tsoom

  about 3 kilometres etwa
drei Kilometer **e**tvah

fuse (noun) die Sicherung
z**i**sheroong

  the lights have fused die
Sicherung ist durchgebrannt
d**oo**rsh-gebrannt

fuse box der Sicherungskasten
z**i**sheroongs-kasten

fuse wire der Schmelzdraht

shm**e**lts-draht

future die Zukunft ts**oo**koonft

  in future in Zukunft

G

gallon die Gallone gal**oh**n-uh

game das Spiel shpeel

  (meat) das Wild vilt

garage (fuel) die Tankstelle t**a**nkshtell-uh

  (repairs) die Werkstatt
v**ai**rkshtatt

  (parking) die Garage gar**a**HJ uh

garden der Garten

garlic der Knoblauch
k-n**oh**blow**KH**

gas das Gas gahss

  (US: gasoline) das Benzin bents**ee**n

gas cylinder (camping gas) die
Gasflasche g**a**hss-flash-uh

gasoline das Benzin bents**ee**n

gas permeable lenses
luftdurchlässige Kontaktlinsen
l**oo**ft-doorsh-lessig-uh
kont**a**kt-linzen

gas station die Tankstelle t**a**nkshtell-uh

gate das Tor tohr

  (at airport) der Flugsteig fl**oo**k-
shtike

gay schwul shvool

gay bar die Schwulenkneipe
shv**oo**len-k-nipe-uh

gear (in car etc) der Gang

gearbox das Getriebe getr**ee**b-uh

gear lever der Schaltknüppel
shalt-k-nooppel

general allgemein al-gemine

Geneva Genf

gents' (toilet) die Herrentoilette
hairen-twalett-uh

genuine echt esht

German (*male/female*) der/die
Deutsche doytch-uh
(*adj*) deutsch doytch
(language) Deutsch
the Germans die Deutschen

German measles die Röteln
rurteln

Germany Deutschland
doytch-lant

get (obtain) bekommen
(fetch) holen hohlen
(become) werden vairden

**will you get me another
one, please?** bringen Sie mir
bitte noch eins noKH ine-ss

**do you know where I can
get them?** wissen Sie, wo ich
sie bekommen kann?

can I get you a drink?
möchtest du/möchten Sie
etwas trinken? murshtest
doo/murshten zee etvass

**no, I'll get this one, what
would you like?** nein,
das ich meine Runde, was
möchten Sie? mine-uh
roond-uh

a glass of red wine ein Glas
Rotwein

how do I get to...? wie
komme ich nach...? vee
komm-uh ish naKH

to get old alt werden vairden

get back (return) zurückkommen
tsooroock-kommen

get in (arrive) ankommen
an-kommen

get off aussteigen owss-shtygen

where do I get off? wo
muss ich aussteigen? vo
mooss ish

get on (to train etc) einsteigen
ine-shtygen

get out (of car etc) aussteigen
owss-shtygen

get up (in the morning) aufstehen
owf-shtay-en

gift das Geschenk geshenk

gift shop der Geschenkladen
geshenk-lahden

gin der Gin

a gin and tonic, please
einen Gin Tonic, bitte ine-en

girl das Mädchen maytshen

girlfriend die Freundin froyndin

give geben gayben

I gave it to him ich habe es
ihm gegeben ish hahb-uh ess
eem gegayben

will you give this to...?
bitte geben Sie dies...

give back zurückgeben
tsooroock-gayben

glad froh

glass das Glas glahss

a glass of wine ein Glas Wein

glasses (spectacles) die Brille
br**i**ll-uh

gloves die Handschuhe
h**a**nt-sh00-uh

glue der Klebstoff kl**ay**p-shtoff

go gehen g**ay**-en

(by car, train etc) f**a**hren

we'd like to go to the Black Forest wir möchten zum Schwarzwald fahren veer m**u**rshten tsoom

where are you going? wohin gehen/fahren Sie? voh**i**n

where does this bus go? wohin fährt dieser Bus? fairt

let's go gehen wir

she's gone (left) sie ist gegangen

where has he gone? wohin ist er gegangen?

I went there last week ich war l**e**tzte W**o**che da

hamburger to go Hamburger zum M**i**tnehmen tsoom

go away weggehen v**e**k-gay-en

go away! gehen Sie weg!

go back (return) zurückgehen ts00r**00**ck-gay-en

go down (the stairs etc) hinuntergehen hin**00**nter-gay-en

go in hineingehen hin-**ine**-gay-en

go out (in the evening) ausgehen **ow**ss-gay-en

do you want to go out tonight? möchten Sie heute abend ausgehen? m**u**rshten zee h**oy**t-uh **ah**bent

go through gehen durch g**ay**-en doorsh

go up (the stairs etc) hinaufgehen hin**ow**f-gay-en

goat die Ziege ts**ee**g-uh

God Gott

goggles (ski) die Skibrille sh**ee**brill-uh

gold das Gold gollt

golf Golf

golf course der Golfplatz g**o**lf-plats

good gut g00t

good! gut!

it's no good es hat keinen Zweck ess hat k**i**ne-en tsveck

goodbye auf Wiedersehen owf-v**ee**derzayn

good evening guten Abend g**00**ten **ah**bent

Good Friday der Karfreitag kar-fr**y**tahk

good morning guten Morgen g**00**ten m**o**rgen

good night gute Nacht g**00**t-uh naк**H**t

goose die Gans ganss

got: we've got to... wir müssen... veer m**00**ssen

I've got to... ich muss... mooss

have you got any...? haben Sie...? h**ah**ben zee

government die Regierung reg**ee**roong

gradually allmählich al-m**ay**lish

grammar die Grammatik

gram(me) das Gramm

granddaughter die Enkelin
enk-uh-lin

grandfather der Großvater
grohssfahter

grandmother die Großmutter
grohssmootter

grandson der Enkel

grapefruit die Grapefruit

grapefruit juice der
Grapefruitsaft -zaft

grapes die Trauben trowben

grass das Gras grahss

grateful dankbar

gravy die Soße zohss-uh

great (excellent) großartig
grohss-artish

that's great! das ist toll! tol

a great success ein großer
Erfolg grohss-er

Great Britain Großbritannien
grohss-britannee-en

Greece Griechenland
greeshenlant

greedy gefräßig gefrayssish

Greek griechisch greeshish

green grün groon

green card (car insurance) die
grüne Karte groon-uh kart-uh

greengrocer's der Gemüsehändler gemooz-uh-hentler

grey grau grow

grill (on cooker) der Grill

grilled gegrillt

grocer's der
Lebensmittelhändler
laybensmittel-hentler

ground der Boden bohden

on the ground auf dem
Boden

ground floor das Erdgeschoss
airt-geshoss

group die Gruppe groop-uh

guarantee die Garantie garantee

is it guaranteed? ist darauf
Garantie? darowf

guest der Gast

guesthouse die Pension
pangz-yohn

guide (person) der Reiseleiter
ry-zuh-lyter

guidebook der Reiseführer
ry-zuh-f00rer

guided tour die Rundfahrt
roontfahrt

(on foot) der Rundgang
roontgang

guitar die Gitarre gitarr-uh

gum (in mouth) das Zahnfleisch
tsahn-flysh

gun das Gewehr gevair

gym das Fitness-Studio
fitness-sht00dee-o

H

hair das Haar hahr

hairbrush die Haarbürste
hahrb00rst-uh

haircut der Haarschnitt
hahrshnit

hairdresser der Frisör frizur

hairdryer der Fön furn

hair gel das Haargel hahr-gayl

hairgrip die Haarklemme hahrklem-uh

hair spray das Haarspray hahr-shpray

half halb halp

half an hour eine halbe Stunde ine-uh halb-uh shtoond-uh

half a litre ein halber Liter halber leeter

about half that etwa die Hälfte etvah dee helft-uh

half board die Halbpension halp-pangz-yohn

half-bottle die halbe Flasche halb-uh flash-uh

half fare der halbe Fahrpreis halb-uh fahr-price

half price: at half price zum halben Preis tsoom halben price

hall (in house) die Diele deel-uh

ham der Schinken shinken

hamburger der Hamburger hemburger

hammer der Hammer

hand die Hand hant

handbag die Handtasche hant-tash-uh

handbrake die Handbremse hantbremz-uh

handkerchief das Taschentuch tashen-tooKH

handle (on door) die Klinke klink-uh

(on suitcase etc) der Griff

hand luggage das Handgepäck hant-gepeck

hang-gliding das Drachen-fliegen draKHen-fleegen

hangover der Kater kahter

I've got a hangover ich habe einen Kater ish hahb-uh ine-en

happen geschehen geshay-en

what's happening? was ist los? lohss

what has happened? was ist passiert? passeert

happy glücklich gl**oo**cklish

 I'm not happy about this ich
 bin damit nicht zufrieden ish
 bin d**ah**mit nisht ts**oo**fr**ee**den

harbour der Hafen h**ah**fen

hard hart

 (difficult) schwer shvair

hard-boiled egg ein
 hartgekochtes Ei h**a**rtgek**o**кнtess **ī**

hard lenses harte Kontaktlinsen
 h**a**rt-uh kontakt-linzen

hardly kaum kowm

 hardly ever fast nie fasst nee

hardware shop die
 Eisenwarenhandlung
 īzenvahren-hantloong

hat der Hut h**oo**t

hate (verb) hassen

have haben h**ah**ben

 can I have a…? kann ich
 ein… haben? kan ish

 can we have some…?
 können wir etwas… haben?
 k**u**rnen veer **e**tvass

 do you have…? hast du/
 haben Sie…? d**oo**/… zee

 what'll you have? (drink) was
 möchtest du/möchten Sie? vass
 m**u**rshtest d**oo**/m**u**rshten zee

 I have to leave now ich muss
 jetzt gehen m**oo**ss yetst g**ay**-en

 do I have to…? muss ich…?

hayfever der Heuschnupfen h**oy**-
 shnoopfen

hazelnuts die Haselnüsse h**ah**zel-
 n**oo**ss-uh

he er air

head der Kopf

headache die Kopfschmerzen
 k**o**pf-shmairtsen

headlights die Scheinwerfer
 sh**ine**-vairfer

headphones die Kopfhörer
 k**o**pf-hur-rer

health food shop der Bioladen
 b**ee**-oh-lahden

healthy gesund gez**oo**nt

hear hören h**u**r-ren

DIALOGUE

 can you hear me? können
 Sie mich hören? k**u**rnen
 zee mish

 I can't hear you ich kann
 Sie nicht hören ish kan zee
 nisht

hearing aid das Hörgerät
 h**u**r-gerayt

heart das Herz hairts

heart attack der Herzinfarkt
 h**a**irts-infarkt

heat die Hitze h**i**ts-uh

heater (in room) der Ofen **oh**fen
 (in car) die Heizung h**y**tsoong

heating die Heizung h**y**tsoong

heavy schwer shvair

heel (of foot) die Ferse f**a**irz-uh
 (of shoe) der Absatz **a**pzats

 could you heel these?
 können Sie mir hier die Absätze
 erneuern? k**u**rnen zee meer heer
 dee **a**psets-uh airn**oy**ern

heelbar die Absatzbar **a**pzatsbar

height (of mountain) die Höhe
 h**u**r-uh
 (of person) die Größe gr**u**rss-uh

helicopter der Hubschrauber h00p-shrowber

hello hallo

helmet (for motorcycle) der Helm

help die Hilfe hilf-uh

(verb) helfen

help! Hilfe!

can you help me? können Sie mir helfen? kurnen zee meer

thank you very much for your help vielen Dank für Ihre Hilfe feelen dank f00r eer-uh

helpful hilfreich hilf-rysh

hepatitis die Hepatitis hepateetiss

her: I haven't seen her ich habe sie nicht gesehen zee

give it to her geben Sie es ihr eer

with her mit ihr

for her für sie

that's her das ist sie

that's her towel das ist ihr Handtuch

herbal tea der Kräutertee kroyter-tay

herbs die Kräuter kroyter

here hier heer

here is/are... hier ist/sind zint

here you are (offering) bitte bitt-uh

hers: that's hers das gehört ihr dass gehurt eer

hey! he! hay

hi! hallo!

hide verstecken fairshtecken

high hoch hohKH

highchair der Hochstuhl hohKH-sht00l

highway die Autobahn owtobahn

hill der Berg bairk

him: I haven't seen him ich habe ihn nicht gesehen een

give it to him geben Sie es ihm eem

with him mit ihm

for him für ihn

that's him das ist er air

hip die Hüfte h00ft-uh

hire: for hire zu vermieten ts00 fairmeeten

(verb) mieten meeten

where can I hire a bike? wo kann ich ein Fahrrad mieten? vo kan ish ine fahr-raht

his: it's his car es ist sein Auto zine

that's his das ist seins zine-ss

hit (verb) schlagen shlahgen

hitch-hike trampen trempen

hobby das Hobby

hold (verb) halten

hole das Loch loKH

holiday der Urlaub 00rlowp

on holiday im Urlaub

Holland Holland hol-lant

home das Zuhause ts00howz-uh

at home (in my house etc) zu Hause

(in my country) bei uns by oonss

we go home tomorrow wir fahren morgen nach Hause veer fahren morgen naKH

honest ehrlich airlish

honey der Honig h**o**hnish

honeymoon die Flitterwochen
fl**i**ttervoкнen

hood (US: of car) die Haube
h**o**wb-uh

hope h**o**ffen

  I hope so hoffentlich
h**o**ffentlish

  I hope not hoffentlich nicht
nisht

hopefully hoffentlich
h**o**ffentlish

horn (of car) die Hupe h**oo**p-uh

horrible schr**e**cklich

horse das Pferd pfairt

horse riding Reiten r**y**ten

hospital das Krankenhaus
kr**a**nken-howss

hospitality die Gastfreundschaft g**a**st-froynt-shafft

  **thank you for your
  hospitality** vielen Dank für
  Ihre Gastfreundschaft f**ee**len
  dank f**oo**r **ee**r-uh

hot heiß hice

  (spicy) scharf sharf

  I'm hot mir ist heiß meer

  it's hot today es ist heiß heute

h**oy**t-uh

hotel das Hotel

hotel room: in my hotel room
in meinem Hotelzimmer
m**i**ne-em hotel-tsimmer

hot spring die Thermalquelle
tairm**ah**l-kvell-uh

hour die Stunde sht**oo**nd-uh

house das Haus howss

house wine der Tafelwein
t**ah**fel-vine

hovercraft das Luftkissenboot
l**oo**ft-kissenboht

how wie vee

  how many? wie viele? f**ee**l-uh

  how do you do? guten Tag!
g**oo**ten tahk

DIALOGUE

  how are you? wie geht es
  dir/Ihnen? gayt ess deer/
  eenen

  fine, thanks, and you?
  danke, gut, und dir/Ihnen?
  dank-uh g**oo**t

  how much is it? was kostet
  das?

  75 euros fünfundsiebzig
  Euro

  I'll take it ich nehme es ish
  n**ay**m-uh ess

---

humid feucht foysht

humour der Humor hoom**oh**r

Hungarian ungarisch
oongahrish

Hungary Ungarn **oo**ngarn

hungry hungrig h**oo**ngrish

I'm hungry ich habe Hunger ish ha**h**buh h**oo**ng-er

are you hungry? hast du/ haben Sie Hunger? d**oo**/ha**h**ben zee

hurry (*verb*) sich beeilen zish buh-**ī**len

I'm in a hurry ich habe es eilig ish ha**h**b-uh ess **ī**lish

there's no hurry es eilt nicht **ī**lt nisht

hurry up! beeilen Sie sich!

hurt (*verb*) weh tun vay t**oo**n

it really hurts es tut echt weh t**oo**t esht vay

husband der Mann

hydrofoil das Tragflächenboot tra**h**kfleshenboht

hypermarket der Verbrauchermarkt fair-br**ow**KHer-markt

I ich ish

ice das Eis ice

with ice mit Eis

no ice, thanks kein Eis, danke kine ice, d**a**nk-uh

ice cream das Eis ice

ice-cream cone die Tüte Eiskrem t**oo**t-uh **ice**-kraym

ice lolly das Eis am Stiel ice am shteel

ice rink die Schlittschuhbahn shl**i**tt-sh**oo**-bahn

ice skates die Schlittschuhe shl**i**tt-sh**oo**-uh

idea die Idee eed**a**y

idiot der Idiot eedee-**oh**t

if wenn ven

ignition die Zündung ts**oo**ndoong

ill krank

I feel ill ich fühle mich krank ish f**oo**l-uh mish

illness die Krankheit kr**a**nkhite

imitation (leather etc) nachgemacht na**KH**-gemak**H**t

immediately sofort zof**o**rt

important wichtig v**i**shtish

it's very important es ist sehr wichtig ist zair

it's not important es ist nicht wichtig nisht

impossible unmöglich oon-mu**r**glish

impressive beeindruckend be-**ine**-droockent

improve verbessern fair-b**e**ssern

I want to improve my German ich möchte mein Deutsch aufbessern ish m**u**rsht-uh mine doytch **ow**f-bessern

in: it's in the centre es ist im Z**e**ntrum

in my car in m**ei**nem Auto

in Munich in M**ü**nchen

in two days from now in zwei Tagen ta**h**gen

in May im Mai

in English auf Englisch owf **e**ng-lish

in German auf Deutsch doytch

is he in? ist er da?

in five minutes in fünf Minuten min**oo**ten

inch der Zoll tsoll

include enthalten ent-h**a**lten

does that include meals? ist das einschließlich der Mahlzeiten? **ine**-shleeslish dair m**ah**l-tsyten

is that included? ist das im Preis enthalten? price

inconvenient ungünstig **oo**ng**oo**nstish

incredible (very good, amazing) unglaublich oon-gl**ow**plish

Indian indisch **i**ndish

indicator (on car) der Blinker

indigestion die Magenverstimmung m**ah**gen-fair-shtimmoong

indoor pool das Hallenbad h**a**llenbaht

indoors dr**i**nnen

inexpensive billig b**i**llish

infection die Infektion infekts-y**oh**n

infectious ansteckend **a**nshteckent

inflammation die Entzündung ent-ts**oo**ndoong

informal (clothes, occasion, meeting) zwanglos tsv**a**ng-lohss

information die Information informats-y**oh**n

do you have any information about...? haben Sie Informationen über...? h**ah**ben zee informats-y**oh**nnen **oo**ber

information desk der Informationsschalter informats-y**oh**ns-shalter

injection die Spritze shpr**i**ts-uh

injured verletzt fairl**e**tst

she's been injured sie ist verletzt zee

in-laws die Schwiegereltern shv**ee**ger-eltern

inner tube der Schlauch shlowᴋʜ

innocent unschuldig **oo**n-shooldish

insect das Insekt ins**e**kt

insect bite der Insektenstich ins**e**kten-shtish

do you have anything for insect bites? haben Sie etwas für Ins**e**ktenstiche? h**ah**ben zee **e**tvass f**oo**r

insect repellent das Insektenbekämpfungsmittel ins**e**kten-bek**e**mpfoongs-mittel

inside **i**nnen

inside the hotel im Hotel

let's sit inside setzen wir uns nach dr**i**nnen z**e**tsen veer oonss naᴋʜ

insist: **I insist** ich bestehe darauf ish besht**ay**-uh dar**ow**f

insomnia die Schlaflosigkeit shl**ah**f-lohzish-kite

instant coffee der Pulverkaffee p**oo**lver-kaffay

instead statt d**e**ssen shtatt

instead of... anstelle von... ansht**e**ll-uh fon

give me that one instead geben Sie mir statt dessen das

gay ben zee meer shtatt dessen dass

insulin das Insulin inz00leen

insurance die Versicherung fairzisheroong

intelligent intelligent intelligent

interested: I'm interested in... ich interessiere mich für... ish interesseer-uh mish f00r

interesting interessant

    that's very interesting das ist sehr interessant zair

international international internats-yonahl

Internet das Internet

interpret dolmetschen dolmetchen

interpreter (*male/female*) der Dolmetscher dolmetcher/die Dolmetscherin

intersection (US) die Kreuzung kroytsoong

interval (at theatre) die Pause powz-uh

into in

    I'm not into... ich stehe nicht auf... ish shtay-uh nisht owf

introduce vorstellen for-shtellen

    may I introduce...? darf ich Ihnen... vorstellen? ish eenen

invitation die Einladung ine-lahdoong

invite einladen ine-lahden

Ireland Irland eerlant

Irish irisch eerish

    I'm Irish (*male/female*) ich bin Ire/Irin ish bin eer-uh/eerin

iron (for ironing) das Bügeleisen b00gel-īzen

can you iron these for me? könnten Sie diese Sachen für mich bügeln? kurnten zee deez-uh zaKHen f00r mish b00geln

is ist

island die Insel inzel

it es ess

    (*nouns with der*) er air

    (*nouns with die*) sie zee

    it is... es ist...

    is it...? ist es...?

    where is it? wo ist es? vo

    it's him er ist es

    it was... es war... vahr

Italian (*adj*) italienisch ital-yaynish

    (language) Italienisch

Italy Italien itahlee-en

itch: it itches es juckt ess yoockt

J

jack (for car) der Wagenheber vahgen-hayber

jacket die Jacke yackuh

jam die Marmelade marm-uh-lahd-uh

jammed: it's jammed es klemmt

January der Januar yan00ar

jar das Glas glahss

jaw der Kiefer keefer

jazz der Jazz

jealous eifersüchtig īferz00shtish

jeans die Jeans

jellyfish die Qualle kvall-uh

jersey der Pullover poollohver

jetty der Steg shtayk

Jewish jüdisch y**oo**dish

jeweller's das Juweliergeschäft yoov-uh-l**ee**r-gesheft

jewellery der Schmuck shmoock

job die Arbeit **a**rbite

jogging das Joggen

   I'm going jogging ich gehe joggen ish g**ay**-uh

joke der Witz vits

journey die Reise r**i**ze-uh

   have a good journey! gute Reise! g**oo**t-uh

jug die Kanne k**a**nn-uh

   a jug of water ein Krug mit Wasser kr**oo**k mit v**a**sser

juice der Saft zaft

July der Juli y**oo**lee

jump (*verb*) springen shpr**i**ngen

jumper der Pullover pooll**oh**ver

jump leads das Starthilfekabel sht**a**rt-hilf-uh-k**ah**bel

junction die Kreuzung kr**oy**tsoong

June der Juni y**oo**nee

just (only) nur n**oo**r

   just two nur zwei

   just for me nur für mich f**oo**r mish

   just here genau hier gen**ow** heer

   not just now nicht jetzt nisht yetst

   we've just arrived wir sind gerade angekommen veer zint ger**ah**d-uh **a**n-gekommen

K

keep behalten

   keep the change der Rest ist für Sie dair rest ist f**oo**r zee

   can I keep it? kann ich es behalten?

   please keep it bitte behalten Sie es

kettle der Wasserkessel v**a**sser-kessel

key der Schlüssel shl**oo**ssel

   the key for room 201, please den Schlüssel für Zimmer zweihunderteins, bitte dayn – f**oo**r ts**i**mmer

key ring der Schlüsselring shl**oo**ssel-ring

kidneys die Nieren n**ee**ren

kill töten t**u**rten

kilo das Kilo k**ee**lo

kilometre der Kilometer keelo-m**ay**ter

   how many kilometres is it to…? wieviel Kilometer sind es nach…? v**ee**feel

kind (generous) nett

   that's very kind das ist sehr nett zair

DIALOGUE

   which kind do you want? welche möchtest du/ möchten Sie? v**e**lsh-uh m**u**rshtest d**oo**/m**u**rshten zee

   I want this/that kind ich möchte diese hier/die da ish m**u**rsht-uh d**ee**z-uh heer/ dee da

king der König k**u**rnish

kiosk der Kiosk

kiss der Kuss k**oo**ss

(*verb*) küssen k**oo**ssen

kitchen die Küche k**oo**sh-uh

kitchenette die Kochnische
ko**KH**neesh-uh

Kleenex die Papiertücher papeer-
t**oo**sher

knee das Knie k-nee

knickers das Höschen h**u**rss-shen

knife das Messer

knitwear die Strickwaren
shtrick-vahren

knock (*verb*) kl**o**pfen

knock down anfahren

he's been knocked down
er ist angefahren worden air ist
an-gefahren v**o**rden

knock over (object) umstoßen
oom-shtohssen

(pedestrian) anfahren

know (somebody, a place) k**e**nnen

(something) wissen v**i**ssen

I don't know ich weiß nicht
ish vice nisht

I didn't know that das wusste
ich nicht v**oo**st-uh

**do you know where I can
find...?** wissen Sie, wo ich...
f**i**nden kann?

L

label das Etik**e**tt

ladies' (toilets) die
Damentoilette d**ah**men-twalett-uh

ladies' wear die Damenkleidung
d**ah**men-klydoong

lady die Dame d**ah**m-uh

lager das helle Bier h**e**ll-uh beer

lake der See zay

Lake Constance der Bodensee
b**oh**denzay

Lake Lucerne der
Vierwaldstätter See f**ee**rvalt-
shtetter zay

lamb das Lamm

lamp die Lampe l**a**mp-uh

lane (on motorway) die Spur shp**oo**r

(small road) die Gasse g**a**ss-uh

language die Sprache shpr**ah**KH-uh

language course der
Sprachkurs shpr**ah**KH-koors

laptop der Laptop l**e**p-top

large groß grohss

last letzter l**e**tster

last week letzte Woche l**e**tst-
uh v**o**KH-uh

last Friday letzten Freitag
l**e**tsten

last night gestern abend
g**e**stern **ah**bent

**what time is the last train
to Hamburg?** wann fährt der
letzte Zug nach Hamburg?
vann fairt

late spät shpayt

sorry I'm late tut mir Leid,
dass ich zu spät komme t**oo**t
meer lite dass ish ts**oo** shpayt
k**o**mm-uh

the train was late der Zug
hatte Verspätung dair ts**oo**k
h**a**tt-uh fairshp**a**ytoong

we must go, we'll be late
wir müssen gehen, sonst
kommen wir zu spät veer
mOOssen gay-en zonst kommen
veer tsOO

it's getting late es wird spät
ess veert

later später shpayter

I'll come back later ich
komme später wieder ish
komm-uh – veeder

see you later bis später

later on nachher naKH-hair

latest spätester shpaytester

by Wednesday at the latest
spätestens bis Mittwoch
shpaytestens biss

Latvia Lettland lettlant

laugh (*verb*) lachen laKHen

launderette der Waschsalon
vash-zallong

laundromat der Waschsalon

laundry (clothes) die Wäsche
vesh-uh

(place) die Wäscherei vesherī

lavatory die Toilette twalett-uh

law das Gesetz gezets

lawn der Rasen rahzen

lawyer der Rechtsanwalt
reshts-anvallt

laxative das Abführmittel
apfOOr-mittel

lazy faul fowl

lead (electrical) das Kabel kahbel

lead (*verb*) führen fOOren

**where does this road
lead to?** wohin führt diese
Straße? vohin fOOrt deez-uh
shtrahss-uh

leaf das Blatt

leaflet der Prospekt

leak die undichte Stelle
OOndisht-uh shtell-uh

(*verb*) lecken

the roof leaks das Dach ist
undicht

learn lernen lairnen

least: not in the least nicht im
mindesten nisht

at least mindestens

leather das Leder layder

leave verlassen fairlassen

I am leaving tomorrow ich
reise morgen ab ish rize-uh
morgen ap

he left yesterday er ist
gestern abgereist ap-geryst

may I leave this here? kann
ich das hierlassen? heerlassen

I left my coat in the bar ich
habe meinen Mantel in der Bar
gelassen hahb-uh mine-en

**when does the bus for
Saarbrücken leave?**
wann fährt der Bus nach
Saarbrücken? vann fairt dair
booss naкн

leek der Lauch lowкн

left links

on the left links

to the left nach links naкн

turn left biegen Sie links ab
beegen zee – ap

there's none left es ist alle aluh

left-handed linkshändig
links-hendish

left luggage (office) die
Gepäckaufbewahrung
gepeck-owfbevahroong

leg das Bein bine

lemon die Zitrone tsitrohn-uh

lemonade die Limonade
limonahd-uh

lemon tea der Zitronentee
tsitrohnentay

lend leihen ly-en

will you lend me your... ?
könnten Sie mir Ihr... leihen?
kurnten zee meer eer

lens (of camera) das Objektiv
ob-yekteef

lesbian die Lesbierin lesbee-erin

less weniger vayniger

less than weniger als

less expensive nicht so teuer
nisht zoh

lesson die Stunde shtoond-uh

let (allow) lassen

will you let me know?
können Sie mir Bescheid sagen?
kurnen zee meer beshite zahgen

I'll let you know ich werde
Ihnen Bescheid sagen ish
vaird-uh eenen

**let's go for something to
eat** gehen wir etwas essen
gay-en veer etvass

let off absetzen apzetsen

will you let me off at...?
können Sie mich in...
absetzen? kurnen zee mish

letter der Brief breef

**do you have any letters
for me?** ist ein Brief für mich
angekommen? ine breef foor
mish an-gekommen

letterbox der Briefkasten
breefkasten

lettuce der Kopfsalat kopfzalaht

lever der Hebel haybel

library die Bücherei boosherī

licence die Genehmigung
genaymigoong

(driving) der Führerschein foorer-shine

lid der Deckel

lie (tell untruth) lügen loogen

lie down sich hinlegen zish hinlaygen

life das Leben layben

lifebelt der Rettungsgürtel rettoongs-goortel

lifeguard (on beach) der Rettungsschwimmer rettoongs-shvimmer

life jacket die Schwimmweste shvimm-vest-uh

lift (in building) der Aufzug owf-tsook

could you give me a lift? könnten Sie mich mitnehmen? kurnten zee mish mitnaymen

would you like a lift? kann ich Sie mitnehmen?

lift pass (for ski lift) der Liftpass liftpas

a daily/weekly lift pass ein Liftpass für einen Tag/eine Woche foor ine-en tahk/ine-uh voкн-uh

light das Licht lisht

(not heavy) leicht lysht

do you have a light? (for cigarette) haben Sie Feuer? hahben zee foyer

light green hellgrün hellgroon

light bulb die Glühbirne gloobeern-uh

I need a new light bulb ich brauche eine neue Birne noy-uh

lighter (cigarette) das Feuerzeug foyer-tsoyk

lightning der Blitz blits

like mögen murgen

I like it es gefällt mir ess gefelt meer

I don't like it es gefällt mir nicht nisht

I like going for walks ich gehe gern spazieren ish gay-uh gairn

I like you ich mag dich ish mahk dish

do you like…? magst du/mögen Sie…? mahkst doo/murgen zee

I'd like a beer ich möchte gern ein Bier mursht-uh gairn

I'd like to go swimming ich würde gern schwimmen gehen voord-uh

would you like a drink? möchtest du/möchten Sie etwas trinken?

would you like to go for a walk? möchtest du/möchten Sie einen Spaziergang machen?

what's it like? wie ist es? vee

I want one like this ich möchte so eins zoh ine-ss

lime die Limone limohn-uh

lime cordial der Limonensaft limohnenzaft

line (on paper) die Linie leenee-uh

(telephone) die Leitung lytoong

could you give me an outside line? könnten Sie mir ein Amt geben? kurnten zee meer ine amt gayben

lips die Lippen

lip salve der Lippen-Fettstift fett-shtift

lipstick der Lippenstift lippen-shtift

liqueur der Likör likur

listen zuhören ts00-hur-ren

Lithuania Litauen litowen

litre der Liter leeter

  a litre of white wine ein Liter Weißwein

little klein kline

  just a little, thanks danke, nur ein bisschen dank-uh n00r ine biss-shen

  a little milk etwas Milch etvass

  a little bit more ein bisschen mehr mair

live leben layben

  we live together wir wohnen zusammen veer vohnen tsoozammen

  where do you live? wo wohnen Sie? vo vohnen zee
  I live in London ich wohne in London

lively lebhaft layp-haft

liver die Leber layber

loaf das Brot broht

lobby (in hotel) das Foyer foy-yay

lobster der Hummer hoommer

local örtlich urtlish

  can you recommend a local restaurant? können Sie ein Restaurant am Ort empfehlen? kurnen zee ine restorong am ort empfaylen

lock das Schloss shloss

  (verb) abschließen ap-shleessen

  it's locked es ist abgeschlossen ap-geshlossen

lock in einschließen ine-shleessen

lock out ausschließen owss-shleessen

  I've locked myself out ich habe mich ausgesperrt ish hahb-uh mish owss-geshpairt

locker (for luggage etc) das Schließfach shleessfaкН

lollipop der Lutscher l00tcher

London London lon-don

long lang

  how long will it/does it take? wie lange dauert es? vee lang-uh dowert ess

  a long time eine lange Zeit ine-uh lang-uh tsite

  one day/two days longer ein Tag/zwei Tage länger leng-er

long distance call das Ferngespräch fairn-geshpraysh

look: I'm just looking, thanks danke, ich sehe mich nur um dank-uh, ish zay-uh mish n00r oom

  you don't look well du siehst nicht gut aus d00 zeest nisht g00t owss

  look out! passen Sie auf! passen zee owf

  can I have a look? kann ich mal sehen? kann ish mahl zay-en

look after sich kümmern um zish k00mmern oom

look at ansehen anzay-en

look for suchen zooKHen

  I'm looking for... ich suche... ish zooKH-uh

look forward to sich freuen auf zish froyen owf

  I'm looking forward to it ich freue mich darauf ish froy-uh mish darowf

loose (handle etc) lose lohz-uh

lorry der Lastwagen lasst-vahgen

lose verlieren fairleeren

  I've lost my way ich habe mich verlaufen ish hahb-uh mish fairlowfen

  I'm lost, I want to get to... ich weiß nicht, wo ich bin, ich möchte nach... vice nisht vo ish bin ish mursht-uh naKH

  I've lost my handbag ich habe meine Handtasche verloren fairlohren

lost property (office) das Fundbüro foont-booro

lot: a lot, lots viel feel

  not a lot nicht sehr viel nisht zair

  a lot of people viele Leute feel-uh

  a lot bigger viel größer

  I like it a lot ich mag es sehr ish mahk ess zair

lotion die Lotion lohts-yohn

loud laut lowt

lounge (in house) das Wohnzimmer vohn-tsimmer

  (in hotel) die Lounge

  (in airport) der Warteraum vart-uh-rowm

love die Liebe leeb-uh

  (*verb*) lieben leeben

  I love Germany ich liebe Deutschland

lovely herrlich hairlish

low (prices, bridge) niedrig needrish

luck das Glück glOOck

  good luck! viel Glück feel

luggage das Gepäck gepeck

luggage trolley der Kofferkuli koffer-kOOli

lump (on body) die Beule boyl-uh

lunch das Mittagessen mittahkessen

lungs die Lungen loong-en

Luxembourg Luxemburg looksemboork

luxurious luxuriös looksooree-urss

luxury der Luxus looksooss

M

machine die Maschine masheen-uh

mad (insane) verrückt fair-rOOckt

  (angry) böse burz-uh

made: what is it made of? woraus ist es? vohrowss

  (food) was ist da drin? vass

magazine die Zeitschrift tsite-shrift

maid (in hotel) das Zimmermädchen tsimmer-maytshen

maiden name der Mädchenname maytshen-nahm-uh

mail die Post posst

is there any mail for me? ist Post für mich da? foor mish

mailbox der Briefkasten breefkasten

main Haupt- howpt

main course das Hauptgericht howpt-gerisht

main post office die Hauptpost howpt-posst

main road die Hauptstraße howpt-shtrahss-uh

mains switch der Hauptschalter howpt-shalter

make (brand name) die Marke mark-uh

(*verb*) machen maKHen

I make it 200 euros nach meiner Rechnung sind das zweihundert Euro naKH mine-er reshnoong zint dass

make-up das Make-up

man der Mann

manager der Geschäftsführer geshefts-foorer

can I see the manager? kann ich den Geschäftsführer sprechen? dayn – shpreshen

manageress die Geschäftsführerin geshefts-foorerin

manual (car) ein Auto mit Handschaltung owto mit hant-shaltoong

many viele feel-uh

not many nicht viele nisht

map (of city) der Stadtplan shtatt-plahn

(road map) die Straßenkarte shtrahssen-kart-uh

(geographical) die Landkarte lantkart-uh

March der März mairts

margarine die Margarine margareen-uh

market der Markt

marmalade die Orangenmarmelade oronJen-marmelahd-uh

married: I'm married ich bin verheiratet ish bin fairhyrahtet

are you married? sind Sie verheiratet? zint zee

mascara die Wimperntusche vimpern-toosh-uh

match (football etc) das Spiel shpeel

matches die Streichhölzer shtrysh-hurltser

material (fabric) der Stoff shtoff

matter: it doesn't matter das macht nichts maKHt nishts

what's the matter? was ist los? vass ist lohss

mattress die Matratze matrats-uh

May der Mai my

may: may I have another one? kann ich noch eins haben? ish noKH ine-ss hahben

may I come in? darf ich hereinkommen? hairine-kommen

may I see it? kann ich es sehen? zay-en

maybe vielleicht feelysht

mayonnaise die Mayonnaise my-oh-nayz-uh

me mich mish

  that's for me das ist für mich

  send it to me schicken Sie es mir meer

  me too ich auch ish owKH

meal die Mahlzeit mahltsite

did you enjoy your meal? hat es Ihnen geschmeckt? eenen geshmeckt

it was excellent, thank you es war ausgezeichnet, danke vahr owss-getsyshnet, dank-uh

mean (*verb*) bedeuten bedoyten

  what do you mean? was meinen Sie damit? vass mine-en zee

what does this word mean? was bedeutet dieses Wort? vass bedoytet deezess vort

it means... in English auf Englisch bedeutet es... owf eng-lish

measles die Masern mahzern

meat das Fleisch flysh

mechanic der Mechaniker meshahniker

medicine die Medizin meditseen

medium (size) mittlerer

medium-dry (wine) halbtrocken halp-trocken

medium-rare (steak) medium maydee-oom

medium-sized mittelgroß mittelgrohss

meet treffen

  nice to meet you freut mich froyt mish

  where shall I meet you? wo treffen wir uns? vo – veer oonss

meeting die Besprechung beshpreshoong

meeting place der Treffpunkt treff-poonkt

melon die Melone melohn-uh

memory stick der Memory-Stick

men die Männer menner

mend reparieren repareeren

  could you mend this for me? können Sie das reparieren? kurnen zee

menswear die Herrenkleidung hairen-klydoong

mention erwähnen airvaynen

  don't mention it gern geschehen gairn geshay-en

menu die Speisekarte shpize-uh-kart-uh

  may I see the menu, please? kann ich bitte die Speisekarte haben? bitt-uh

  see **Menu Reader**

message die Nachricht naKHrisht

  are there any messages for me? ist eine Nachricht für mich hinterlassen worden? ine-uh – foor mish

  I want to leave a message for... ich möchte eine Nachricht für... hinterlassen ish mursht-uh

metal das Metall

metre der Meter m**ay**ter

microwave (oven) der Mikrowellenherd m**ee**krovellen-hairt

midday der Mittag

at midday mittags m**i**ttahgs

middle: in the middle in der Mitte dair m**i**tt-uh

in the middle of the night mitten in der Nacht

the middle one der mittlere m**i**ttler-uh

midnight die Mitternacht m**i**tter-naкнt

at midnight um Mitternacht oom

might: I might vielleicht feel**y**sht

I might not vielleicht nicht nisht

I might want to stay another day vielleicht bleibe ich noch einen Tag länger bl**i**be-uh ish noкн **i**ne-en tahk l**e**ng-er

migraine die Migräne migr**ay**n-uh

mild (taste, weather) mild milt

mile die Meile m**i**le-uh

milk die Milch milsh

milkshake der Milchshake

millimetre der Millimeter m**i**llimayter

minced meat das Hackfleisch h**a**ckflysh

mind: never mind macht nichts maкнt nishts

I've changed my mind ich habe es mir anders überlegt ish h**ah**b-uh ess meer **a**nders ∞berl**ay**kt

DIALOGUE

do you mind if I open the window? macht es Ihnen etwas aus, wenn ich das Fenster öffne? maкнt ess **ee**nen **e**tvass owss venn ish

no, I don't mind nein, das ist mir gleich meer gl**y**sh

mine: it's mine es gehört mir geh**u**rt meer

mineral water das Mineralwasser miner**ah**lvasser

mint (sweet) das Pfefferminz pfefferm**i**nts

minute die Minute min**oo**t-uh

in a minute gleich gl**y**sh

just a minute Moment mal mohm**e**nt mahl

mirror der Spiegel shp**ee**gel

Miss Frau frow

Miss! (waitress etc) Fräulein fr**oy**line

miss (bus, train) verpassen fairp**a**ssen

(regret absence of) vermissen fairm**i**ssen

I missed the bus ich habe den Bus verpasst ish h**ah**b-uh dayn booss fairp**a**sst

missing: to be missing fehlen f**ay**len

there's a suitcase missing ein Koffer fehlt

mist der Nebel n**ay**bel

mistake der Fehler f**ay**ler

I think there's a mistake ich glaube, da ist ein Fehler ish gl**ow**b-uh

sorry, I've made a mistake tut mir Leid, ich habe einen Fehler gemacht t00t meer lite ish hahb-uh ine-en

misunderstanding das Missverständnis miss-fairshtentniss

mix-up: sorry, there's been a mix-up tut mir Leid, etwas ist schiefgelaufen t00t meer lite, etvass ist sheef-gelowfen

mobile phone das Handy hendi

modern modern modairn

modern art gallery die Galerie für moderne Kunst gal-eree f00r modairn-uh koonst

moisturizer die Feuchtigkeitscreme foyshtishkites-kraym

moment: I'll be back in a moment ich bin gleich wieder da glysh veeder

Monday Montag mohntahk

money das Geld gelt

> **Travel tip** The bureaux de change (*Wechselstuben*) at the main train stations in the cities tend to offer better exchange rates than the banks, and they're open outside normal banking hours, usually 8a.m.–8p.m., including weekends.

month der Monat mohnaht

monument das Denkmal denkmahl

moon der Mond mohnt

moped das Moped mohpet

more mehr mair

can I have some more water, please? kann ich bitte noch etwas Wasser haben? ish bitt-uh noкн etvass

more expensive/interesting teurer/interessanter toyrer

more than 50 über fünfzig oober

more than that mehr als das

a lot more viel mehr feel

DIALOGUE

would you like some more? möchten Sie noch etwas? murshten zee noкн etvass

no, no more for me, thanks nein danke, das ist genug nine dank-uh dass ist genook

how about you? und Sie? oont zee

I don't want any more, thanks ich möchte nichts mehr, danke nishts

morning der Morgen

this morning heute morgen hoyt-uh

in the morning am Morgen

most: I like this one most of all dies gefällt mir am besten deess gefellt meer

most of the time die meiste Zeit dee myst-uh tsite

most tourists die meisten Touristen mysten

mostly meistens mystens

mother die Mutter mootter

motorbike das Motorrad motohr-raht

motorboat das Motorboot motohr-boht

motorway die Autobahn owtobahn

mountain der Berg bairk

in the mountains in den Bergen dayn bairgen

mountaineering das Bergsteigen bairk-shtygen

mouse die Maus mowss

moustache der Schnurrbart shnoorr-bart

mouth der Mund moont

mouth ulcer die Mundfäule moont-foyl-uh

move bewegen bevaygen

(move house) umziehen oom-tsee-en

he's moved to another room er ist in ein anderes Zimmer gezogen air ist in ine anderess tsimmer getsohgen

could you move your car? könnten Sie Ihr Auto wegfahren? kurnten zee eer owto veckfahren

could you move up a little? könnten Sie etwas aufrücken? etvass owf-roocken

where has it moved to? (shop, gallery) wo ist es jetzt? vo

movie der Film

movie theater das Kino keeno

MP3 format das MP3-Format em-pay-dry-formaht

Mr Herr hair

Mrs Frau frow

Ms Frau frow

much viel feel

  much better/worse viel besser/schlechter shlesht**er**

  much hotter viel heißer

  not much nicht viel nisht

  not very much nicht sehr viel zair

  I don't want very much ich möchte nicht so viel

mud der Dreck

mug (for drinking) die Tasse tass-uh

  I've been mugged ich bin überfallen worden ish bin ᴕberfallen vorden

mum die Mutter moott**er**

mumps der Mumps moomps

Munich München moonshen

museum das Museum moozay**oo**m

Travel tip Infuriatingly, tourism is strictly a Tuesday to Sunday, 9a.m. to 6p.m. business. Only a handful of museums and tourist attractions are open on Mondays, and some also close at lunchtimes. Many museums are also closed from November to March, as are sights in tourist-orientated regions such as the Moselle and Rhine valleys.

mushrooms die Pilze pilts-uh

music die Musik moozeek

musician der Musiker mooziker

Muslim moslemisch moslaymish

mussels die Muscheln moosheln

must: I must ich muss… ish mooss

  I mustn't drink alcohol ich darf keinen Alkohol trinken kine-en

mustard der Senf zenf

my: my room mein Zimmer mine

  my family meine Familie mine-uh

  my parents meine Eltern

myself: I'll do it myself ich mache es selbst ish maKH-uh ess zelpst

  by myself allein alline

N

nail (finger, metal) der Nagel nahgel

nail varnish der Nagellack nahgel-lack

name der Name nahmuh

  my name's John ich heiße John ish hice-uh

  what's your name? wie heißen Sie? vee hice-en zee

  what is the name of this street? wie heißt diese Straße? vee hysst

napkin die Serviette zairvee-ett-uh

nappy die Windel vindel

narrow eng

nasty (person) gemein gemine (weather, accident) furchtbar foorshtbar

national national nats-yohnahl

nationality die
Staatsangehörigkeit sht**ah**ts-an-
gehurishkite

natural natürlich nat**oo**rlish

nausea die Übelkeit **oo**belkite

navy (blue) marineblau
mar**ee**n-uh-blow

near nah

   is it near the city centre?
ist es nahe dem St**a**dtzentrum?
n**ah**-uh daym

   **do you go near the
Brandenburg Gate?**
fahren Sie in die Nähe des
Brandenburger T**o**res? f**ah**ren
zee in dee n**ay**-uh

   where is the nearest...? wo
ist der nächste...? vo ist dair
n**ay**kst-uh

nearby in der Nähe dair n**ay**-uh

nearly fast fasst

necessary notwendig
n**oh**tvendish

neck der Hals halss

necklace die Halskette h**a**lskett-uh

necktie die Krawatte krav**a**tt-uh

need: I need... ich brauche...
ish br**ow**KH-uh

   do I need to pay? muss ich
bez**ah**len? mooss

needle die Nadel n**a**hdel

neither: neither (one) of them
keiner (von ihnen) k**i**ne-er fon
eenen

   neither... nor... weder...
noch... v**ay**der... n**o**KH

nephew der Neffe n**e**ff-uh

net (in sport) das Netz

Netherlands die Niederlande
n**ee**derland-uh

network map der
Nahverkehrsplan n**ah**fairkairs-
plahn

never nie nee

DIALOGUE

   **have you ever been to
Mainz?** waren Sie schon
einmal in Mainz? v**ah**ren zee
shohn **i**ne-mahl

   **no, never, I've never been
there** nein, ich war noch
nie da n**o**KH

new neu noy

news (radio, TV etc) die
Nachrichten n**a**KHrishten

newsagents der
Zeitungshändler
ts**y**toongs-hentler

newspaper die Zeitung ts**y**toong

newspaper kiosk der
Zeitungskiosk ts**y**toongs-kee-osk

New Year Neujahr n**oy**-yahr

   Happy New Year! frohes
neues Jahr fr**oh**-ess n**oy**ess yar

New Year's Eve Silvester
zilv**e**ster

New Zealand Neuseeland
noyz**ay**lant

**New Zealander: I'm a New
Zealander** (*male/female*) ich
bin Neuseeländer noyz**ay**lender/
Neeseeländerin

next nächster n**ay**kster

   **the next turning/street
on the left** die nächste

Abzweigung/Straße links naykst-uh

at the next stop an der nächsten Haltestelle nayksten

next week nächste Woche

next to neben nayben

nice (food) gut g00t

(looks, view etc) hübsch h00psh

(person) nett

niece die Nichte nisht-uh

night die Nacht naкнт

at night nachts

good night gute Nacht g00t-uh

DIALOGUE

do you have a single room for one night? haben Sie ein Einzelzimmer für eine Nacht? hahben zee ine ine-tsel-tsimmer f00r ine-uh

yes ja yah

how much is it per night? was kostet es pro Nacht?

it's 150 euros for one night eine Übernachtung kostet hundertfünfzig Euro 00ber-naкнtoong

thank you, I'll take it danke, ich nehme es naym-uh

nightclub der Nachtklub naкнtkloob

nightdress das Nachthemd naкнt-hemt

night porter der Nachtportier naкнt-port-yay

no nein nine

I've no change ich habe kein Kleingeld kine

there's no... left es ist kein... übrig 00brish

no way! auf keinen Fall owf kine-en fal

oh no! (upset) nein!

nobody keiner kine-er

there's nobody there es ist keiner da

noise der Lärm lairm

noisy: it's too noisy es ist zu laut ts00 lowt

non-alcoholic alkoholfrei alkoh**ohl**fry

none keiner kine-er

nonsmoking... Nichtraucher... nishtr0wкнer

noon der Mittag mittahk

no-one keiner kine-er

nor: nor do I ich auch nicht owкн nisht

normal normal normahl

north der Norden

in the north im Norden

north of Leipzig nördlich von Leipzig nurtlish fon

northeast der Nordosten nort-osten

northern nördlich nurtlish

North Sea die Nordsee nortzay

northwest der Nordwesten nortvesten

Northern Ireland Nordirland nort-eerlant

Norway Norwegen norvaygen

Norwegian (*adj*) norwegisch
norvaygish

nose die Nase na**h**z-uh

nosebleed Nasenbluten
na**h**zen-blooten

not nicht nisht

  no, I'm not hungry nein, ich
habe keinen Hunger k**i**ne-en

  **I don't want any, thank
you** ich möchte keine, danke
mursht-uh k**i**ne-uh d**a**nk-uh

  it's not necessary es ist nicht
nötig

  I didn't know that das wusste
ich nicht v**oo**st-uh

  not that one – this one nicht
den – diesen dayn – d**ee**zen

note (banknote) der Geldschein
gelt-shine

notebook das Notizbuch
noht**ee**ts-bookh

notepaper (for letters) das
Briefpapier br**ee**f-papeer

nothing nichts nishts

  nothing for me, thanks
nichts für mich, d**a**nke

  nothing else sonst nichts zonst

novel der Roman rom**ah**n

November der November

now jetzt yetst

number die Nummer n**oo**mmer

  I've got the wrong number
ich habe mich verwählt
h**a**hb-uh mish fairv**ay**lt

  **what is your phone
number?** was ist Ihre Telefonnummer? **ee**r-uh telef**oh**n-
noommer

number plate das
Nummernschild n**oo**mmern-
shilt

Nuremburg Nürnberg n**oo**rn-bairk

nurse (female) die
Krankenschwester
kranken-shvester

  (male) der Krankenpfleger
kranken-pflayger

nursery slope der
Anfängerhügel **a**nfenger-h**oo**gel

nut (for bolt) die Schraubenmutter
shr**ow**benmootter

nuts die Nüsse n**oo**ss-uh

O

occupied (toilet) besetzt bez**e**tst

o'clock: it's nine o'clock es ist
neun Uhr **oo**r

October der Okt**o**ber

odd (strange) merkwürdig m**ai**rk-
v**oo**rdish

of von fon

  the name of the hotel der
Name des Hotels

off (lights) aus **o**wss

  it's just off Goethestraße
es ist ganz in der Nähe der
Goethestraße gants in dair
n**ay**-uh

  we're off tomorrow wir
reisen morgen ab veer r**y**zen

offensive anstößig **a**n-shturssish

office das Büro b**oo**ro

often oft

  not often nicht oft nisht

how often are the buses?
wie oft fahren die Busse? vee
oft fahren dee boossuh

oil (for car, for salad) das Öl url

ointment die Salbe zalb-uh

OK okay

are you OK? sind Sie okay?

is that OK with you? ist das
in Ordnung? ordnoong

is it OK if I...? kann ich... ?

that's OK thanks (it doesn't
matter) danke, das ist in
Ordnung

I'm OK (nothing for me, I've got
enough) nein, danke nine
(I feel OK) mir geht's gut meer
gayts goot

is this train OK for...? fährt
dieser Zug nach...?

I said I'm sorry, OK ich habe
doch gesagt, es tut mir Leid
hahb-uh doKH gezahkt

old alt

how old are you? wie alt
bist du/sind Sie? vee alt bist
doo/zint zee

I'm twenty-five ich bin
fünfundzwanzig

and you? und du/Sie? oont

old-fashioned altmodisch
altmohdish

old town (old part of town) die
Altstadt alt-shtatt

in the old town in der
Altstadt

olive oil das Olivenöl oleeven-url

olives die Oliven oleeven

omelette das Omelette omlett

on auf owf

on the street/beach auf der
Straße/am Strand

is it on this road? ist es auf
dieser Straße?

on the plane im Flugzeug

on Saturday am Samstag

on television im Fernsehen

I haven't got it on me ich
habe es nicht bei mir hahb-uh
ess nisht by meer

this one's on me (drink) diese
Runde ist auf meine Rechnung
deez-uh roond-uh ist owf mine-uh
reshnoong

the light wasn't on das Licht
war nicht an

what's on tonight? was gibt
es heute abend? vass geept ess

once (one time) einmal ine-mahl

at once (immediately) sofort
zofort

one ein ine
(nouns with die) eine ine-uh
(as figure) eins ine-ss

the white one der weiße dair

one-way ticket die einfache
Fahrkarte ine-faKH-uh fahr-kart-uh

onion die Zwiebel tsveebel

online (book, check) online

only nur noor

only one nur einer

it's only 6 o'clock es ist erst
sechs Uhr airst

I've only just got here ich
bin gerade erst angekommen
gerahd-uh airst

on/off switch der Ein/Aus-
Schalter ine-**ow**ss-shalter

open (*adj*) offen

open (*verb*) öffnen **ur**fnen

when do you open? wann
machen Sie auf? van ma**к**нen
zee owf

I can't get it open ich
bekomme es nicht auf
bek**o**mm-uh

in the open air im Freien fry-en

opening times die
Öffnungszeiten **ur**fnoongs-tsyten

open ticket die unbeschränkte
Fahrkarte **oo**nbeshrenkt-uh
fahrkart-uh

opera die Oper **oh**per

operation (medical) die
Operation operats-y**oh**n

operator (telephone) die
Vermittlung fair**mit**tloong

**opposite: the opposite
direction** die entgegengesetzte
Richtung entg**ay**gen-gezetst-uh
r**i**shtoong

the bar opposite die Kneipe
gegenüber gaygen-**oo**ber

opposite my hotel gegenüber
m**ei**nem Hotel

optician der Augenarzt
owgenartst

or oder **oh**der

orange (fruit) die Apfelsine
apfelz**ee**n-uh, die Orange
or**o**nJ-uh

(colour) orange

orange juice der Orangensaft
or**o**nJen-zaft

orchestra das Orchester ork**e**ster

order: can we order now?
können wir jetzt bestellen?
k**u**rnen veer yetst besht**e**llen

**I've already ordered,
thanks** danke, ich habe schon
bestellt hah**b**-uh shohn

I didn't order this das habe
ich nicht bestellt

out of order außer Betrieb
owsser betr**ee**p

ordinary normal norm**ah**l

other andere **a**nder-uh

the other one der andere

the other day (recently)
neulich n**oy**lish

I'm waiting for the others
ich w**a**rte auf die anderen
dee **a**nderen

do you have any others?
haben Sie noch andere? ha**h**ben
zee n**o**кн

otherwise sonst zonst

our unser **oo**nzer

ours unserer **oo**nzerer

out: he's out (not at home) er ist
nicht da air ist nisht

**three kilometres out
of town** drei Kilom**e**ter
außerhalb der Stadt **ow**sserhalp
dair shtatt

outdoors draußen dr**ow**ssen

outside... außerhalb...
owsser-halp

can we sit outside?
können wir draußen sitzen?
dr**ow**ssen

oven der Backofen b**a**ck-ohfen

over: over here hier heer

over there dort drüben dr**oo**ben

over 500 über fünfhundert **oo**ber

it's over (finished) es ist vorbei for-b**y**

overcharge: you've overcharged me Sie haben mir zuviel berechnet zee h**ah**ben meer ts**oo**f**eel** ber**esh**net

overcoat der Mantel

overnight (travel) über Nacht **oo**ber n**a**ĸHt

overtake überholen **oo**ber**hoh**len

owe: how much do I owe you? was bin ich Ihnen schuldig? vass bin ish **ee**nen sh**oo**ldish

own: my own... mein eigener... mine **I**gener

are you on your own? sind Sie allein hier? zint zee all**ine** heer

I'm on my own ich bin allein hier

owner (male/female) der Besitzer bez**I**tser/die Besitzerin

P

pack (verb) packen

pack: a pack of... (food, drink etc) eine Packung... **ine**-uh p**a**ckoong

package das Paket pak**ay**t

package holiday die Pauschalreise powsh**ah**lrize-uh

packed lunch das Lunchpaket -pak**ay**t

packet: a packet of cigarettes eine Schachtel Zigaretten sh**a**ĸHtel tsigar**e**tten

padlock das Vorhängeschloss f**o**rheng-uh-shloss

page (of book) die Seite z**I**te-uh

could you page Mr...? können Sie Herrn... ausrufen lassen? k**u**rnen zee hairn... **ow**ssroofen

pain der Schmerz shmairts

I have a pain here ich habe hier Schmerzen ish h**ah**b-uh heer

painful schmerzhaft shm**ai**rts-haft

painkillers das Schmerzmittel shm**ai**rts-mittel

paint die Farbe f**a**rb-uh

painting (picture) das Gemälde gem**e**ld-uh

pair: a pair of... ein Paar... ine pahr

Pakistani (adj) pakistanisch pakist**ah**nish

palace der Palast

pale blass

pale blue zartblau ts**a**rtblow

pan die Pfanne pf**a**nn-uh

panties das Höschen h**u**rs-shen

pants (underwear: men's) die Unterhose **oo**nter-hohz-uh

(women's) das Höschen h**u**rs-shen

(US) die Hose h**oh**z-uh

pantyhose die Strumpfhose shtr**oo**mpf-hohz-uh

paper das Papier pap**ee**r

(newspaper) die Zeitung ts**y**toong

a piece of paper ein Stück Papier ine sht00ck

paper handkerchiefs die Papiertaschentücher papeer-tashent00sher

parcel das Paket pakayt

pardon?, pardon me? (didn't understand) wie bitte? vee bitt-uh

parents: my parents meine Eltern mine-uh eltern

parents-in-law die Schwiegereltern shveeger-eltern

park der Park

(verb) parken

can I park here? kann man hier parken? heer

parking lot der Parkplatz parkplats

part ein Teil tile

partner (boyfriend, girlfriend) der Partner/die Partnerin

party (group) die Gruppe gr00pp-uh

(celebration) die Fete fayt-uh

pass (in mountains) der Pass pas

passenger der Passagier passaJeer

passport der Pass pas

password das Passwort pas-vort

past: in the past in der Vergangenheit dair fairgangen-hite

just past the information office kurz hinter dem Auskunftsbüro koorts

path der Weg vayk

pattern das Muster m00ster

pavement der Bürgersteig b00rgershtike

on the pavement auf dem Bürgersteig

pay (verb) zahlen tsahlen

can I pay, please? kann ich zahlen, bitte? bitt-uh

it's already paid for es ist schon bezahlt shohn betsahlt

pay phone der Münzfernsprecher m00nts-fairnshpresher

peaceful friedlich freetlish

peach der Pfirsich pfeerzish

peanuts die Erdnüsse airtn00ss-uh

pear die Birne beern-uh

peas die Erbsen airpsen

peculiar eigenartig Igen-artish

pedestrian crossing der Fußgängerüberweg f00ssgeng-er-00bervayk

pedestrian precinct die Fußgängerzone f00ssgeng-er-tsohn-uh

peg (for washing) die Wäscheklammer vesh-uh-klammer

(for tent) der Hering hairing

pen der Stift shtift**

pencil der Bleistift bly-shtift

penicillin das Penizillin penitsilleen

penknife das Taschenmesser tashen-messer

pensioner (*male/female*) der Rentner/die Rentnerin

people die Leute loyt-uh

the other people in the hotel die anderen Leute im Hotel

too many people zu viele Leute tsoo feel-uh

pepper (spice) der Pfeffer (vegetable) die Paprikaschote paprika-shoht-uh

peppermint (sweet) das Pfefferminz pfeffermints

per: per night pro Nacht naкнт

how much per day? was kostet es pro Tag? tahk

per cent Prozent protsent

perfect perfekt pairfekt

perfume das Parfüm parfOOm

perhaps vielleicht feelysht

perhaps not vielleicht nicht

period (of time) die Zeit tsite (menstruation) die Periode pairee-**ohd**-uh

perm die Dauerwelle dowervell-uh

permit die Genehmigung genay-migoong

person die Person pairzohn

petrol das Benzin bentseen

petrol can der Reservekanister rezairv-uh-kanister

petrol station die Tankstelle tank-shtell-uh

pharmacy die Apotheke apotayk-uh

phone das Telefon telefohn (*verb*) anrufen an-rOOfen

phone book das Telefonbuch telefohn-bOOKH

phonecard die Telefonkarte
telef**ohn**-kart-uh

phone charger das Handy-
Ladegerät hendi-**lahd**-uh-gerayt

phone number die
Telefonnummer
telef**ohn**-noommer

photo das F**o**to

**excuse me, could you take
a photo of us?** entsch**u**ldigen
Sie, könnten Sie ein F**o**to von
uns m**a**chen? k**u**rnten zee ine

phrase book der Sprachführer
shprah**KH**-f**oo**rer

piano das Klavier klav**ee**r

pickpocket der Taschendieb
t**a**shen-deep

**pick up: will you be there to
pick me up?** w**e**rden Sie da
sein, um mich abzuholen? oom
mish apts**oo**-hohlen

picnic das P**i**cknick

picture das Bild b**i**lt

pie (meat) die Pastete past**ay**t-uh

(fruit) der Kuchen k**oo**KHen

piece das Stück sht**oo**ck

a piece of... ein Stück… ine

pill die Pille p**i**ll-uh

I'm on the pill ich nehme die
P**i**lle ish n**ay**m-uh dee

pillow das K**o**pfkissen

pillow case der
Kopfkissenbezug
k**o**pfkissen-bets**oo**k

pin die Nadel n**a**hdel

pineapple die Ananas **a**nanas

pineapple juice der Ananassaft
ananas-zaft

pink rosa r**oh**za

pipe (for smoking) die Pfeife
pf**i**fe-uh

(for water) das Rohr

pipe cleaner der Pfeifenreiniger
pf**y**fen-ryniger

pity: it's a pity das ist schade
sh**ah**d-uh

pizza die Pizza p**ee**tsa

place der Platz plats

is this place taken? ist dieser
Platz besetzt? d**ee**zer – bez**e**tst

at your place bei dir/Ihnen
by deer/**ee**nen

at his place bei ihm eem

plain (not patterned) uni **oo**nee

plane das Flugzeug fl**oo**ktsoyk

by plane mit dem Flugzeug
daym

plant die Pflanze pfl**a**nts-uh

plaster (for cut) das H**e**ftpflaster

plaster cast der Gipsverband
g**i**ps-fairbant

plastic das Plastik

(credit cards) die Kreditkarten
kred**ee**t-karten

plastic bag die Plastiktüte
plastik-t**oo**t-uh

plate der T**e**ller

platform der Bahnsteig
b**ah**nshtike

**which platform is it,
please?** welches Gleis, bitte?
v**e**lshess glice b**i**tt-uh

play (verb) spielen shp**ee**len

(noun: in theatre) das Stück
sht**oo**ck

playground der Spielplatz
shpeel-plats

pleasant angenehm an-genaym

please bitte bitt-uh

yes please ja bitte yah

could you please…?
könnten Sie bitte…? kurnten zee

please don't bitte nicht nisht

pleased to meet you! freut
mich! froyt mish

pleasure die Freude froyd-uh

my pleasure ganz meinerseits
gants mine-er-zites

plenty: plenty of… viel… feel

we've plenty of time wir
haben viel Zeit

that's plenty, thanks das
reicht, danke rysht

pliers die Zange tsang-uh

plug (electrical) der Stecker
shtecker

(for car) die Zündkerze
tsoontkairts-uh

(in sink) der Stöpsel shturpsel

plumber der Klempner

p.m. (in the afternoon) nachmittags
naKHmittahks

(in the evening) abends ahbents

poached egg das pochierte Ei
posheert-uh ī

pocket die Tasche tash-uh

point: two point five zwei
Komma fünf

there's no point es hat keinen
Sinn kine-en zin

points (in car) die Kontakte
kontakt-uh

poisonous giftig giftish

Poland Polen

Polish polnisch

police die Polizei politsī

call the police! rufen Sie die
Polizei! roofen zee dee

policeman der Polizist politsist

police station die Polizeiwache
politsī-vaKH-uh

policewoman die Polizistin
politsistin

polish die Creme kraym

polite höflich hurflish

polluted verschmutzt fairshmootst

pony der Pony ponnee

pool (for swimming) das
Schwimmbecken
shvimm-becken

poor (not rich) arm

(quality) schlecht shlesht

pop music die Popmusik
pop-moozeek

pop singer (male/female) der
Popsänger popzenger/die
Popsängerin

population die Bevölkerung
befurlkeroong

pork das Schweinefleisch
shvine-uh-flysh

port (for boats) der Hafen hahfen

(drink) der Portwein portvine

porter (in hotel) der Portier
port-yay

portrait das Porträt portray

posh (restaurant, people) vornehm
fornaym

possible möglich murglish

is it possible to…? ist es möglich, zu…?

as… as possible so… wie möglich zo… vee

post (mail) die Post posst

(verb) absenden

could you post this for me? könnten Sie das für mich aufgeben? kurnten zee dass foor mish owf-gayben

postbox der Briefkasten breefkasten

postcard die Postkarte posstkart-uh

poster das Plakat plakaht

post office die Post

poste restante postlagernd posst-lahgernt

pots and pans das Kochgeschirr koKHgesheer

potato die Kartoffel

potato chips die Chips chips

potato salad der Kartoffelsalat kartoffel-zalaht

pottery (objects) die Töpferwaren turpfer-vahren

pound (money, weight) das Pfund pfoont

power cut der Stromausfall shtrohm-owssfal

power point die Steckdose shteck-dohz-uh

practise: I want to practise my German ich will mein Deutsch üben ish vill mine doytch ooben

prawns die Krabben

prefer: I prefer… ich mag

lieber… ish mahk leeber

pregnant schwanger shvang-er

prescription (for chemist) das Rezept raytsept

present (gift) das Geschenk geshenk

president der Präsident prezeedent

pretty hübsch hoopsh

it's pretty expensive es ist ganz schön teuer gants shurn toyer

price der Preis price

priest der Geistliche gystlish-uh

prime minister der Premierminister premyay-minister

printed matter die Drucksache droock-zaKH-uh

priority (in driving) die Vorfahrt forfahrt

prison das Gefängnis gefeng-niss

private privat privaht

private bathroom das eigene Bad īgen-uh baht

private room das Einzelzimmer ine-tseltsimmer

probably wahrscheinlich vahrshine-lish

problem das Problem problaym

no problem! kein Problem kine

program(me) das Programm

promise: I promise ich verspreche es fairshrpesh-uh

pronounce: how is this

pronounced? wie spricht man das aus? vee shprisht man dass owss

properly (repaired, locked etc) richtig rishtish

protection factor der Lichtschutzfaktor lisht-shoots-faktor

Protestant evangelisch ayvangaylish

public convenience die öffentliche Toilette urfentlish-uh twalett-uh

public holiday der gesetzliche Feiertag gezetslish-uh fire-tahk

pudding (dessert) der Nachtisch naкнtish

pull ziehen tsee-en

pullover der Pullover poollohver

puncture die Reifenpanne ryfen-pann-uh

purple violett vee-oh-lett

purse (for money) das Portemonnaie port-monay (US) die Handtasche hant-tash-uh

push schieben sheeben

pushchair der Sportwagen shport-vahgen

put tun toon

   where can I put...? wo kann ich... hinstellen? hin-shtellen

   could you put us up for the night? könnten Sie uns heute nacht unterbringen? oonss hoyt-uh naкнt oonterbringen

pyjamas der Schlafanzug shlahf-antsook

Q

quality die Qualität kvalitayt

quarantine die Quarantäne kvarantayn-uh

quarter das Viertel feertel

quayside: on the quayside am Kai ky

question die Frage frahg-uh

queue die Schlange shlang-uh

quick schnell shnell

   that was quick das war schnell vahr

   what's the quickest way there? wie komme ich am schnellsten dorthin? vee komm-uh ish am shnellsten dort-hin

   fancy a quick drink? wollen wir schnell einen trinken gehen? vollen veer – ine-en trinken gay-en

quickly schnell shnell

quiet (place, hotel) ruhig rooish

   quiet! Ruhe! roo-uh

quite (fairly) ziemlich tseemlish (very) ganz gants

   that's quite right ganz recht resht

   quite a lot eine ganze Menge ine-uh gants-uh meng-uh

R

rabbit das Kaninchen kaneenshen

race (for runners, cars) das Rennen

racket (squash, tennis etc) der Schläger shl**ay**ger

radiator (in room) der Heizkörper h**i**tes-kurper

(of car) der Kühler k**oo**ler

radio das Radio r**ah**dee-o

on the radio im Radio

rail: by rail per Bahn pair

railway die Eisenbahn **ī**zenbahn

rain der Regen r**ay**gen

in the rain im Regen

it's raining es regnet r**ay**gnet

raincoat der Regenmantel r**ay**genmantel

rape die Vergewaltigung fairgeval-tigoong

rare (steak) englisch **e**ng-lish

rash (on skin) der Ausschlag **ow**ss-shlahk

raspberry die Himbeere h**i**mbair-uh

rat die Ratte r**a**tt-uh

rate (for changing money) der Wechselkurs v**e**ksel-koorss

rather: it's rather good es ist ganz gut gants g**oo**t

I'd rather... ich würde lieber... ish v**oo**rd-uh l**ee**ber

razor (electric) der Rasierapparat raz**ee**r-apparaht

razor blades die Rasierklingen raz**ee**r-klingen

read lesen l**ay**zen

ready fertig f**ai**rtish

are you ready? bist du/sind Sie fertig?

I'm not ready yet ich bin noch nicht fertig noKH nisht

when will it be ready? wann ist es fertig? vann

it should be ready in a couple of days es müßte in ein paar Tagen fertig sein m**oo**sst-uh

DIALOGUE

real echt esht

really wirklich v**ee**rklish

that's really great das ist echt toll esht tol

rearview mirror der Rückspiegel r**oo**ck-shpeegel

reasonable (prices etc) vernünftig fairn**oo**nftish

receipt die Quittung kv**i**ttoong

recently kürzlich k**oo**rtslish

reception (in hotel, for guests) der Empfang

at reception am Empfang

reception desk die Rezeption retsepts-y**oh**n

receptionist die Empfangsperson empf**a**ngs-pairzohn

recognize erkennen airk**e**nnen

recommend: could you recommend...? könnten Sie... empfehlen? k**u**rnten zee... empf**ay**len

record (music) die Schallplatte sh**a**llplat-uh

red rot roht

red wine der Rotwein r**oh**tvine

refund (*verb*) erstatten air-sht**atten**

can I have a refund?
kann ich das Geld
zurückbekommen? kan ish dass
gelt tsoor**oo**ck-bekommen

region das Gebiet geb**ee**t

registered: by registered
mail per Einschreiben pair
ine-shryben

registration number die
Autonummer **ow**to-noommer

relative (*male/female*) der/die
Verwandte fairv**a**nt-uh

religion die Religion relig-y**oh**n

> **Travel tip** Access to church-
> es is generally excellent, and
> most are open all day and
> all week, though you should
> respect services. Churches
> in the Catholic south tend to
> observe longer hours than
> their northern counterparts.

remember: I don't remember
ich kann mich nicht
erinnern ish kan mish nisht
air-**i**nnern

I remember ich erinnere mich
air-**i**nner-uh

do you remember? erinnern
Sie sich? zee zish

rent die Miete m**ee**t-uh
(*verb*) mieten m**ee**ten

for rent zu vermieten ts00
fairm**ee**ten

rented car das Mietauto m**ee**t-
owto

repair (*verb*) reparieren repar**ee**ren

can you repair it? können Sie
es reparieren? k**u**rnen zee

repeat wiederholen veederh**oh**len

could you repeat that?
können Sie das noch einmal
wiederholen? k**u**rnen zee dass
noKH **ine**-mahl

reservation die Reservierung
rezairv**ee**roong

I'd like to make a
reservation ich möchte eine
Reservierung vornehmen
m**u**rsht-uh **ine**-uh – for-naymen

I have a reservation ich
habe eine Reservierung ish
h**ah**b-uh

yes sir, what name
please? auf welchen
Namen, bitte? owf velshen
n**ah**men

---

reserve reservieren rezairv**ee**ren

---

can I reserve a table for
tonight? kann ich für
heute abend einen Tisch
reservieren? kan ish f00r
h**oy**t-uh **ah**bent **ine**-en tish

yes madam, for how many
people? ja, für wieviele
Personen? f00r vee v**ee**l-uh
pairz**oh**nen

for two für zwei tsvy

and for what time? und für
welche Zeit? velsh-uh tsite

for eight o'clock für acht
Uhr 00r

---

and could I have your name please? und kann ich bitte Ihren Namen haben? *eeren nahmen*

rest: I need a rest ich brauche Erholung *ish browkH-uh airhohloong*

the rest of the group der Rest der Gruppe

restaurant das Restaurant *restorong*

rest room die Toilette *twalett-uh*

retired: I'm retired ich bin im Ruhestand *ish bin im roo-uh-shtant*

return (ticket) die Rückfahr-karte *rōock-fahrkart-uh*

DIALOGUE

a return to Heilbronn eine Rückfahrkarte nach Heilbronn

coming back when? wann soll die Rückfahrt sein? *rōock-fahrt*

reverse charge call das R-Gespräch *air-geshpraysh*

reverse gear der Rückwärtsgang *rōockvairtsgang*

revolting ekelhaft *aykelhaft*

Rhine der Rhein *rine*

rib die Rippe *ripp-uh*

rice der Reis *rice*

rich (person) reich *rysh*

(food) schwer *shvair*

ridiculous lächerlich *lesherlish*

right (correct) richtig *rishtish*

(not left) rechts *reshts*

you were right Sie hatten recht *resht*

that's right das stimmt *shtimmt*

this can't be right das kann nicht stimmen *nisht shtimmen*

right! okay!

is this the right road for…? ist dies die Straße nach…? *deess*

on the right rechts

turn right biegen Sie rechts ab *beegen zee – ap*

right-hand drive die Rechtssteuerung *reshts-shtoyeroong*

ring (on finger) der Ring

I'll ring you ich rufe Sie an *ish roof-uh zee*

ring back zurückrufen *tsoorōock-rōofen*

ripe (fruit) reif *rife*

rip-off: it's a rip-off das ist Wucher *vookHer*

rip-off prices Wucherpreise *vookHer-prize-uh*

risky riskant

river der Fluss *flooss*

road die Straße *shtrahss-uh*

is this the road for…? ist dies die Straße nach…? *deess dee – nakH*

down the road die Straße entlang

road accident der Verkehrsunfall fairk**ai**rss-oonfal

road map die Straßenkarte
shtr**ah**ssen-kart-uh

roadsign das Verkehrszeichen
fairk**ai**rs-tsyshen

rob: I've been robbed ich
bin bestohlen worden ish bin
besht**oh**len v**o**rden

rock der Felsen f**e**lzen

(music) der Rock

on the rocks (with ice) mit Eis
ice

roll (bread) das Brötchen br**ur**tchen

roof das Dach daKH

roof rack der Dachgepäckträger
daKH-gepeck-trayger

room das Zimmer ts**i**mmer

in my room in meinem
Zimmer m**ine**-em

room service der Zimmerservice ts**i**mmer-service

rope das Seil zile

rosé (wine) der Roséwein rohz**ay**-
vine

roughly (approximately) ungefähr
oongef**ai**r

round: it's my round das ist
meine Runde m**ine**-uh r**oo**nd-uh

roundabout (for traffic) der
Kreisverkehr kr**ice**-fairkair

round trip ticket die
Rückfahrkarte r**oo**ck-
fahrkart-uh

route die Strecke shtr**e**ck-uh

what's the best route?
welches ist der beste Weg?
v**e**lshess ist dair b**e**st-uh vayk

rubber (material) das Gummi
g**oo**mmee

(eraser) der Radiergummi
rad**ee**r-goommee

rubber band das Gummiband
g**oo**mmee-bant

rubbish (waste) der Abfall **a**p-fal

(poor quality goods) der Mist

rubbish! (nonsense) Quatsch!
kvatch

rucksack der Rucksack
r**oo**ckzack

rude unhöflich **oo**n-hurflish

ruins die Ruinen roo-**ee**nen

rum der Rum roomm

rum and coke ein Rum mit
Cola k**oh**la

run (person) r**e**nnen, laufen l**ow**fen

how often do the buses run? wie oft fahren die Busse? vee oft **fahren** dee **booss**-uh

I've run out of money ich habe kein Geld mehr ish hahb-uh kine gelt mair

rush hour die Rush-hour

S

sad traurig tr**ow**rish

saddle der Sattel z**a**ttel

safe (not in danger) sicher z**i**sher

(not dangerous) ungefährlich **oo**n-gefairlish

safety pin die Sicherheitsnadel z**i**sher-hites-nahdel

sail das Segel z**ay**gel

sailboard das Windsurfbrett v**i**nt-surfbrett

sailboarding das Windsurfen v**i**nt-surfen

salad der Salat zal**aht**

salad dressing die Salatsoße zal**aht**-zohss-uh

sale: for sale zu verkaufen ts**oo** fairk**ow**fen

salmon der Lachs lacks

salt das Salz zalts

same: the same derselbe dairz**e**lb-uh

the same man/woman derselbe Mann/dieselbe Frau deez**e**lb-uh

the same as this dasselbe wie das dass**e**lb-uh vee

the same again, please dasselbe nochmal, bitte noKHm**ahl** bitt-uh

it's all the same to me das ist mir ganz egal meer gants ayg**ahl**

sand der Sand zant

sandals die Sandalen zand**ah**len

sandwich das belegte Brot bel**ay**kt-uh broht

sanitary napkin die Damenbinde d**ah**menbind-uh

sanitary towel die Damenbinde d**ah**menbind-uh

sardines die Sardinen zard**ee**nen

Saturday Samstag z**a**mstahk

sauce die Soße z**oh**ss-uh

saucepan der Kochtopf k**o**KHtopf

saucer die Untertasse **oo**nter-tass-uh

sauna die Sauna z**ow**nah

sausage die Wurst voorst

say: how do you say... in German? was heißt... auf Deutsch? vass hyst... owf doytch

what did he say? was hat er gesagt? gez**ah**kt

I said... ich sagte... z**ah**kt-uh

he said... er sagte...

could you say that again? könnten Sie das wiederholen? k**u**rnten zee dass veeder-h**oh**len

scarf (for neck) der Schal shahl

(for head) das Kopftuch k**o**pft00KH

scenery die Landschaft l**a**nt-shafft

schedule (US) der Fahrplan

fahrplahn

scheduled flight der Linienflug leen-yenflook

school die Schule shool-uh

scissors: a pair of scissors eine Schere shair-uh

scotch der Scotch

Scotch tape der Tesafilm tayzahfilm

Scotland Schottland shottlant

Scottish schottisch shottish

I'm Scottish (*male/female*) ich bin Schotte shott-uh/Schottin

scrambled eggs die Rühreier roor-ier

scratch der Kratzer kratser

screw die Schraube shrowb-uh

screwdriver der Schrau- benzieher shrowben-tsee-er

scrubbing brush (for hands) die Handbürste hant-boorst-uh (for floors) die Scheuerbürste shoyer-boorst-uh

sea das Meer mair

by the sea am Meer

seafood die Meeresfrüchte mairess-froosht-uh

seafood restaurant das Fischrestaurant fish-restorong

seafront die Strandpromenade shtrant-promenahd-uh

seagull die Möwe murv-uh

search (*verb*) suchen zooKHen

seashell die Muschel mooshel

seasick: I feel seasick ich bin seekrank ish bin zaykrank

I get seasick ich werde leicht

seekrank **vaird-**uh lysht

seaside: by the seaside am Meer mair

seat der Sitzplatz **zitsplats**

is this anyone's seat? sitzt hier jemand? zitst heer **yay**mant

seat belt der Sicherheitsgurt **zi**sherhites-goort

seaweed der Tang

secluded abgelegen ap-gelaygen

second (*adj*) zweiter tsv**y**ter (of time) die Sekunde zek**oo**nd-uh

just a second! Moment mal! mahl

second class zweiter Klasse tsv**y**ter klass-uh

second-hand gebraucht gebrowKHt

see sehen z**ay**-en

can I see? kann ich mal sehen?

have you seen...? haben Sie... gesehen? h**ah**ben zee... gez**ay**-en

I saw him this morning ich habe ihn heute morgen gesehen

see you! bis später! shp**ay**ter

I see (I understand) ich verstehe fairst**ay**-uh

self-catering apartment die Ferienwohnung f**ay**ree-en-vohnoong

self-service die Selbstbedienung z**e**lpst-bedeenoong

sell verkaufen fairk**ow**fen

do you sell...? haben Sie...? h**ah**ben zee

Sellotape der Tesafilm t**ay**zahfilm

send senden z**e**nden

I want to send this to England ich möchte dies nach England senden ish m**u**rsht-uh deess

senior citizen (*male/female*) der R**e**ntner/die R**e**ntnerin

separate getr**e**nnt

separated: I'm separated ich lebe getr**e**nnt ish l**ay**b-uh

separately (pay, travel) getr**e**nnt

September der September zept**e**mber

septic vereitert fair-**ī**tert

serious ernst **a**irnst

service charge (in restaurant) die Bedienung bed**ee**noong

service station die Tankstelle (mit Werkstatt) t**a**nkshtell-uh mit v**a**irkshtatt

serviette die Serviette zairvee-**e**tt-uh

set menu die Tageskarte t**a**hgess-kart-uh

several mehrere m**a**irer-uh

sew nähen n**ay**-en

could you sew this back on? können Sie das wieder annähen? k**u**rnen zee dass v**ee**der **a**n-nay-en

sex der Sex

sexy s**e**xy

shade: in the shade im Schatten sh**a**tten

shake: let's shake hands geben wir uns die Hand g**ay**ben

veer oonss dee hant

shallow (water) seicht z**y**sht

shame: what a shame! wie schade! vee sh**a**hd-uh

shampoo das Shampoo

can I have a shampoo and set? können Sie mir die Haare waschen und legen? k**u**rnen zee meer dee h**a**hr-uh v**a**shen oont l**ay**gen

share (room, table etc) sich teilen zish t**y**len

sharp (knife, taste) scharf sharf (pain) stechend sht**e**shent

shattered (very tired) todmüde t**o**htmood-uh

shaver der Rasierapparat razeer-apparaht

shaving foam die Rasierseife razeer-zife-uh

shaving point die Steckdose für Rasierapparate sht**e**ckdohz-uh foor razeer-apparaht-uh

she sie zee

is she here? ist sie hier? heer

sheet (for bed) das Laken l**a**hken

shelf das Brett

shellfish die Schaltiere sh**a**hl-teer-uh

sherry der Sherry

ship das Schiff shiff

by ship mit dem Schiff

shirt das Hemd hemt

shit! Scheiße! sh**i**ce-uh

shock der Schock shock

I got an electric shock from... ich habe einen

elektrischen Schlag von…
bekommen ish hahb-uh ine-en
aylektrishen shlahk fon

shock-absorber der
Stoßdämpfer shtohss-dempfer

shocking (behaviour, prices)
skandalös skandalurss

(custom etc) schockierend
shockeerent

shoe der Schuh shoo

a pair of shoes ein Paar
Schuhe pahr shoo-uh

shoelaces die Schnürsenkel
shnoor-zenkel

shoe polish die Schuhcreme
shoo-kraym

shoe repairer der Schuhmacher
shoo-maKHer

shop das Geschäft gesheft

shopping: I'm going shopping
ich gehe einkaufen ish gay-uh
ine-kowfen

shopping centre das
Einkaufszentrum ine-kowfss-
tsentroom

shop window das Schaufenster
showfenster

shore (of sea) der Strand
shtrant

(of lake) das Ufer oofer

short (time, journey) kurz koorts

(person) klein kline

shortcut die Abkürzung
ap-koortsoong

shorts die Shorts

should: what should I do? was
soll ich machen? vass zoll ish
maKHen

he shouldn't be long er
kommt sicher bald air kommt
zisher balt

you should have told me
das hätten Sie mir sagen sollen
hetten zee meer zahgen zollen

shoulder die Schulter shoolter

shout (verb) schreien shry-en

show (in theatre) die Vorstellung
for-shtelloong

could you show me?
könnten Sie mir das zeigen?
kurnten zee meer dass tsygen

shower (in bathroom) die Dusche
doosh-uh

with shower mit Dusche

shower gel das Duschgel
doosh-gayl

shut (verb) schließen shleessen

when do you shut? wann
machen Sie zu? vann maKHen
zee tsoo

when do they shut? wann
machen sie zu?

they're shut sie sind
geschlossen geshlossen

I've shut myself out ich habe
mich ausgesperrt ish hahb-uh
mish owss-geshpairt

shut up! halt den Mund! dayn
moont

shutter (on camera) der
Verschluss fairshlooss

shutters (on window) die
Fensterläden fenster-layden

shy (person) schüchtern shooshtern

(animal) scheu shoy

sick (ill) krank

I'm going to be sick (vomit)
ich muss mich übergeben ish
mooss mish ooberg**ay**ben

side die Seite z**ite**-uh

the other side of town das
andere Ende der Stadt **a**nder-uh
end-uh dair shtatt

side lights das Standlicht
sht**a**ntlisht

side salad die Salatbeilage
zal**a**ht-bylahg-uh

side street die Seitenstraße
z**y**ten-shtrass-uh

sidewalk der Bürgersteig
b**oo**rgershtike

sight: the sights of... die
Sehenswürdigkeiten von...
z**ay**-ens-v**oo**rdish-kyten fon

**sightseeing: we're going
sightseeing** wir machen eine
Rundfahrt veer m**a**kHen **ine**-uh
r**oo**nt-fahrt

(on foot) wir machen einen
Rundgang **ine**-en r**oo**nt-gang

sightseeing tour die Rundfahrt
r**oo**nt-fahrt

sign das Schild shilt

(roadsign) das Verkehrszeichen
fairk**a**irs-tsyshen

signal: he didn't give a signal
(driver) er hat nicht geblinkt

(cyclist) er hat keine Richtung
angezeigt k**ine**-uh r**i**shtoong
an-getsykt

signature die Unterschrift
oonter-shrift

signpost der Wegweiser
v**ay**k-vyzer

silence die Ruhe r**oo**-uh

silk die Seide z**y**duh

silly (person) albern **a**l-bairn

(thing to do etc) dumm doomm

silver das Silber z**i**lber

silver foil die Alufolie
ahloo-fohl-yuh

similar ähnlich **ay**nlish

simple (easy) einfach **ine**-faKH

since: since yesterday seit
g**e**stern zite

since I got here seit ich hier
bin heer

sing singen z**i**ngen

singer (male/female) der Sänger
z**e**nger/die Sängerin

single (not married) unverheiratet
oon-fair-hyrahtet

a single to... eine einfache
Fahrt nach... **ine**-uh **ine**-faKH-uh
fahrt naKH

single bed das Einzelbett
ine-tsel-bett

single room das Einzelzimmer
ine-tsel-tsimmer

sink (in kitchen) die Spüle
shp**oo**l-uh

sister die Schwester shv**e**ster

sister-in-law die Schwägerin
shv**ay**gerin

sit: can I sit here? kann ich
mich hier hinsetzen? ish mish
heer h**i**nzetsen

is anyone sitting here? sitzt
hier jemand? zitst heer y**ay**mant

sit down sich hinsetzen zish
h**i**nzetsen

do sit down nehmen Sie Platz
naymen zee plats

size die Größe grurss-uh

ski der Ski shee

(*verb*) skifahren sheefahren

a pair of skis ein Paar Skier
pahr shee-er

ski boots die Skistiefel
shee-shteefel

skiing das Skifahren sheefahren

we're going skiing wir gehen
Skilaufen veer gay-en
shee-lowfen

ski instructor (*male/female*)
der Skilehrer shee-lairer/die
Skilehrerin

ski-lift der Skilift sheelift

skin die Haut howt

skinny dünn dɷnn

ski-pants die Skihose
shee-hohz-uh

ski-pass der Skipass sheepas

ski pole der Skistock sheeshtock

skirt der Rock

ski run die Skipiste shee-pist-uh

ski slope die Skipiste
shee-pist-uh

ski wax das Skiwachs
sheevacks

sky der Himmel

sleep schlafen shlahfen

did you sleep well? haben
Sie gut geschlafen? hahben zee
gɷot geshlahfen

I need a good sleep ich
muss mich mal richtig
ausschlafen rishtish
owss-shlahfen

sleeper (on train) der Schlafwagen
shlahfvahgen

sleeping bag der Schlafsack
shlahfzack

sleeping car der Schlafwagen
shlahfvahgen

sleeping pill die Schlaftablette
shlahf-tablett-uh

sleepy: I'm feeling sleepy ich
bin müde ish bin mɷod-uh

sleeve der Ärmel airmel

slide (photographic) das Dia dee-ah

slip (under dress) der Unterrock
ɷonter-rock

slippery glatt

Slovak (*adj*) slowakisch slovahkish

Slovak Republic die
Slowakische Republik
slovahkish-uh repɷobleek

slow langsam langzahm

slow down! etwas langsamer
bitte etvass

slowly langsam langzahm

could you say it slowly?
könnten Sie das etwas
langsamer sagen? kurnten zee
dass etvass langzahmer zahgen

very slowly ganz langsam
gants

small klein kline

smell: it smells es stinkt shtinkt

smile (*verb*) lächeln lesheln

smoke der Rauch rowKH

do you mind if I smoke?
macht es Ihnen etwas aus,
wenn ich rauche? maKHt ess
een-en etvass owss venn ish
rowKH-uh

I don't smoke ich bin Nichtraucher nishtrowкнer

do you smoke? rauchen Sie? rowкнen zee

snack: I'd just like a snack ich möchte nur eine Kleinigkeit ish mursht-uh noor ine-uh klynish-kite

sneeze (*verb*) niesen neezen

snorkel der Schnorchel shnorshel

snow der Schnee shnay

it's snowing es schneit shnite

so: it's so good es ist so gut zo goot

not so fast nicht so schnell

so am I ich auch ish owкн

so do I ich auch

so-so einigermaßen ine-iger-mahssen

soaking solution (for contact lenses) die Aufbewahrungslösung owfbevahroongs-lurzoong

soap die Seife zyf-uh

soap powder das Waschpulver vashpoolver

sober nüchtern nooshtern

sock die Socke zock-uh

socket (electrical) die Steckdose shteck-dohz-uh

soda (water) das Sodawasser zohda-vasser

sofa das Sofa zohfa

soft (material etc) weich vysh

soft-boiled egg das weichgekochte Ei vysh-gekoкнt-uh ī

soft drink das alkoholfreie Getränk alkohohlfry-uh getrenk, der Soft drink

soft lenses die weichen Kontaktlinsen vyshen kontakt-linzen

sole die Sohle zohl-uh

could you put new soles

on these? können Sie diese Schuhe neu besohlen? **kurnen zee** deez-uh shoo-uh noy bezohlen

some: can I have some water/rolls? kann ich etwas Wasser/ein paar Brötchen haben? **etvass vasser/ine pahr brurt-shen hahben**

can I have some of those? kann ich ein paar davon haben? da-fon

somebody, someone jemand yaymant

something etwas etvass

something to drink etwas zu trinken

sometimes manchmal manshmahl

somewhere irgendwo eergentvo

son der Sohn zohn

song das Lied leet

son-in-law der Schwiegersohn shveeger-zohn

soon bald balt

I'll be back soon ich bin bald zurück ish bin balt tsooroock

as soon as possible so bald wie möglich vee murglish

sore: it's sore es tut weh toot vay

sore throat die Halsschmerzen hals-shmairtsen

sorry: (I'm) sorry tut mir Leid toot meer lite

sorry? (didn't understand) wie bitte? vee bitt-uh

sort: what sort of...? welche Art von...? velsh-uh art fon

soup die Suppe zoop-uh

sour (taste) sauer zower

south der Süden zooden

in the south im Süden

to the south nach Süden

South Africa Südafrika zoot-afrika

South African (adj) südafrikanisch zoot-afrikahnish

I'm South African (male/female) ich bin Südafrikaner zoot-afrikahner/Südafrikanerin

southeast der Südosten zoot-osten

southwest der Südwesten zoot-vesten

souvenir das Souvenir

spa der Kurort koor-ort

spanner der Schraubenschlüssel shrowben-shloosel

spare part das Ersatzteil airzats-tile

spare tyre der Ersatzreifen airzats-ryfen

spark plug die Zündkerze tsoont-kairts-uh

speak: do you speak English? sprechen Sie Englisch? shpreshen zee eng-lish

I don't speak... ich spreche kein... ish shpresh-uh kine

I'm sorry, he's not in, can I take a message? tut mir Leid, er ist nicht da, kann ich etwas ausrichten?
toot meer lite, air ist nisht da, kann ish **etvass owss**-rishten

no thanks, I'll call back later nein danke, ich rufe später nochmal an nine dank-uh, ish roof-uh shpayter noKHmahl an

please tell him I called bitte sagen Sie ihm, dass ich angerufen habe zahgen zee eem, dass ish an-geroofen hahb-uh

speciality die Spezialität shpets-yalitayt

spectacles die Brille brill-uh

speed die Geschwindigkeit geshvindish-kite

speed limit die Geschwindig-keitsbeschränkung geshvindishkites-beshrenkoong

speedometer der Tachometer taKHomayter

spell: how do you spell it? wie schreibt man das? vee shrypt man dass
see **alphabet**

spend ausgeben owssgayben
(time) verbringen fairbring-en

spider die Spinne shpinn-uh

spin-dryer die Schleuder shloyder

splinter der Splitter shplitter

spoke (in wheel) die Speiche shpysh-uh

spoon der Löffel lurfel

sport der Sport shport

sprain: I've sprained my... ich habe mein... verstaucht ish hahb-uh mine... fair-shtowKHt

spring (season) der Frühling frooling
(of car, seat) die Feder fayder

square (in town) der Platz plats

stairs die Treppe trepp-uh

stale (bread) alt
(drink) abgestanden ap-geshtanden

stall: the engine keeps stalling der Motor geht dauernd aus dair mohtohr gayt dowernt owss

stamp die Briefmarke breefmark-uh

a stamp for England, please eine Marke nach England bitte ine-uh mark-uh naKH England bitte

what are you sending? was möchten Sie senden? vass murshten zee zenden

this postcard diese Postkarte deez-uh posstkart-uh

standby: standby ticket das Standby-Ticket

star der Stern shtairn
(in film) der Star

start der Anfang anfang

(*verb*) anfangen

when does it start?
wann fängt es an? van
fengt ess an

the car won't start das Auto
springt nicht an dass **ow**to
shpringt nisht an

starter (of car) der **A**nlasser
(food) die Vorspeise for-shpize-uh

state (in country) das Land lant

the States (USA) die USA
00-ess-**ah**

station der Bahnhof ba**h**nhohf

statue die Statue sht**ah**-t00-uh

stay: where are you staying?
wo wohnen Sie? vo v**oh**nen zee

I'm staying at... ich wohne
in... ish v**oh**n-uh

**I'd like to stay another two
nights** ich möchte gern noch
zwei Tage bleiben m**ur**sht-uh
gairn no**KH** – t**ah**g-uh bl**y**ben

steak das Steak

steal stehlen sht**ay**len

my bag has been stolen
meine T**a**sche ist gestohlen
worden gesht**oh**len v**o**rden

steep (hill) steil shtile

steering die Lenkung l**e**nkoong

step: on the steps auf den
Stufen owf dayn sht**oo**fen

stereo die Stereoanlage
sht**ay**ray-oh-anlahg-uh

sterling das Pfund St**e**rling pfoont

steward (on plane) der Steward

stewardess die Stewardess

sticking plaster das

H**e**ftpflaster

still: I'm still waiting ich warte
immer noch v**a**rt-uh – no**KH**

is he still there? ist er noch
da?

keep still! stillhalten!
sht**i**ll-halten

sting: I've been stung ich bin
gestochen worden gesht**o**KHen
v**o**rden

stockings die Strümpfe
shtr**oo**mpf-uh

stomach der Magen m**ah**gen

stomach ache die
Magenschmerzen
m**ah**gen-shmairtsen

stone (rock) der Stein shtine

stop (*verb*) anhalten

please, stop here (to taxi
driver etc) bitte halten Sie hier
b**i**tt-uh hal-ten zee heer

do you stop near...? halten
Sie in der Nähe von...? n**ay**-uh

stop doing that! hören Sie
auf damit! h**ur**-ren zee owf damit

stopover die Zwischenstation
tsv**i**shen-shtats-yohn

storm der Sturm sht**oo**rm

straight: it's straight ahead es
ist geradeaus ger**ah**d-uh-**ow**ss

a straight whisky ein Whisky
pur p**oo**r

straightaway sofort zof**o**rt

strange (odd) seltsam z**e**ltzahm

stranger (*male/female*) der/die
Fr**e**md-uh

I'm a stranger here ich bin
hier fremd heer fremt

strap (on watch) das Band bant
  (on dress) der Träger trayger
  (on suitcase) der Riemen reemen
strawberry die Erdbeere
  airtbair-uh
stream der Bach baкн
street die Straße shtrahss-uh
  on the street auf der Straße
  owf dair
streetmap der Stadtplan
  shtattplahn
string die Schnur shnoor
strong (person, drink) stark shtark
  (taste) kräftig kreftish
stuck: the key's stuck der
  Schlüssel steckt fest shteckt
student (*male/female*) der Student
  shtoodent/die Studentin
stupid dumm doomm
suburb die Vorstadt for-shtatt
subway (US) die U-Bahn
  00-bahn
suddenly plötzlich plurtslish
suede das Wildleder vilt-layder
sugar der Zucker tsoocker
suit der Anzug antsook
  it doesn't suit me (jacket etc)
  es steht mir nicht shtayt meer
  nisht
  it suits you es steht Ihnen
  eenen
suitcase der Koffer
summer der Sommer zommer
  in the summer im Sommer
sun die Sonne zonn-uh
  in the sun in der Sonne
  out of the sun im Schatten

shatten
sunbathe sonnenbaden zonnenbahden
sunblock (cream) die Sun-Block-
  Creme -kraym
sunburn der Sonnenbrand
  zonnen-brant
sunburnt: to get sunburnt
  einen Sonnenbrand bekommen
  ine-en zonnen-brant
Sunday Sonntag zonntahk
sunglasses die Sonnenbrille
  zonnen-brill-uh
sun lounger der Ruhesessel
  r00-uh-zessel
sunny: it's sunny die Sonne
  scheint dee zonn-uh shynt
sun roof (in car) das Schiebedach
  sheeb-uh-daкн
sunset der Sonnenuntergang
  zonnen-oontergang
sunshade der Sonnenschirm
  zonnen-sheerm
sunshine der Sonnenschein
  zonnen-shine
sunstroke der Sonnenstich
  zonnen-shtish
suntan die Sonnenbräune
  zonnen-broyn-uh
suntan lotion die Sonnenmilch
  zonnen-milsh
suntanned braungebrannt
  brown-gebrannt
suntan oil das Sonnenöl
  zonnen-url
super fantastisch
  fantastish
supermarket der Supermarkt

zoopermarkt

supper das Abendessen **ah**bent-essen

supplement (extra charge) der Zuschlag ts**oo**shlahk

sure: are you sure? bist du/ sind Sie sicher? bist d**oo**/zint zee z**i**sher

sure! klar!

surname der Nachname na**kh**nahm-uh

swearword der Kraftausdruck kraft-**ow**ssdroock

> Travel tip Although far more
> relaxed than even a decade
> ago, German etiquette is
> generally more formal and
> politer than you might per-
> haps expect. Swearing or
> shouting in public is frowned
> upon – met with a dismissive
> shrug at best and barely
> concealed disdain at worst.

sweater der Pullover pool**oh**ver

sweatshirt das Sweatshirt

Sweden Schweden shv**ay**den

Swedish schwedisch shv**ay**dish

sweet (taste) süß z**oo**ss

(noun: dessert) der Nachtisch na**kh**tish

sweets die Süßigkeiten z**oo**ssish-kyten

swelling die Schwellung shv**e**lloong

swim (verb) schwimmen shv**i**mmen

I'm going for a swim ich gehe schwimmen g**ay**-uh

let's go for a swim gehen wir schwimmen g**ay**-en veer

swimming costume der Badeanzug b**ah**d-uh-antsook

swimming pool das Schwimmbad shv**i**mmbaht

swimming trunks die Badehose b**ah**d-uh-hohz-uh

Swiss (male/female) der Schweizer shv**y**tser/die Schweizerin

(adj) schweizerisch shv**y**tserish

the Swiss die Schweizer

Swiss Alps die Schweizer Alpen shv**y**tser

switch der Schalter sh**a**lter

switch off (TV, lights) ausschalten **ow**ss-shalten

(engine) abstellen **a**p-shtellen

switch on (TV, lights) einschalten **ine**-shalten

(engine) **a**nlassen

Switzerland die Schweiz shv**i**tes

swollen geschwollen geshv**o**llen

T

table der Tisch tish

a table for two ein Tisch für zwei Personen f**oo**r tsvy pairts**oh**nen

tablecloth das Tischtuch t**i**sht00kh

table tennis das Tischtennis t**i**shtennis

table wine der Tafelwein

tahfelvine

tailback (of traffic) der Rückstau roock-shtow

tailor der Schneider shnyder

take (lead) bringen

(accept) nehmen naymen

can you take me to the airport? können Sie mich zum Flughafen bringen? kurnen zee mish tsoom

do you take credit cards? nehmen Sie Kreditkarten?

fine, I'll take it gut, ich nehme es goot, ish naym-uh ess

can I take this? (leaflet etc) kann ich das mitnehmen? mitnaymen

how long does it take? wie lange dauert es? vee lang-uh dowert ess

it takes three hours es dauert drei Stunden

is this seat taken? ist dieser Platz besetzt? deezer plats bezetst

hamburger to take away Hamburger zum Mitnehmen tsoom

can you take a little off here? (to hairdresser) können Sie hier etwas kürzen? kurnen zee heer etvass koortsen

talcum powder der Körperpuder kurper-pooder

talk (verb) sprechen shpreshen

tall (person) groß grohss

(building) hoch hohкн

tampons die Tampons

tan die Bräune broyn-uh

to get a tan braun werden brown vairden

tank (of car) der Tank

tap der Wasserhahn vasserhahn

tape (for cassette) das Band bant

(sticky) das Klebeband klayb-uh-bant

tape measure das Bandmaß bantmahss

tape recorder der Kassettenrecorder

taste der Geschmack geshmack

can I taste it? kann ich es probieren? probeeren

taxi das Taxi

will you get me a taxi? können Sie mir ein Taxi bestellen? kurnen zee meer

where can I find a taxi? wo bekomme ich ein Taxi? vo bekomm-uh ish

to the airport/to Hotel… please zum Flughafen/ zum Hotel… bitte tsoom

how much will it be? was kostet das?

thirty euros dreißig Euro

that's fine right here thanks bis hierhin, danke heer-hin

taxi-driver der Taxifahrer

taxi rank der Taxistand taksi-shtant

tea (drink) der Tee tay

tea for one/two please Tee für eine Person/zwei Personen bitte foor **ine**-uh pairz**ohn**/tsvy pairz**oh**nen b**i**tt-uh

teabag der Teebeutel **tay**boytel

teach: could you teach me? könnten Sie es mir beibringen? **ku**rnten zee ess meer b**y**bringen

teacher (*male/female*) der Lehrer l**ai**rer/die Lehrerin

team das Team

teaspoon der Teelöffel **tay**-lurfel

tea towel das Geschirrtuch gesh**ee**r-t00KH

teenager der Teenager

telephone das Telefon telef**oh**n

television das Fernsehen f**ai**rn-zay-en

tell: could you tell him...? können Sie ihm sagen...? **ku**rnen zee eem z**ah**gen

temperature (weather) die Temperatur temperat**00**r

(fever) das Fieber f**ee**ber

tennis das Tennis

tennis ball der Tennisball t**e**nnis-bal

tennis court der Tennisplatz t**e**nnis-plats

tennis racket der Tennis-schläger t**e**nnis-shl**ay**ger

tent das Zelt tselt

term (at school) das Halbjahr h**a**lp-yar

(at university) das Semester zem**e**ster

terminus (rail) die Endstation **e**nt-shtats-yohn

terrible furchtbar f**00**rshtbar

terrific sagenhaft z**ah**genhaft

text (message) die SMS ess-em-**e**ss

(*verb*) simsen z**i**mzen

than als alss

smaller than kleiner als

thanks, thank you danke d**a**nk-uh

thank you very much vielen Dank f**ee**len

thanks for the lift danke fürs Mitnehmen f**00**rs m**i**tnaymen

no thanks nein danke nine

that: that man dieser Mann d**ee**zer

that woman diese Frau d**ee**z-uh

that one das da

I hope that... ich hoffe, dass... dass

that's nice das ist schön

is that...? ist das...?

that's it (that's right) genau gen**ow**

the (*singular*) der/die/das dair/dee/dass

(*plural*) die dee

theatre das Theater tay**ah**ter

their ihr **ee**r

theirs ihrer **ee**r-er

them sie zee

for them für sie foor

with them mit ihnen een-en

I gave it to them ich habe es
ihnen gegeben hahb-uh

then (at that time) damals dahmalss

(after that) dann

there da, dort

over there dort drüben
drooben

up there da oben

is there…? gibt es…? geept

are there…? gibt es…?

there is… es gibt…

there are… es gibt…

there you are (giving
something) bitte bitt-uh

thermometer das Thermometer
tairmo-mayter

thermos flask die
Thermosflasche tairmoss-
flash-uh

these: these men diese Männer
deez-uh

these women diese Frauen

can I have these? kann ich
diese hier haben? heer

they sie zee

thick dick

(stupid) blöd blurt

thief der Dieb deep

thigh der Schenkel shenkel

thin dünn doon

thing das Ding

my things meine Sachen
mine-uh zakHen

think denken

I think so ich glaube ja glowb-

uh ya

I don't think so ich glaube
nicht nisht

I'll think about it ich werde
darüber nachdenken vaird-uh
daroober nakHdenken

third party insurance die
Haftpflichtversicherung
haft-pflisht-fairzisheroong

thirsty: I'm thirsty ich habe
Durst hahb-uh doorst

this: this man dieser Mann
deezer

this woman diese Frau
deez-uh

this one dieser/diese/dieses
deezess

this is my wife das ist meine
Frau mine-uh frow

is this…? ist das…?

those: those men diese
Männer deez-uh

those women diese Frauen

which ones? – those
welche? – diese velsh-uh

thread der Faden fahden

throat der Hals halss

throat pastilles die
Halstabletten halss-tabletten

through durch doorsh

does it go through…? (train,
bus) fährt er über…? fairt air
oober

throw (verb) werfen vairfen

throw away (verb) wegwerfen
vekvairfen

thumb der Daumen dowmen

thunderstorm das Gewitter

gevitter

Thursday Donnerstag
donnerstahk

ticket (train, bus, boat) die
Fahrkarte fahrkart-uh

(plane) das Ticket

(theatre, cinema) die
Eintrittskarte ine-trittskart-uh

(cloakroom) die
Garderobenmarke
garderohben-mark-uh

**a return ticket to
Heidelberg** eine
Rückfahrkarte nach
Heidelberg

coming back when? wann
soll die Rückfahrt sein?
rOOck-fahrt

today/next Tuesday heute/
nächsten Dienstag

that will be ninety euros
das macht neunzig Euro

ticket office (bus, rail) der
Fahrkartenschalter
fahrkarten-shalter

tide: high tide die Flut flOOt

low tide die Ebbe ebb-uh

tie (necktie) die Krawatte
kravatt-uh

tight (clothes etc) eng

it's too tight es ist zu eng tsOO

tights die Strumpfhose
shtrOOmpf-hohz-uh

till (cash desk) die Kasse kass-uh

time die Zeit tsite

what's the time? wie spät ist
es? vee shpayt ist ess

this time diesmal deessmahl

last time letztes Mal
letstess mahl

next time nächstes Mal
naykstess

four times viermal feermahl

timetable der Fahrplan fahrplahn

tin (can) die Dose dohz-uh

tinfoil die Alufolie ahlOO-fohl-yuh

tin opener der Dosenöffner
dohzen-urfner

tiny winzig vintsish

tip (to waiter etc) das Trinkgeld
trinkgelt

tired müde mOOd-uh

I'm tired ich bin müde

tissues die Papiertücher
papeer-tOOsher

to: to Freiburg/London nach
Freiburg/London naKH

to Germany/England nach
Deutschland/England

to the post office zum
Postamt tsoom

to the bank zur Bank tsOOr

toast (bread) der Toast

today heute hoyt-uh

toe der Zeh tsay

together zusammen tsoozammen

we're together (in shop etc)
wir sind zusammen veer zint

can we pay together?
können wir zusammen
bezahlen? kurnen veer –
betsahlen

toilet die Toilette twal**e**tt-uh

where is the toilet? wo ist
die Toilette? vo

I have to go to the toilet ich
muss zur Toilette ts**oo**r

toilet paper das Toilettenpapier
twal**e**tten-pap**ee**r

tomato die Tomate tom**ah**t-uh

tomato juice der Tomatensaft
tom**ah**tenzaft

tomato ketchup der
Tomatenketchup

tomorrow m**o**rgen

tomorrow morning m**o**rgen
früh fr**oo**

the day after tomorrow
übermorgen **oo**bermorgen

toner (cosmetic) die
Tönungslotion t**u**rnoongs-lohts-
yohn

tongue die Zunge ts**oo**ng-uh

tonic (water) das Tonic

tonight heute abend h**oy**t-uh
ahbent

tonsillitis die Mandelentzündung m**a**ndel-ent-
ts**oo**ndoong

too (excessively) zu ts**oo**

(also) auch owKH

too hot zu heiß hice

too much zuviel ts**oo**f**ee**l

me too ich auch ish

tooth der Zahn tsahn

toothache die Zahnschmerzen
ts**ah**n-shmairtsen

toothbrush die Zahnbürste
ts**ah**n-b**oo**rst-uh

toothpaste die Zahnpasta
ts**ah**npasta

top: on top of... oben auf...
ohben owf

at the top oben

top floor der oberste Stock
ohberst-uh shtock

topless oben ohne **oh**ben **oh**n-uh

torch die Taschenlampe
t**a**shenlamp-uh

total die Endsumme **e**ntzoom-uh

what's the total? was macht
das zusammen? vass maKHt dass
ts**oo**z**a**mmen

tour (journey) die Reise r**ize**-uh

is there a tour of...? gibt es
eine Führung durch...? geept
ess **ine**-uh f**oo**roong doorsh

tour guide der Reiseleiter
r**ize**-uh-lyter

tourist (*male/female*) der Tourist
t**oo**rist/die Touristin

tourist information office das
Fremdenverkehrsbüro
fr**e**mden-fairkairs-b**oo**ro

Travel tip You'll find a
walk-in tourist office almost
wherever you go. They typi-
cally stock a good spread of
pamphlets and brochures,
usually in English in larger
towns and cities, where one
member of staff will be near-
fluent.

---

tour operator der
Reiseveranstalter r**ize**-uh-
fair**a**nshtalter

towards nach naKH

towel das Handtuch
hant-tOOKH

town die Stadt shtatt

in town in der Stadt dair

just out of town am
Stadtrand shtattrant

town centre die Innenstadt
innen-shtatt

town hall das Rathaus raht-howss

toy das Spielzeug shpeel-tsoyk

track (US: at train station) der
Bahnsteig bahnshtike

tracksuit der Trainingsanzug
trainings-antsOOk

traditional traditionell tradits-
yohnell

traffic der Verkehr fairkair

traffic jam der Stau shtow

traffic lights die Ampel

trailer (for carrying tent etc) der
Anhänger anheng-er
(US: caravan) der Wohnwagen
vohnvahgen

trailer park der Wohnwagenplatz
vohnvahgen-plats

train der Zug tsOOk

by train mit dem Zug daym

is this the train for...? fährt
dieser Zug nach...? fairt
deezer tsOOk naKH

sure ja yah

**no, you want that platform
there** nein, gehen Sie zu
dem Bahnsteig da nine, gay-
en zee tsOO daym bahnshtike

trainers (shoes) die Turnschuhe
toornshOO-uh

train station der Bahnhof
bahnhohf

tram die Straßenbahn
shtrahssen-bahn

translate übersetzen OOber-zetsen

could you translate that?
könnten Sie das übersetzen?
kurnten zee

translation die Übersetzung
OOber-zetsoong

translator (*male/female*) der
Übersetzer OOber-zetser/die
Übersetzerin

trash (waste) der Abfall ap-fal
(poor quality goods) der Mist

trashcan die Mülltonne
mOOlltonn-uh

travel reisen ryzen

we're travelling around wir
machen eine Rundreise veer
maKHen ine-uh roont-rize-uh

travel agent's das Reisebüro
rize-uh-bOOro

traveller's cheque der
Reisescheck rize-uh-sheck

tray das Tablett

tree der Baum bowm

tremendous fantastisch
fantastish

trendy schick shick

trim: just a trim please (to
hairdresser) nur etwas kürzen,
bitte nOOr etvass kOOrtsen bitt-uh

trip (excursion) der Ausflug
owssflOOk

I'd like to go on a trip to… ich möchte gern eine Reise nach… machen m**u**rsht-uh gairn **ine**-uh r**i**ze-uh naкн… m**a**кнen

trolley (in supermarket) der Einkaufswagen **ine**-kowfs-vahgen

(in station) der Kofferkuli k**o**ffer-k00lee

trouble die Schwierigkeiten shv**ee**rish-kyten

I'm having trouble with… ich habe Schwierigkeiten mit… h**a**hb-uh

sorry to trouble you tut mir Leid, Sie zu belästigen t00t meer lite zee ts00 bel**e**stigen

trousers die Hose h**oh**z-uh

true wahr vahr

that's not true das stimmt nicht shtimmt nisht

trunk (US: of car) der Kofferraum k**o**ffer-rowm

trunks (swimming) die Badehose b**ah**d-uh-hohz-uh

try (*verb*) versuchen fairz**00**кнen

can I have a try? kann ich es versuchen?

try on: can I try it on? kann ich es anprobieren? **a**n-probeeren

T-shirt das T-Shirt

Tuesday Dienstag d**ee**nstahk

tuna der Thunfisch t**00**nfish

tunnel der Tunnel t**00**nnel

Turkey die Türkei t00rk**ī**

Turkish (*adj*) türkisch t**00**rkish

(language) Türkisch

turn: turn left/right biegen Sie links/rechts ab b**ee**gen zee links/ reshts ap

turn off: where do I turn off? wo muss ich abbiegen? vo mooss ish **a**p-beegen

can you turn the heating off? können Sie die Heizung abstellen? k**u**rnen zee dee h**y**tsoong ap-shtellen

turn on: can you turn the heating on? können Sie die Heizung anstellen? k**u**rnen zee dee h**y**tsoong **a**n-shtellen

turning (in road) die Abzweigung **a**p-tsvygoong

TV das Fernsehen f**a**irnzay-en

tweezers die Pinzette pin-ts**e**tt-uh

twice zweimal tsv**y**mahl

twice as much zweimal soviel zof**ee**l

twin beds zwei Einzelbetten tsvy **ine**-tsel-betten

twin room das Zweibettzimmer tsv**y**bett-tsimmer

twist: I've twisted my ankle ich habe mir den Fuß vertreten ish h**a**hb-uh meer dayn f00ss fairtr**ay**ten

type die Art

a different type of… eine andere Art von… **ine**-uh **a**nder-uh

typical typisch t**00**pish

tyre der Reifen r**y**fen

U

ugly hässlich hesslish

UK das Vereinigte Königreich fair-**ine**-isht-uh **kur**nish-rysh

ulcer das Geschwür geshv**oo**r

umbrella der Schirm sheerm

uncle der **O**nkel

unconscious bewusstlos bev**oo**st-lohss

under unter **oo**nter

underdone (meat) nicht gar nisht

underground (railway) die U-Bahn **oo**-bahn

underpants die Unterhose **oo**nter-hohz-uh

understand: I understand ich verstehe ish fairsht**ay**-uh

  I don't understand das verstehe ich nicht nisht

  do you understand? verstehen Sie? fairsht**ay**-en zee

unemployed arbeitslos **ar**bites-lohss

United States die Vereinigten Staaten fair-**ine**-ishten sht**ah**ten

university die Universität **oo**nivairzi-**tayt**

unleaded petrol das bleifreie Benzin bly-fry-uh bents**een**

unlimited mileage ohne Kilometerbeschränkung ohn-uh keelo-**may**ter-beshr**e**nkoong

unlock aufschließen **owf**-shleessen

unpack auspacken **ow**ss-packen

until bis biss

unusual ungewöhnlich **oo**n-gevurnlish

up oben **oh**ben

  up there da oben

  he's not up yet (not out of bed) er ist noch nicht auf noкн nisht owf

  what's up? (what's wrong?) was ist los? vass ist lohss

upmarket (restaurant, hotel, goods etc) anspruchsvoll **a**nshprooкнsfoll

upset stomach die Magenverstimmung m**ah**gen-fairsht**i**mmoong

upside down verkehrt herum fairk**ai**rt hair**oo**m

upstairs oben **oh**ben

urgent dringend dr**i**ng-ent

us uns oonss

  with us mit uns

  for us für uns f**oo**r

USA die USA 00-ess-**ah**

use (verb) benutzen ben**oo**tsen

  may I use…? kann ich… benutzen?

useful nützlich n**oo**tslish

user id die Nutzer-ID n**oo**tser-īdee

usual üblich **oo**plish

  the usual (drink etc) dasselbe wie immer dass**e**lb-uh vee

V

vacancy: do you have any vacancies? (hotel) haben

Sie Zimmer frei? ha**h**ben zee
tsi**m**mer fry

vacation der Urlaub **oo**rlowp

(from university) die
Semesterferien zem**e**ster-
fairee-en

vaccination die Impfung
impfoong

vacuum cleaner der
Staubsauger sht**ow**p-zowger

valid (ticket etc) gültig g**oo**ltish

how long is it valid for?
wie lange ist es gültig?
vee l**a**ng-uh

valley das Tal tahl

valuable (*adj*) wertvoll v**a**irtfol

**can I leave my valuables
here?** kann ich meine
Wertsachen hierlassen? m**i**ne-
uh v**a**irtzakHen h**ee**rlassen

value der Wert vairt

van der Lieferwagen l**ee**fervahgen

vanilla die Vanille van**i**ll-uh

a vanilla ice cream ein
Vanilleeis van**i**ll-uh-ice

vary: it varies es ist
unterschiedlich
oonter-sheetlish

vase die Vase v**ah**z-uh

veal das Kalbfleisch k**a**lp-flysh

vegetables das Gemüse
gem**oo**z-uh

vegetarian (*male/female*) der
Vegetarier vegayt**ah**ree-er/die
Veget**a**rierin

vending machine der Automat
owtom**ah**t

very sehr zair

very little for me nur eine
Kleinigkeit für mich n**oo**r **i**ne-uh
kl**i**ne-ishkite f**oo**r mish

I like it very much ich mag es
sehr gern gairn

vest (under shirt) das Unterhemd
oonterhemt

via über **oo**ber

video (film) das Video

(recorder) der Videorecorder

Vienna Wien veen

view der Blick

villa die Villa

village das Dorf

vinegar der Essig **e**ssish

vineyard der Weinberg v**i**ne-bairk

visa das Visum v**ee**zoom

visit (*verb*) besuchen bez**oo**kHen

I'd like to visit... ich
möchte... besuchen m**u**rsht-uh

vital: it's vital that... es ist
unbedingt notwendig, dass...
oon-bedingt n**oh**tvendish

vodka der Wodka v**o**dka

voice die Stimme sht**i**mm-uh

voltage die Spannung
shp**a**nnoong

vomit erbrechen airbr**e**shen

W

waist die Taille t**a**l-yuh

waistcoat die Weste v**e**st-uh

wait warten v**a**rten

wait for me warten Sie auf
mich zee owf mish

don't wait for me warten Sie nicht auf mich nisht

can I wait until my wife/ partner gets here? (eg as said to waiter) kann ich warten, bis meine Frau/Partnerin kommt?

can you do it while I wait? kann ich darauf warten? dar**owf**

could you wait here for me? (eg as said to taxi driver) können Sie hier warten? **kur**nen zee heer

waiter der Ober **oh**ber

waiter! Herr Ober! hair

waitress die Kellnerin

waitress! Fräulein! **froy**line

wake: can you wake me up at 5.30? können Sie mich um 5.30 Uhr wecken? **kur**nen zee mish oom – **veck**en

wake-up call der Weckanruf **veck**-anroof

Wales Wales

walk: is it a long walk? geht man lange dorthin? gayt man lang-uh

Travel tip Germany has an abundance of scenic walks and long-distance hikes, and no matter where you go there'll be a well-marked trail or pleasant short stroll. The most popular is the Rennsteig (168 km) in the Thuringian Forest, but the Malerweg (112 km) in Saxon Switzerland is the prettiest.

it's only a short walk es ist nicht weit zu gehen nisht vite ts00 **gay**-en

I'll walk ich gehe zu Fuß gay-uh ts00 f00ss

I'm going for a walk ich gehe spazieren shpats**ee**ren

wall die Wand vant

(external) die Mauer **mow**er

wallet die Brieftasche **breef**tash-uh

wander: I like just wandering around ich wandere gern einfach so durch die Gegend ish **van**der-uh gairn **ine**-faKH zo doorsh dee **gay**gent

want: I want two... ich möchte zwei... ish **mursht**-uh

I don't want any... ich möchte keinen... k**ine**-en

I want to go home ich will nach Hause vill

I don't want to ich will nicht nisht

he wants to... er will...

what do you want? was wollen Sie? vass **voll**en zee

ward (in hospital) die Station shtats-y**oh**n

warm warm varm

I'm so warm mir ist so warm meer

was: I/he/she/it was... ich/er/ sie/es war... vahr

wash (*verb*) waschen v**a**shen

can you wash these? können Sie die für mich waschen? **kur**nen zee

washer (for bolt etc) die Dichtung

dishtoong

washhand basin das Handwaschbecken h**a**ntvash-becken

washing (clothes) die Wäsche v**e**sh-uh

washing machine die Waschmaschine v**a**shmasheen-uh

washing powder das Waschpulver v**a**shpoolver

washing-up liquid das Spülmittel shp**oo**lmittel

wasp die Wespe v**e**sp-uh

watch (wristwatch) die Armbanduhr **a**rmbant-00r

   will you watch my things for me? könnten Sie auf meine Sachen aufpassen? k**ur**nten zee owf m**ine**-uh z**a**khen **o**wfpassen

   watch out! p**a**ssen Sie auf!

watch strap das Uhrarmband 00r-armbant

water das Wasser v**a**sser

   may I have some water? kann ich etwas Wasser haben? **e**tvass – h**ah**ben

waterproof (*adj*) wasserfest v**a**sserfest

waterskiing Wasserskilaufen v**a**ssershee-lowfen

wave (in sea) die Welle v**e**ll-uh

way: it's this way es ist hier entlang heer

   it's that way es ist dort entlang

   is it a long way to…? ist es weit bis nach…? vite biss n**a**kh

   no way! auf keinen Fall! owf k**ine**-en fal

could you tell me the way to...? können Sie mir sagen, wie ich nach... komme? *kurnen zee meer zahgen vee ish naKH... komm-uh*

go straight on until you reach the traffic lights fahren Sie geradeaus bis zur Ampel *gerahd-uh-owss*

turn left biegen Sie links ab *beegen*

take the first on the right nehmen Sie die erste Straße rechts *naymen zee dee airst-uh shtrahss-uh reshts*

see also **where**

we wir *veer*

weak schwach *shvaKH*

weather das Wetter *vetter*

what's the weather forecast? wie ist die Wettervorhersage? *vee ist dee vetter-forhairzahg-uh*

it's going to be fine es gibt schönes Wetter geept *shurness*

it's going to rain es gibt Regen *raygen*

it'll brighten up later es wird sich später aufklären *veert zish shpayter owf-klairen*

website die Website *vep-site*

wedding die Hochzeit *hoKH-tsite*

---

wedding ring der Ehering *ay-uh-ring*

Wednesday Mittwoch *mittvoKH*

week die Woche *voKH-uh*

a week (from) today heute in einer Woche *hoyt-uh in ine-er*

a week (from) tomorrow morgen in einer Woche *morgen*

weekend das Wochenende *voKHen-end-uh*

at the weekend am Wochenende

weight das Gewicht *gevisht*

weird seltsam *zeltzahm*

weirdo der Verrückte *fair-rOOckt-uh*

welcome: welcome to... willkommen in... *villkommen*

you're welcome (don't mention it) keine Ursache *kine-uh OOrzaKH-uh*

well: I don't feel well ich fühle mich nicht wohl *ish fOOl-uh mish nisht vohl*

how are you? wie geht es dir? *vee gayt ess deer*

very well, thanks sehr gut, danke *zair gOOt dank-uh*

and you? und dir? *oont deer*

she's not well sie fühlt sich nicht wohl *zee*

you speak English very well Sie sprechen sehr gut Englisch *shpreshen zair gOOt eng-lish*

well done! gut gemacht! *gemaKHt*

this one as well diesen auch d**ee**zen owKH

well well! (surprise) na so was! zo vass

well-done (meat) gut durchgebraten g**oo**t d**oo**rsh-gebrahten

Welsh walisisch val-**ee**zish

I'm Welsh (*male/female*) ich bin Waliser val**ee**zer/Waliserin

were: you were du warst varst/ Sie waren zee v**ah**ren

we/they were wir/sie waren

west der Westen v**e**sten

in the west im Westen

West Indian (*adj*) westindisch v**e**st**i**ndish

wet nass

what? was? vass

what's that? was ist das?

what should I do? was soll ich tun? zoll ish t**oo**n

what a view! was für ein Blick! vass f**oo**r ine

what bus is it? welcher Bus ist das? v**e**lsher

wheel das Rad raht

wheelchair der Rollstuhl r**o**l-sht**oo**l

when? wann? van

when's the train/ferry? wann fährt der Zug/die Fähre? van fairt dair ts**oo**k/dee f**ai**r-uh

when we get back wenn wir zurückkommen ven veer tsoor**oo**ck-kommen

when we got back als wir zurückkamen alss

where? wo? vo

I don't know where it is ich weiß nicht, wo es ist vice nisht

where is the cathedral? wo ist der Dom?

it's over there er ist dort drüben dr**oo**ben

could you show me where it is on the map? können Sie ihn mir auf der Karte zeigen? k**u**rnen zee een meer – ts**y**gen

it's just here er ist da

see also **way**

which: which bus? welcher Bus? v**e**lsher

which house? welches Haus?

which bar? welche Bar?

which one? welcher?

that one dieser d**ee**zer

this one? dieser?

no, that one nein, dieser nine

while: while I'm here während ich hier bin v**ai**rent ish heer

whisky der Whisky

white weiß vice

white wine der Weißwein v**i**ce-vine

who? wer? vair

who is it? (reply to knock at door etc) wer ist da?

the man who... der Mann, der... dair

whole: the whole week die
ganze Woche dee gants-uh
voKH-uh

the whole lot das Ganze

whose: whose is this? wem
gehört das? vaym gehurt

why? warum? varoom

why not? warum nicht? nisht

wide breit brite

wife: my wife meine Frau
mine-uh frow

Wi-Fi der WLAN-Zugang vay-
lahn-tsoogang

will: will you do it for me?
können Sie es für mich tun?
kurnen zee ess foor mish toon

wind der Wind vint

window das Fenster

near the window am Fenster

in the window (of shop) im
Schaufenster show-fenster

window seat der Fensterplatz

windscreen die
Windschutzscheibe vint-shoots-
shybuh

windscreen wiper der
Scheibenwischer shyben-visher

windsurfing das Windsurfen
vintzurfen

windy: it's so windy es ist so
windig zo vindish

wine der Wein vine

**can we have some more
wine?** können wir noch etwas
Wein haben? kurnen veer noKH
etvass – hahben

wine list die Weinkarte vine-
kart-uh

winter der Winter vinter

in the winter im Winter

winter holiday der
Winterurlaub vinter-oorlowp

wire die Draht

(electric) die Leitung lytoong

wish: best wishes mit besten
Wünschen voonshen

with mit

I'm staying with... ich wohne
bei... vohn-uh by

without ohne ohn-uh

witness (male/female) der Zeuge
tsoyg-uh/die Zeugin

**will you be a witness for
me?** würden Sie für mich als
Zeuge zur Verfügung stehen?
voorden zee foor mish – tsoor
fairfoogoong shtay-en

woman die Frau frow

wonderful wundervoll
voonder-fol

won't: it won't start es will
nicht anspringen vill nisht
an-shpringen

wood (material) das Holz
holts

woods (forest) der Wald valt

wool die Wolle voll-uh

word das Wort vort

work die Arbeit arbite

it's not working es
funktioniert nicht foonkts-
yohneert nisht

I work in... ich arbeite in...
arbite-uh

world die Welt velt

worry: I'm worried ich mache mir Sorgen ish ma<small>KH</small>-uh meer z**o**rgen

worse: it's worse es ist schlimmer shl**i**mmer

worst am schlimmsten shl**i**mmsten

worth: is it worth a visit? lohnt sich ein Besuch dort? zish ine bez**OO**<small>KH</small>

would: would you give this to...? könnten Sie dies... geben? k**u**rnten zee – g**ay**ben

wrap: could you wrap it up? können Sie es einpacken? k**u**rnen zee ess **i**ne-packen

wrapping paper das Packpapier p**a**ck-papeer

wrist das Handgelenk h**a**ntgelenk

write schreiben shr**y**ben

could you write it down? könnten Sie es aufschreiben? k**u**rnten zee ess **ow**f-shryben

how do you write it? wie schreibt man das? vee shrypt

writing paper das Schreibpapier shr**i**pe-papeer

wrong: it's the wrong key es ist der falsche Schlüssel dair f**a**lsh-uh

this is the wrong train dies ist der falsche Zug

the bill's wrong in der Rechnung ist ein Fehler dair r**e**shnoong ist ine f**a**yler

sorry, wrong number tut mir Leid, falsch verbunden t**OO**t meer lite falsh fairb**oo**nden

sorry, wrong room tut mir leid, ich habe mich im Zimmer geirrt ish h**a**hb-uh mish im ts**i**mmer guh-**ee**rrt

there's something wrong with... mit... stimmt etwas nicht sht**i**mmt **e**tvass nisht

what's wrong? was ist los? vass ist l**oh**ss

X-ray die Röntgenaufnahme r**u**rntgen-owfnahm-uh

yacht die Jacht ya<small>KH</small>t

yard das Yard

year das Jahr yahr

yellow gelb gelp

yes ja yah

you don't smoke, do you? – yes Sie rauchen nicht, oder? – doch zee r**ow**<small>KH</small>en nisht **oh**der – do<small>KH</small>

yesterday g**e**stern

yesterday morning gestern m**o**rgen

the day before yesterday vorgestern f**o**rgestern

yet noch no<small>KH</small>

DIALOGUE

is he here yet? ist er schon
hier? air shohn heer

no, not yet nein, noch nicht
nine noKH nisht

**you'll have to wait a little
longer yet** Sie müssen
noch etwas warten zee
moossen

yoghurt der Joghurt yohg-hoort

you (*familiar: singular*) du doo
(*familiar: plural*) ihr eer
(*polite: singular and plural*) Sie zee

this is for you das ist für dich/
euch oysh/Sie

with you mit dir/euch/Ihnen
eenen

young jung yoong

your (*familiar: singular*) dein dine
(*familiar: plural*) euer oyer

(*polite*) Ihr eer

your camera deine/Ihre
Kamera dine-uh/eer-uh

yours (*familiar: singular*) deiner
dine-er
(*familiar: plural*) eurer oyrer
(*polite*) Ihrer eerer

youth hostel die Jugendherberge
yoogent-hairbairg-uh

Z

zero null nooll

zip der Reißverschluß rice-
fairshlooss

**could you put a new zip
on?** könnten Sie einen neuen
Reißverschluß anbringen?
kurnten zee ine-en noy-en

zoo der Zoo tsoh

GERMAN

→ **ENGLISH**

Colloquialisms

The following are words you might well hear. You shouldn't be tempted to use any of the stronger ones unless you are sure of your audience.

Arschloch *n* arshloKH arsehole

aufs Kreuz legen to screw, to lay; to take for a ride

blau blow pissed, smashed

Bulle *m* bool-uh cop

bumsen boomss-en to bonk

Bumslokal *n* boomss-lohkahl dive

das ist Jacke wie Hose yack-uh vee hohz-uh it doesn't make any difference

das ist mir scheißegal meer shice-aygahl I couldn't give a shit

du kannst mich mal fuck off, go to hell

du spinnst ja you're off your head

einen Scheißdreck werd' ich tun ine-en shice-dreck vaird ish toon no fucking way

ficken to fuck

geil gile brilliant; horny

kotzen to puke

leck mich am Arsch fuck off; fuck it

Mensch! mensh wow!, hey!

Mist *m* crap, rubbish

Nutte *f* noot-uh hooker, whore

Puff *m* poof brothel

Scheißdreck *m* shice-dreck shit

Scheiße *f* shice-uh shit

Scheißkerl *m* shice-kairl bastard, son-of-a-bitch

scheißvornehm shice-fornaym bloody posh, swanky

Spinner *m* shpinner crazy guy, nutcase

stark shtark great

verdammte Scheiße fairdammt-uh shice-uh bloody hell, fucking hell

verdammt noch mal bloody hell

verpiss dich fairpiss piss off, fuck off

A

ab ap from; off; down

abbiegen ap-beegen to turn off

Abblendlicht *n* ap-blent-lisht dipped/dimmed headlights

Abend *m* ahbent evening

zu Abend essen to have dinner

Abendessen *n* ahbent-essen dinner

Abendkleid *n* ahbent-klite evening dress

abends ahbents in the evening

aber ahber but

Abf. (Abfahrt) dept, departure

Abfahrt *f* ap-fahrt departure(s)

Abfall *m* ap-fal litter; rubbish, garbage

Abfälle litter

Abfalleimer *m* apfal-ime-er
rubbish bin, trashcan

Abfertigung *f* ap-fairtigoong
check-in

Abflug *m* ap-flook departure(s)

Abführmittel *n* ap-foor-mittel
laxative

abgefüllt in... bottled in...

abgezähltes Geld ap-getsayltess
gelt exact fare

abheben ap-hayben to take off;
to withdraw

Abhebung *f* ap-hayboong
withdrawal

abholen ap-hohlen to pick up

Abkürzung *f* ap-koortsoong
abbreviation; shortcut

ablehnen ap-laynen to refuse

abnehmen ap-naymen to lift
(the receiver); to remove; to
lose weight

abreisen ap-rize-en to leave

abschließen ap-shleessen
to lock

Absender *m* ap-zender sender

absichtlich ap-zishtlish
deliberately

absolutes Halteverbot waiting
strictly prohibited

absolutes Parkverbot parking
strictly prohibited

absolutes Rauchverbot
smoking strictly prohibited

Abstand *m* ap-shtant distance

Abtei *f* ap-tī abbey

Abteil *n* ap-tile compartment

Abteilung *f* ap-tyloong
department

Abtreibung *f* ap-tryboong
abortion

abtrocknen ap-trocknen to dry
the dishes

Abwasch *m* ap-vash washing-up

abwaschen ap-vashen to do the
dishes

Achse *f* aks-uh axle

ach so! аkн zo I see

acht aкнt eight

Achtung! aкнtoong look out!;
attention

Achtung! Straßenbahn
beware of trams

achtzehn aкн-tsayn eighteen

achtzig aкн-tsish eighty

**ADAC (Allgemeiner
Deutscher Automobil-
Club)** ah-day-ah-tsay German
motoring organization

Adressbuch *n* adressbooкн
address book

Affe *m* aff-uh monkey

Agentur *f* agentoor agency

ähneln ayneln to look like

ähnlich aynlish similar

Aktentasche *f* akten-tash-uh
briefcase

Aktie *f* aktsee-uh share

Akzent *m* aktsent accent

akzeptieren aktsepteeren
to accept

albern silly

alle al-uh all; everybody; finished,
all gone

allein aline alone

alle Kassen all health insurance schemes accepted

alle Rechte vorbehalten all rights reserved

Allergie *f* alairgee allergy

allergisch gegen alairgish gaygen allergic to

Allerheiligen *n* allerhyligen All Saints' Day (1 November)

alles al-ess everything

alles Gute al-ess gOOt-uh best wishes; all the best

alles klar! al-ess klar fine!, great!

allgemein al-gemine general; generally

Alpen Alps

als alss when; than; as

also alzo therefore

als ob alss op as if

alt old

Altbau *m* altbow old building

Altenheim *n* alten-hime old people's home

Alter *n* age

Altersheim *n* alters-hime old people's home

altmodisch alt-mohdish old-fashioned

Altstadt *f* alt-shtatt old (part of) town

Alufolie *f* ahlOO-fohlee-uh silver foil

a.M. (am Main) on the Main

am at the; on (the)

  am schnellsten (the) fastest

am Apparat am apparaht speaking

Ambulanz *f* ambOOlants out-patients

Ameise *f* ahmize-uh ant

Amerikaner *m* amairee-kahner, **Amerikanerin** *f* American

amerikanisch amairee-kahnish American

Ampel *f* traffic lights

amüsieren: sich amüsieren zish amOOzeeren to have fun

an at; to; on

anbieten anbeeten to offer

Andenken *n* souvenir

andere ander-uh other(s)

andere Orte other destinations

anderthalb andert-halp one and a half

Änderung *f* enderoong change; alteration

Anfall *m* anfal attack; fit

Anfang *m* beginning

anfangen to begin

Anfänger *m* anfenger, **Anfängerin** *f* beginner

Anfassen der Waren verboten do not touch the merchandise

Angeklagte *m/f* an-geklahkt-uh defendant

Angeln *m* ang-eln fishing

Angeln verboten no fishing

angenehm an-genaym pleasant; pleased to meet you

Angestellte *m/f* an-geshtellt-uh employee

Angst *f* fear

anhalten to stop

Anhalter: per Anhalter fahren
  to hitchhike

Anhänger *m* anhenger trailer;
  pendant; follower

Ank. (Ankunft) arr, arrival

Ankauf... we buy...

ankommen to arrive

ankreuzen ankroytsen to cross

Ankunft *f* ankoonft arrival(s)

Ankunftshalle *f* ankoonfts-hal-uh
  arrivals (area)

Anlieger frei residents only

Anmeldung *f* an-meldoong
  reception

anprobieren anprobeeren to
  try on

Anruf *m* anr00f call

anrufen anr00fen to phone, to ring

ans anss to the

anschalten an-shalten to
  switch on

Anschluss *m* an-shlooss
  connection

Anschluss an... connects
  with...

Anschrift *f* an-shrift address

ansehen anzay-en to look (at)

Ansicht *f* anzisht view; opinion

Ansichtskarte *f* anzishts-kart-uh
  picture postcard

anstatt an-shtatt instead of

ansteckend an-shteckent
  contagious

Antenne *f* antenn-uh aerial;
  antenna

Antiquitäten anti-kvitayten
  antiques

Antwort *f* antvort answer

antworten antvorten to answer

Anwalt *m* anvalt, **Anwältin**
  anveltin *f* lawyer

Anwohner frei residents only

Anzahlung *f* an-tsahloong deposit

anziehen antsee-en to dress

  sich anziehen zish
  to get dressed

Anzug *m* ants00k suit

anzünden an-ts00nden to light

**AOK (Allgemeine
  Ortskrankenkasse)** ah-oh-
  kah German health insurance
  scheme

Apotheke *f* apotayk-uh chemist's,
  pharmacy

Apparat *m* apparaht telephone;
  apparatus

Appetit *m* appeteet appetite

a.R. (am Rhein) on the Rhine

Arbeit *f* arbite work; job

arbeiten arbite-en to work

Arbeiter *m* arbyter, **Arbeiterin**
  f worker

arbeitslos arbites-lohss
  unemployed

**ARD (Arbeitsgemeinschaft
  der Rundfunkanstalten
  Deutschlands)** ah-air-day first
  German television channel

Ärger *m* airger annoyance;
  trouble; hassle

ärgerlich airgerlish annoying

ärgern: sich ärgern zish airgern
  to be/get annoyed

arm poor

Arm *m* arm

Armaturenbrett *n* armat**oo**ren-brett dashboard

Armband *n* armbant bracelet

Armbanduhr *f* armbant-**oo**r watch

Arschloch! arshlo**KH** bastard!

Art *f* sort, kind

Arzt *m* artst doctor

Ärztin *f* airtstin doctor

Ärztlicher Notdienst *m* airtst-lisher n**o**ht-deenst emergency medical service

Asche *f* ash-uh ash

Aschenbecher *m* ashenbesher ashtray

Aschermittwoch *m* asher-mittvo**KH** Ash Wednesday

aß ahss, **aßen** ahssen, **aßt** ahsst ate

atmen aht-men to breathe

Attentat *n* atten-taht assassination

Attest *n* certificate

auch ow**KH** too, also

auf owf on; to; open

   auf deutsch in German

Aufbewahrungslösung *f* owf-bevahroongs-lurzoong soaking solution

Aufenthalt *m* owf-ent-hallt stay

Aufenthaltsraum *m* owf-ent-hallts-rowm lounge

Aufführung *f* owf-f**oo**roong performance

aufgeben owf-gayben to give up; to post, to mail

aufhören owf-hur-ren to stop

aufpassen owf-passen to pay attention

aufpassen auf owf to take care of; to watch out for

aufregend owf-raygent exciting

aufs owfs on the; onto the

Aufsicht *f* owf-zisht supervision

aufstehen owf-shtay-en to get up

aufwachen owf-va**KH**en to wake up

Aufzug *m* owf-ts**oo**k lift, elevator

Auge *n* owg-uh eye

Augenarzt *m* owgen-artst ophthalmologist, optician

Augenblick *m* owgenblick moment

Augenbraue *f* owgen-brow-uh eyebrow

Augenoptiker *m* owgen-optiker optician

Augenzeuge *m* owgen-tsoyg-uh, **Augenzeugin** *f* eye witness

aus owss from; off; out; out of; made of; finished

Ausfahrt *f* owssfahrt exit

Ausfahrt freihalten keep exit clear

Ausfahrt Tag und Nacht freihalten keep exit clear day and night

Ausflug *m* owssfl**oo**k trip

ausfüllen owssf**oo**llen to fill in

Ausgang *m* owssgang exit, way out; gate; departure

ausgeben owssgayben to spend

ausgenommen owss-genommen except

ausgezeichnet owss-gets**y**shnet excellent

Auskunft *f* owsskoonft
information; information desk;
directory enquiries

Ausland *n* owsslant international;
overseas, abroad

Ausländer *m* owsslender,
Ausländerin *f* foreigner

ausländisch owsslendish foreign

ausländisches Erzeugnis
foreign produce

ausländische Währungen
owsslendish-uh vairoongen
foreign currencies

Ausland: im/ins Ausland
owsslant abroad

Auslandsflüge international
departures

Auslandsgespräche
international calls

Auslandsporto *n* owsslants-porto
overseas postage

Ausnahme *f* owssnahm-uh
exception

auspacken owsspacken
to unpack

Auspuff *m* owsspooff exhaust

ausruhen: sich ausruhen zish
owssr00-en to relax; to take
a rest

ausschalten owss-shalten
to switch off

ausschl. (ausschließlich) excl.,
exclusive

aussehen owss-zay-en to look

Aussehen *n* look; appearance

außen owssen outside

außer owsser except

außer Betrieb out of order

außerhalb owsser-halp
outside (of)

äußerlich anzuwenden
not to be taken internally

außer sonntags Sundays
excepted

Aussicht *f* owss-zisht view

Aussichtspunkt *m* owss-
zishts-poonkt viewpoint

aussprechen owss-shpreshen to
pronounce

aussteigen owss-shtygen
to get off

Ausstellung *f* owss-shtelloong
exhibition

Australien *n* owstrahlee-en
Australia

australisch owstrahlish
Australian

Ausverkauf *m* owss-fairkowf sale

ausverkauft owss-fairkowft
sold out

Auswahl *f* owssvahl choice;
selection

Ausweis *m* owssvice pass,
identity card; identification

Auszahlungen withdrawals;
cash desk, cashier

ausziehen: sich ausziehen zish
owss-tsee-en to undress

Auto *n* owto car

mit dem Auto by car

Autobahn *f* owto-bahn motorway,
highway, freeway

Autobahndreieck motorway
junction; motorways merge

Autobahnkreuz motorway
junction

Autobahnraststätte
service station

Autobus *m* owtobooss bus

Autofähre *f* owto-fair-uh car-ferry

Autofahrer *m* owtofahrer,
Autofahrerin *f* car driver,
motorist

Automat *m* vending machine

**dieser Automat nimmt
folgende Banknoten an**
this machine will accept the
following banknotes/bills

automatisch owtomahtish
automatic

Autoradio *n* owto-rahdee-o
car radio

Autoreparaturen auto repairs

Autotelefon *n* owto-telefohn
car phone

Autounfall *m* owto-oonfal
car accident

Autovermietung *f* owto-
fairmeetoong car rental

Autowäsche *f* owtovesh-uh
car wash

B

Babyartikel babywear, items for
babies

Bach *m* baKH stream

Bäcker *m* becker baker

Bäckerei *f* beckerī baker's, bakery

Bad *n* baht bath; bathroom

Badeanzug *m* bahd-uh-antsook
swimming costume

Badehose *f* bahd-uh-hohz-uh
swimming trunks

> **Travel tip** Since pre-Roman
> times, Germany has sworn
> by the curative powers
> of spa waters, and towns
> that have Bad as a prefix
> or include Baden (baths) in
> their titles (Baden-Baden,
> Wiesbaden etc) offer a
> baffling array of restorative
> spa facilities.

Bademantel *m* bahd-uh-mantel
dressing gown

baden bahden to have a bath

Badesalz *n* bahd-uh-zalts bath
salts

Badewanne *f* bahd-uh-vann-uh
bathtub

Badezimmer *n* bahd-uh-tsimmer
bathroom

Badezimmerartikel bathroom
furniture and fittings

Badezimmerbedarf for the
bathroom

Bahnhof *m* bahn-hohf station

Bahnhofsmission *f* bahnhohfs-
miss-yohn office providing help
for travellers in difficulty

Bahnhofspolizei railway police

Bahnkilometer kilometres by
rail

Bahnsteig *m* bahn-shtike
platform, (US) track

Bahnsteigkarte *f* bahn-shtike-
kart-uh platform ticket

Bahnübergang *m* bahn-
oobergang level crossing

bald balt soon

Balkangrill *m* balkahn-grill restaurant serving dishes from Balkan countries

Balkon *m* balkohn balcony

Band *n* bant tape

Bank *f* bank; bench

Bankkonto *n* bank account

Bankleitzahl *f* banklite-tsahl sort code

Bankomat *m* bankomaht cash dispenser, ATM

bar cash

Bardame *f* bardahm-uh barmaid

Bargeld *n* bargelt cash

Barmann *m* barmann barkeeper

Bart *m* beard

Basel *n* bahzel Basle

bat baht, **baten** bahten asked

Bauch *m* bowKH stomach; belly

Bauer *m* bower farmer

Bauernhof *m* bowern-hohf farm

Baum *m* bowm tree

Baumwolle *f* bowmvoll-uh cotton

Baustelle *f* building site; roadworks

Baustellenausfahrt works exit; building site exit

Bayern by-ern Bavaria

bayrisch by-rish Bavarian

Beamter *m* buh-amter, **Beamtin** *f* civil servant; official

Bedarf *m* needs, requirements; demand

bedeuten bedoyten to mean

bedeutend bedoytent important

bedienen bedeenen to serve

bedienen Sie sich! zee zish help yourself

Bedienung *f* bedeenoong service (charge)

Bedienung inbegriffen service included

Bedienungsanleitung instructions for use

Bedingung *f* bedingoong condition

beeilen: sich beeilen zish buh-īlen to hurry

beeilen Sie sich! zee zish hurry up!

beenden buh-enden to finish

Beerdigung *f* buh-airdigoong funeral

Beerdigungsunternehmen undertaker, mortician

befehlen befaylen to order

Beginn der Vorstellung um... dair forshtelloong oom performance begins at...

begleiten beglyten to accompany

behalten behalten to keep

behandeln to treat

Behandlung *f* behantloong treatment

behaupten behowpten to claim

Behauptung *f* behowptoong claim

behindert behindert disabled

Behinderte *m/f* behindert-uh handicapped person

bei by by; at; next to; near

bei Peter at Peter's

beide bide-uh both (of them)

Bei Frost Glatteisgefahr icy in cold weather

beim at the

Bein *n* bine leg

Beinbruch *m* bine-brooкн broken leg

Beispiel *n* by-shpeel example

zum Beispiel tsoom for example

Bei Störung Taste drücken press key in case of technical fault

bekannt known

Bekannte *m/f* bekannt-uh acquaintance

Bekleidung *f* beklydoong clothing

bekloppt bekloppt crazy

bekommen to get

belegt belaykt occupied, busy; no vacancies; full

beleidigen belydigen to offend

Beleuchtung *f* beloyshtoong lights

Beleuchtungsartikel lamps and lighting

Belgien *n* belgee-en Belgium

belgisch belgish Belgian

Belichtungsmesser *m* belishtoongs-messer light meter

bellen to bark

Belohnung *f* belohnoong reward

bemerken bemairken to notice; to remark

Bemerkung *f* bemairkoong remark

Benehmen *n* benaymen behaviour

benehmen: sich benehmen zish benaymen to behave

Benutzung *f* benootsoong use

Benutzung auf eigene Gefahr use at own risk

Benzin *n* bentseen petrol, gas(oline)

Benzinkanister *m* bentseen-kanister petrol/gasoline can

Benzinuhr *f* bentseen-oor fuel gauge

beobachten buh-ohbaкнten to watch

bequem bekvaym comfortable

bereit berite ready

Bereitschaftsdienst *m* berite-shaftsdeenst duty doctor; duty pharmacy

Berg *m* bairk mountain

Bergsteigen *n* bairk-shtygen mountaineering

Bergwacht *f* bairk-vaKHt mountain rescue

Bericht *m* berisht report

beruhigen: sich beruhigen zish beroo-igen to calm down

Beruhigungsmittel *n* beroo-igoongs-mittel tranquillizer

berühmt beroomt famous

berühren berooren to touch

Berühren der Waren verboten do not touch

Besatzung *f* bezatsoong crew

beschädigen beshaydigen to damage

Bescheid *m* beshite information

Bescheid sagen to tell

Bescheid wissen to know

Bescheinigung *f* beshynigoong certificate

bescheuert beshoyert crazy, daft

beschreiben beshryben to describe

Beschreibung *f* description

beschweren: sich beschweren zish beshvairen to complain

besetzt bezetst busy; engaged, occupied

Besetztzeichen *n* bezetst-tsyshen engaged tone

Besichtigung *f* bezishtigoong tour

Besitzer *m* bezitser owner

besoffen bezoffen pissed, smashed

besonders bezonders especially

besorgt bezorkt worried

besser better

Bestandteile ingredients; component parts

bestätigen beshtaytigen to confirm

Bestattungen funeral director's

beste best-uh best

Bestechung *f* beshteshoong bribery

Besteck *n* beshteck cutlery

bestellen beshtellen to order

Bestellung *f* beshtelloong order

Bestimmungsort *m* beshtim-moongs-ort destination

bestrafen beshtrahfen to punish

Besuch *m* bezooKH visit

besuchen bezooKHen to visit

Besuchszeit *f* bezooKHs-tsite visiting time

Besuchszeiten *fpl* bezooKHs-tsyten visiting hours

Betäubung *f* betoyboong anaesthetic

Beton *m* baytong concrete

Betrag *m* betrahk amount

Betreten auf eigene Gefahr enter at own risk, keep off/out

Betreten der Baustelle verboten no admission to building site

Betreten der Eisfläche verboten keep off the ice**

Betreten des Rasens nicht gestattet keep off the grass

Betreten verboten keep out

Betrieb *m* betreep company, firm; operation, running; bustle

außer Betrieb out of order

betriebsbereit ready to use

Betriebsferien betreeps-fairee-en works' holidays/vacation

Betrug *m* betrook fraud

betrunken betroonken drunk

Bett *n* bed

Bettdecken bedding

Betteln und Hausieren verboten no beggars, no hawkers

Bettwäsche *f* bettvesh-uh bed linen

Bettzeug *n* bett-tsoyk bedding

Be- und Entladen erlaubt loading and off-loading permitted

bevor befor before

bewegen: sich bewegen zish bevaygen to move

Beweis *m* bevice proof

Bewohner *m* bevohner, **Bewohnerin** *f* inhabitant

bewölkt bevurlkt cloudy

bezahlen betsahlen to pay

Bezahlung *f* betsahloong payment

Bezahlung mit Kreditkarte möglich credit cards welcome

beziehungsweise or

Bf. (Bahnhof) station

BH (Büstenhalter) *m* bay-hah bra

Bierkeller *m* beer-keller beer cellar

Bild *n* bilt picture

billig billish cheap, inexpensive

Billigpreise reduced prices

bin am

Bindemittel starch

Bio-Laden *m* bee-oh-lahden health food shop

biologisch abbaubar biodegradable

Birne *f* beern-uh light bulb; pear

bis until; by

bis morgen see you tomorrow

bis später shpayter see you later

Biss *m* bis bite

bisschen: ein bisschen ine biss-shen a little bit (of)

bist are

bitte bitt-uh please; you're welcome

bitte? pardon (me)?; can I help you?

bitte anschnallen fasten seat belt

bitte einordnen get in lane

bitte eintreten ohne zu läuten please enter without ringing

bitte einzeln eintreten please enter one at a time

bitte entwerten please stamp your ticket

bitte Karte einführen please insert card

bitte klingeln please ring

bitte klopfen please knock

bitten to ask

bitte nicht... please do not…

bitte nicht stören please do not disturb

bitte schließen please close the door

bitte schön/sehr bitt-uh shurn/zair here you are; you're welcome

bitte schön/sehr? what will it be?; can I help you?

bitte Schuhe abtreten please wipe your shoes

bitte warten please wait

Blase f blahz-uh bladder; blister

blass pale

Blatt n leaf

blau blow blue

blauer Fleck m blower bruise

Blei n bly lead

bleiben blyben to stay, to remain

bleiben Sie am Apparat zee am apparaht hold the line

Bleichmittel n blysh-mittel bleach

bleifrei blyfry unleaded

Bleistift m bly-shtift pencil

Blick m look; view

mit Blick auf... owf overlooking…

blieb bleep, **bliebst, blieben** stayed

Blinddarmentzündung f blint-darm-ent-ts00ndoong appendicitis

blinder Passagier m blinnder passaJeer stowaway

Blinker m indicator

Blitz m blits flash; lightning

blockiert blockeert blocked

Blödmann m blurtmann twit

Blödsinn m blurt-zinn nonsense, rubbish

Blume f bl00m-uh flower

Blumenhandlung f bl00men-hantloong florist

Bluse f bl00z-uh blouse

Blut n bl00t blood

Blutdruck m bl00t-droock blood pressure

bluten bl00ten to bleed

Blutgruppe f bl00t-groopp-uh blood group

Blutübertragung f bl00t-00bertrahgoong blood transfusion

BLZ (Bankleitzahl) sort code

Boden m bohden bottom; floor

Bodenpersonal n bohden-pairzonahl ground crew

Bodensee: der Bodensee bohdenzay Lake Constance

Bohrer m drill

Boje f boh-yuh buoy

Bolzen m boltsen bolt

Boot n boht boat

Bootsverleih m bohts-fairlī boat hire/rental

Bordkarte f bortkart-uh boarding card

böse burz-uh angry

Botschaft f bohtshafft embassy

brachte braKHt-uh, **brachtest, brachten** brought

Branchenverzeichnis *n* brangshen-fairtsy**s**hniss yellow pages

Brand *m* brant fire

Brandstiftung *f* brant-shtiftoong arson

Bratpfanne *f* bra**h**t-pfann-uh frying pan

Bräu *n* broy brew

Brauch *m* brow**KH** custom

brauchen brow**KH**en to need

Brauerei *f* brewery

Brauereiabfüllung bottled in the brewery

braun brown brown

braungebrannt brown-gebrannt tanned

BRD (Bundesrepublik Deutschland) bay-air-**day** FRG (Federal Republic of Germany)

breit brite wide

Breite *f* bryt-uh width

Bremse *f* bremz-uh brake

bremsen bremzen to brake

Bremsflüssigkeit *f* brems-fl**oo**ssishkite brake fluid

brennbar combustible

brennen to burn

Brief *m* breef letter

Brieffreund *m* breef-froynt, **Brieffreundin** *f* pen pal

Briefkasten *m* breefkasten letterbox, mailbox

Briefmarke *f* breefmark-uh stamp

Brieftasche *f* breeftash-uh wallet

Briefträger *m* breeftrayger postman

Briefträgerin *f* breeftraygerin postwoman

Brille *f* brill-uh glasses, eyeglasses

bringen to bring

Brosche *f* brosh-uh brooch

Broschüre *f* brosh**oo**r-uh brochure

Bruch *m* broo**KH** fracture

Brücke *f* br**oo**ck-uh bridge

Bruder *m* br**oo**der brother

Brunnen *m* bro**oo**nnen fountain

Brust *f* broost breast; chest

Buch *n* boo**KH** book

buchen boo**KH**en to book

Bücherei *f* boosher**ī** library

Bücher und Zeitschriften books and magazines

Buchhandlung *f* boo**KH**-hantloong bookshop, bookstore

Bucht *f* boo**KH**t bay

Bügeleisen *n* b**oo**gel-izen iron

Bügelfalte *f* b**oo**gel-falt-uh crease

bügeln b**oo**geln to iron

Bühne *f* b**oo**n-uh stage

Bundesautobahn federal motorway/highway

Bundesgesundheitsminister *m* German Minister of Health

   Der Bundesgesundheits- minister: Rauchen gefährdet Ihre Gesundheit government warning: smoking can damage your health

Bundeskanzler *m* boondess-kantsler chancellor

Bundesrepublik Deutschland *f* boondess-rep**oo**bleek

doytchlant Federal Republic of
Germany

Bundesstraße f boondess-
shtrahss-uh major road, A-road

Bundestag m boondess-tahk
German parliament

Burg f boork castle

Bürgersteig m boorger-shtike
pavement, sidewalk

Büro n booro office

Büroartikel office supplies

Bürste f boorst-uh brush

Busbahnhof m booss-bahnhohf
bus station

Bushaltestelle f booss-halt-uh-
shtell-uh bus stop

bzw. (beziehungsweise) or

C

Café n kaffay café, serving mainly
cakes, coffee and tea etc

Campingbedarf camping
equipment

Campingliege f kemping-leeg-uh
campbed

Campingplatz m kempingplats
campsite; caravan site,
trailer park

CD-Spieler m tsay-day-shpeeler
CD player

Charterflug m charter-flook
charter flight

Chauvi m shohvee male
chauvinist pig

Chef m shef, **Chefin** f boss

chemische Reinigung f
shaymish-uh rynigoong
dry cleaner's

Chinarestaurant n sheena-
restorong Chinese restaurant

chinesisch sheenayzish Chinese

Chirurg m sheeroork, **Chirurgin**
f surgeon

Coiffeur m kwaffur hairdresser

D

da there; as; since

Dach n dakH roof

Dachboden m dakHbohden attic

Dachgepäckträger m
dakH-gepeck-trayger roof rack

dafür dafoor for that; on that;
in that; in favour; then again;
considering

daher dahair from there; that's why

Datei f da-ty file

Dame f dahm-uh lady

Damen ladies' (toilet), ladies'
room

Damenbinde f dahmenbind-uh
sanitary towel/napkin

Damenkleidung f dahmen-
klydoong ladies' clothing

Damenmoden ladies' fashions

Damensalon m dahmen-zalong
ladies' hairdresser's

Damentoilette f dahmen-twalett-
uh ladies' (toilet), ladies' room

Damenunterwäsche f dahmen-
oontervesh-uh lingerie

damit so that; with it

Dampfer *m* steamer

danach danaкн after that; accordingly

Dänemark *n* dayn-uh-mark Denmark

dänisch daynish Danish

dankbar grateful

danke dank-uh thank you, thanks

danke gleichfalls glyshfals the same to you

danken to thank

dann then

darf am allowed to; is allowed to; may

darfst are allowed to; may

Darlehen *n* dahrlay-en loan

darum daroom about it; that's why

das the; who; that; which

dass that

Datum *n* dahtoom date

Dauerwelle *f* dowervell-uh perm

Daumen *m* dowmen thumb

davon from there; of it; of them; from it; from them

DB (Deutsche (Bundes)bahn) German Railways

Decke *f* deck-uh blanket; ceiling

Deckel *m* lid

defekt out of order; faulty

dein(e) dine(-uh) your

denken to think

Denkmal *n* denkmahl monument

denn for, because; than

deprimiert deprimeert depressed

der dair the; who; that

deshalb dess-halp therefore

Desinfektionsmittel *n* desinfekts-**yoh**ns-mittel disinfectant

deutsch doytch German

Deutsche *m/f* doytch-uh German

deutsches Erzeugnis made in Germany

Deutschland *n* doytchlant Germany

Deutschlandlied *n* doytchlant-leet German national anthem

d.h. (das heißt) i.e.

Dia *n* dee-ah slide

Diabetiker *m* dee-ah-**bay**tiker, **Diabetikerin** *f* diabetic

Diamant *m* dee-ah-mant diamond

Diät *f* dee-**ayt** diet

dich dish you

Dichter *m* dishter poet

dick fat; thick

die dee the; who; that; which

Dieb *m* deep thief

Diebstahl *m* deep-shtahl theft

Dienstag *m* deenstahk Tuesday

dienstbereit deenst-berite on duty

dies deess this (one); that (one)

diese deez-uh this (one); that (one); these (ones); those (ones)

dieser deezer this (one); that (one)

dieses deezess this (one); that (one)

diesseits deess-zites on this side (of)

Ding *n* thing

dir deer (to) you

Direktflug *m* deerekt-flook non-stop flight

diskutieren diskooteeren to discuss

DJH (Deutsche Jugendherberge) German Youth Hostel Association

> Travel tip Budget travellers who want to avoid the large school groups that sometimes seem to take over the official DJH hostels may prefer the communal vibe of the small independent hostel scene. Check out the Backpacker Network Alliance website: www.backpacker-network.de.

DLRG (Deutsche Lebensrettungs-gesellschaft) day-el-air-gay German lifeguards association

doch! dokH oh yes it is!; oh yes I am! etc

Dolmetscher *m* dolmetcher, **Dolmetscherin** *f* interpreter

Dom *m* dohm cathedral

Donau *f* dohnow Danube

Donner *m* thunder

Donnerstag *m* donnerstahk Thursday

doof dohf stupid

Doppelbett *n* double bed

doppelt double

Doppelzimmer *n* doppel-tsimmer double room

Dorf *n* village

dort there

dort drüben drooben over there; up there

dort oben ohben over there; up there

Dose *f* dohz-uh can

Dosenöffner *m* dohzen-urfner tin opener

Dragees *npl* draJayss sugar-coated tablets

Draht *m* wire

Drahtseilbahn *f* drahtzilebahn cable car

Dreck *m* dirt

drehen dray-en to turn

drei dry three

dreimal täglich einzunehmen to be taken three times a day

dreißig dryssish thirty

dreizehn dry-tsayn thirteen

dringend dring-ent urgent

dritte(r,s) dritt-uh,-er,-ess third

Droge *f* drohg-uh drug

Drogerie *f* drohgeree chemist's, toiletries shop

Druck *m* droock pressure

drücken droocken to push

Drucker *m* droocker printer

Drucksache *f* printed matter

DSD (Duales System Deutschland) recycling scheme

du doo you

du lieber Gott! leeber good God!

du liebe Zeit! leeb-uh tsite struth!

Duft *m* dooft smell; fragrance

dumm doomm stupid

Dummheit f doommhite stupidity

Dummkopf m doommkopf idiot

Dünen fpl doonen sand dunes

dunkel doonkel dark

Dunkelheit f doonkelhite darkness

dünn doonn thin; skinny

durch doorsh through; by; well-done

Durcheinander n doorsh-ine-ander mess

Durchfall m doorshfal diarrhoea

Durchgang m doorshgang passage

Durchgangsverkehr through traffic

durchgehend geöffnet open 24 hours

Durchschnitt m doorsh-shnitt average

durchstreichen doorsh-shtryshen to cross out, to delete

Durchsuchung f doorsh-zooKHoong search

Durchwahl direct dialling

dürfen doorfen to be allowed to

Durst m doorst thirst

   Durst haben hahben to be thirsty

Dusche f doosh-uh shower

duschen dooshen to have a shower

Düsenflugzeug n doozen-flooktsoyk jet plane

Dutzend n dootsent dozen

duzen: sich duzen zish dootsen to use the familiar 'du' form

D-Zug day-tsook express train

E

Ebbe *f* ebb-uh low tide

echt esht genuine

Ecke *f* eck-uh corner

Edelstein *m* aydel-shtine precious stone

EG (Europäische Gemeinschaft) ay-gay EC, European Community

ehe ay-uh before

Ehe *f* ay-uh marriage

Ehefrau *f* ay-uh-frow wife

Ehemann *m* ay-uh-man husband

ehrlich airlish honest; sincere

Ehrlichkeit *f* airlishkite honesty

Eiche *f* īsh-uh oak

Eieruhr *f* īer-oor egg timer

eifersüchtig īferzooshtish jealous

eigen īgen own

eigenartig īgen-artish strange

eigentlich īgentlish actual; actually

Eigentümer *m* īgentoomer, **Eigentümerin** *f* owner

Eilzug *m* ile-tsook fast local train

Eimer *m* ime-er bucket

ein ine a; one

Einbahnstraße *f* ine-bahn-shtrahss-uh one-way street

Einbrecher *m* ine-bresher burglar

Einbruch *m* ine-brooKH burglary

einchecken ine-checken to check in

Eindruck *m* ine-droock impression

eine ine-uh a; one

einfach ine-faKH simple; single

einfache Fahrt one-way journey; single; one way

Einfahrt *f* ine-fahrt entrance, way in

Einfahrt freihalten keep entrance clear

Eingang *m* ine-gang entrance, way in

Eingang um die Ecke entrance round corner

eingeschränktes Halteverbot restricted parking

eingetragenes Warenzeichen registered trademark

Einheit *f* ine-hite unit

Einheitspreis flat rate

einige ine-ig-uh a few; some

Einkauf *m* ine-kowf shopping

> Travel tip Most cities have an alternative shopping quarter with a quota of independent boutiques and vintage outlets for local hipsters. Those in Berlin, and to a lesser extent Hamburg, have superb record shops – great places to browse for cutting-edge electronica.

einkaufen: einkaufen gehen ine-kowfen gay-en to go shopping

Einkaufskorb *m* ine-kowfss-korp shopping basket

Einkaufstasche *f* ine-kowfss-tash-uh shopping bag

Einkaufswagen *m* ine-kowfss-vahgen shopping trolley

Einkaufszentrum *n* ine-kowfss-tsentroom shopping centre

einladen ine-lahden to invite

Einladung *f* ine-lahdoong invitation

Einlass *m* ine-lass admission

einmal ine-mahl once

nicht einmal not even

einmalig ine-mahlish unique

einpacken ine-packen to wrap

einreiben ine-ryben to rub in

Einrichtung *f* ine-rishtoong furnishing; organization

eins ine-ss one

einsam ine-zahm lonely

einschalten ine-shalten to switch on

einschenken ine-shenken to pour

einschlafen ine-shlahfen to fall asleep

einschl. (einschließlich) incl., inclusive

einschließlich 15% Bedienung 15% service charge included

Einschreiben *n* ine-shryben registered letter

Einschreibsendungen registered mail

einsteigen ine-shtygen to get in

Einstieg hinten enter at the rear

Einstieg nur mit Fahrausweis obtain a ticket before boarding

Einstieg vorn enter at the front

eintreten in ine-trayten to enter

Eintritt *m* ine-tritt entry

Eintritt frei admission free

Eintrittskarte *f* ine-tritts-kart-uh ticket

Eintrittspreise admission

einverstanden! ine-fair-shtanden OK!; agreed

einwerfen ine-vairfen to insert

Einzahlungen deposits

Einzelbett *n* ine-tselbett single bed

Einzelfahrkarte *f* ine-tsel-fahrkart-uh single/one-way ticket

Einzelhändler *m* ine-tsel-hentler retailer

Einzelheit *f* ine-tselhite detail

Einzelpreis *m* ine-tsel-price (unit) price

Einzelzimmer *n* ine-tsel-tsimmer single room

Eiscafé *n* ice-kaffay ice cream parlour (also serves coffee and liqueurs)

Eisenbahn *f* īzenbahn railway

Eisenwarenhandlung *f* īzenvahren-hantloong hardware store

Eisstadion *n* ice-shtahdee-on ice rink

Eiter *m* ite-er pus

Elektriker *m* aylektriker electrician

Elektrizität *f* aylektritsitayt electricity

Elektroartikel *mpl* aylektro-artikel electrical goods

Elektrogeräte *npl* aylektro-gerayt-uh electrical equipment

elf eleven

Elfmeter *m* elfmayter penalty

Ellbogen *m* ell-bohgen elbow

Eltern parents

Eltern haften für ihre Kinder parents are responsible for their children

Empfang *m* reception

Empfänger *m* emp-fenger addressee; recipient

empfehlen emp-faylen to recommend

Ende der Autobahn end of motorway/highway

Ende der Vorfahrtsstraße end of priority

endlich entlish at last; finally

Endstation *f* ent-shtats-yohn terminus

eng narrow; tight

Engländer *m* eng-lender Englishman

Engländerin *f* eng-lenderin English girl/woman

englisch eng-lish English; rare (meat)

Enkel *m* grandson

Enkelin *f* granddaughter

entdecken to discover

entfernt entfairnt away; distant

Entfernung *f* entfairnoong distance

entführen entf**oo**ren to kidnap, to abduct

Entgleisung *f* ent-gly-zoong derailment

enthält... contains...

entlang along(side)

entscheiden ent-shyden to decide

entschlossen ent-shlossen determined

entschuldigen: sich entschuldigen zish entsh**oo**ldigen to apologize

entschuldigen Sie bitte zee bitt-uh excuse me

Entschuldigung entsh**oo**ldigoong sorry, excuse me

entsetzlich entzetslish appalling

enttäuscht ent-toysht disappointed

Enttäuschung *f* ent-toyshoong disappointment

entweder... oder... entvayder **oh**der either... or...

Entwerter *m* entvairter ticket-stamping machine

entwickeln entvickeln to develop

Entzündung *f* ent-ts**oo**ndoong infection

er air he

Erde *f* aird-uh earth

Erdgeschoss *n* airt-geshoss ground floor, (US) first floor

Erfahrung *f* airfahroong experience

Erfolg *m* airf**o**llk success

Erfrischung *f* airfrishoong refreshment

ergibt die doppelte/dreifache Menge makes twice/three times as much

erhalten airhalten to receive

erholen: sich erholen zish airhohlen to recover

Erholungsgebiet *n* airhohloongsgebeet recreational area

erinnern: sich erinnern an zish air-innern to remember

Erinnerung *f* air-inneroong memory

erkälten: sich erkälten zish airkelten to catch cold

erkältet: erkältet sein airkeltet to have a cold

Erkältung *f* airkeltoong cold

erkennen airkennen to recognize

erklären airklairen to explain

erlauben airlowben to allow

Erlaubnis *f* airlowpniss permission

Erlebnis *n* airlaypniss experience

Ermäßigte Preise reduced prices

Ermäßigungen reductions; concessions

ermorden airmorden to murder

ernst airnst serious

Ersatzreifen *m* airzatz-ryfen spare tyre

Ersatzteile *npl* airzatz-tile-uh spare parts

erschießen airsheessen to shoot (and kill)

Ersparnisse *fpl* airshpahrniss-uh savings

erst airst only just; only

erstatten airshtatten to refund

erstaunlich airshtownlish astonishing

erste(r,s) airst-uh, -er, -es first

Erste Hilfe *f* airst-uh hilf-uh first aid

erste Klasse airst-uh klass-uh first class

erstens airstens first; firstly

erster Stock *m* airster shtock first floor, (US) second floor

ersticken airshticken to suffocate

ertrinken airtrinken to drown

Erwachsene *m/f* airvaksen-uh adult

erwähnen airvaynen to mention

es ess it

essbar essbar edible

essen to eat

Essen *n* food

Esslöffel *m* ess-lurffel tablespoon

Etage *f* aytahJ-uh floor, storey

Etagenbett *n* aytahJen-bett bunk beds

Etat *m* aytah budget

Etikett *n* label

etwa etvah about; perhaps

etwas etvass something; some; somewhat

etwas anderes anderess something else

euch oysh you

euer oyer your

eure oyr-uh your

europäisch oyro-pay-ish European

Euroscheck *m* oyrosheck Eurocheque

ev. (evangelisch) Protestant

evangelisch evang**ay**lish
Protestant

Explosionsgefahr *f* eksploh-
y**oh**ns-gefar danger of
explosion

F

Fabrik *f* fab**ree**k factory

Fach *n* fa**KH** subject; pigeonhole

Facharzt *m* fa**KH**artst specialist

Fachmann *m* fa**KH**mann specialist

Faden *m* f**ah**den string; thread

Fahne *f* f**ah**n-uh flag

Fahrausweis *m* f**ah**r-owssvice
ticket

**Fahrausweise sind auf
Verlangen vorzuzeigen**
tickets must be displayed
on request

Fahrbahn *f* roadway

Fähre *f* f**air**-uh ferry

fahren to drive; to go

Fahrer *m* driver

Fahrgäste passengers

Fahrkarte *f* f**ah**rkart-uh ticket

Fahrkartenautomat *m*
fa**h**rkarten-owtom**ah**t ticket
machine

Fahrkartenschalter *m*
fa**h**rkarten-shalter ticket office

Fahrplan *m* fa**h**rplahn timetable,
(US) schedule

Fahrpreise *mpl* fa**h**rprize-uh fares

Fahrrad *n* fa**h**r-raht bicycle

Fahrräder bicycles

Fahrradkarte *f* fa**h**r-rahtkart-uh
bicycle ticket

Fahrradverleih *m* fa**h**r-raht-fairl**ī**
bicycles for hire/to rent

Fahrradweg *m* fa**h**r-raht-vayk
cycle path

Fahrschein *m* fa**h**r-shine ticket

**Fahrscheinkauf nur beim
Fahrer** buy your ticket from
the driver

Fahrstuhl *m* fa**h**r-sht**oo**l lift,
elevator

Fahrt *f* journey

Fahrtziele destinations

Fahrzeug *n* fa**h**r-tsoyk vehicle

Fall *m* fal fall; case

fallen fal-en to fall

fallenlassen fal-en-lassen to drop

falls falss if

falsch falsh wrong; false

falten to fold

Familie *f* fam**ee**lee-uh family

Familienpackung *f* family pack

fand fant, **fanden** found

fangen to catch

Farbe *f* f**ar**b-uh colour; paint

Farben und Lacke paints

Fasching *m* fa**sh**ing annual
carnival held in the pre-Lent
period with fancy-dress
processions and general
celebrating

Fasse dich kurz! keep it brief!

fast fasst almost, nearly

faul fowl lazy; rotten

Feder *f* f**ay**der feather; spring

Federbett *n* f**ay**derbett quilt

Fehler m fayler mistake; defect

fehlerhaft fayler-haft faulty

Feierabend m fy-erahbent closing time; time to stop

Feiertag m fy-ertahk public holiday

Feinkostgeschäft n fine-kost-gesheft delicatessen

Feinschmecker m fine-shmecker, **Feinschmeckerin** f gourmet

Feld n felt field

Felsen m felzen rock

Fenster n window

Fensterläden mpl fenster-layden shutters

Ferien fpl fairee-en holidays, vacation

Ferienwohnung f fairee-en-vohnoong holiday home

Ferngespräch n fairn-geshpraysh long-distance call

Fernlicht n fairn-lisht full beam

Fernsehen n fairnzay-en television

Fernsprecher m telephone

Ferse f fairz-uh heel

fertig fairtish ready; finished

fest fixed; firm; definite

festnehmen festnaymen to arrest

Fete f fayt-uh party

fett greasy

Fett n fat

Fettgehalt fat content

feucht foysht damp

Feuchtigkeitscreme f foyshtish-kites-kraym moisturizer; cold cream

Feuer n foyer fire

Feuergefahr f foyer-gefahr fire hazard

Feuerlöscher m foyerlursher fire extinguisher

Feuertreppe f foyertrepp-uh fire escape

Feuerwehr f foyervair fire brigade

Feuerwehrausfahrt f fire brigade exit

Feuerwerk n foyervairk fireworks

Feuerzeug n foyer-tsoyk lighter

Fieber n feeber fever

Filmmusik f film-moozeek soundtrack

Filzstift m filts-shtift felt-tip pen

finden fin-den to find

Fingernagel m fing-er-nahgel fingernail

Firma f feerma company

Fischgeschäft n fish-gesheft fishmonger's

FKK ef-kah-kah nudism

flach flakH flat

Flasche f flash-uh bottle

Flaschenöffner m flashen-urfner bottle-opener

Fleck m stain; spot

Fleischerei f flysheri butcher's

Fliege f fleeg-uh fly; bow tie

fliegen fleegen to fly

fließend fleessent fluent

Flitterwochen fpl flittervokHen honeymoon

Flucht f flooKHt escape

flüchten flooshten to escape

Flug m flook flight

Flugdauer f flook-dower flight time

Flügel m floogel wing

Fluggast m flook-gast air passenger

Fluggeschwindigkeit f flook-geshwindish-kite flight speed

Fluggesellschaft f flook-gezellshafft airline

Flughafen m flook-hahfen airport

Flughafenbus m flook-hahfen-booss airport bus

Flughöhe f flook-hur-uh altitude

Flugkarte f flook-kart-uh flight ticket

Fluglinie f flook-leen-yuh airline

Fluglotse m flook-lohts-uh air traffic controller

Flugplan m flookplahn timetable, (US) schedule

Flugsteig m flook-shtike gate

Flugzeug n flook-tsoyk (aero)plane

Flugzeugabsturz m flooktsoyk-apshtoorts plane crash

Flur m floor corridor

Fluss m flooss river

Flut f floot high tide

fl.W. (fließendes Wasser) running water

folgen folgen to follow

folgende folgend-uh next

Fön m furn hair dryer

fönen: sich fönen lassen zish furnen to have a blow-dry

fordern to demand

Formular n formoolahr form

Foto n photo(graph)

Fotoartikel mpl foto-artkel photographic equipment

Fotograf m fotograhf photographer

fotografieren foto-grafeeren to photograph

Fotografin f fotograhfin photographer

Fr. (Frau) Mrs; Ms

Frage f frahg-uh question

fragen frahgen to ask

Frankreich n frank-rysh France

Franzose m frantsohz-uh Frenchman

Französin f frantsurzin French girl; French woman

französisch frantsurzish French

Frau f frow woman; wife; Mrs; Ms

Frauenarzt m frowen-artst gynaecologist

Fräulein n froyline Miss

frech fresh cheeky

frei fry free, vacant

frei von Konservierungsstoffen contains no preservatives

frei von künstlichen Aromastoffen contains no artificial flavouring

Freibad n frybaht outdoor swimming pool

freigegeben ab... Jahren suitable for those over... years of age

Freikörperkultur f fry-kurper-kooltoor nudism

Freitag m frytahk Friday

freiwillig fry-villish voluntary; voluntarily

Freizeichen n fry-tsyshen ringing tone

Freizeit f fry-tsite spare time; leisure

Freizeitzentrum n fry-tsite-tsentroom leisure centre

fremd fremt strange; foreign

Fremde m/f fremd-uh stranger; foreigner

Fremdenzimmer npl fremden-tsimmer room(s) to let/rent

freuen: sich freuen zish froyen to be happy

Freund m froynt friend; boyfriend

Freundin f froyndin friend; girlfriend

freundlich froyntlish kind; friendly

freut mich! froyt mish pleased to meet you!

Frieden m freeden peace

Friedhof m freet-hohf cemetery

frisch frish fresh

frisch gestrichen wet paint

Frischhaltepackung f airtight pack

Friseur m frizur barber; hairdresser

Frisur f frizoor hairstyle

Frittenbude f fritten-bood-uh chip shop

Frl. (Fräulein) Miss

froh glad

frohes neues Jahr froh-ess noy-ess yahr happy New Year!

frohe Weihnachten! froh-uh vynakнten happy Christmas!

Frostschaden m frost-shahden frost damage

Frostschutzmittel n frost-shoots-mittel antifreeze

früh froo early

Frühling m frooling spring

Frühstück n frooshtoock breakfast

frühstücken frooshtoocken to have breakfast

fühlen: (sich) fühlen (zish) foolen to feel

fuhr foor, **fuhren** drove; went; travelled

führen fooren to lead

 wir führen... we stock...

Führer m foorer guide; guidebook

Führerin f foorerin guide

Führerschein m foorer-shine driving licence

fuhrst foorst drove; went

Führung f fooroong guided tour

füllen foollen to fill

Fundbüro n foont-booro lost property office

fünf foonf five

fünfzehn foonf-tsayn fifteen

fünfzig foonf-tsish fifty

Fünfzigeuroschein m foonftsish-oyro-shine fifty-euro note/bill

Funktaxi *n* foonk-taksee
  radio taxi

funktionieren foonkts-yohneeren
  to work

für foor for

Furcht *f* foorsht fear

furchtbar foorshtbar terrible

fürchten: sich fürchten zish
  foorshten to be afraid

fürs foorss for the

Fuß *m* fooss foot

  zu Fuß on foot

Fußball *m* foossbal football

Travel tip Catching a German
premier league match is a
must for any football fan
worth the name, not least
because facilities in club sta-
diums are superb – they were
renovated for the Euro 2006
tournament.

Fußballplatz *m* foossbal-plats
  football ground

Fußballstadion *n* foossbal-
  shtahdee-on football stadium

Fußgänger *m* fooss-geng-er,
  Fußgängerin *f* pedestrian

**Fußgänger bitte andere
  Straßenseite benutzen**
  pedestrians please use other
  side of road

Fußgängerüberweg *m*
  foossgeng-er-oobervayk
  pedestrian crossing

Fußgängerzone *f* foossgeng-er-
  tsohn-uh pedestrian precinct

G

gab gahp gave

Gabel *f* gahbel fork; hook

gaben gahben, **gabst** gahpst
  gave

gähnen gaynen to yawn

Gang *m* corridor; gear; walk;
  course

ganz gants whole; quite; very

  den ganzen Tag all day

  ganz gut goot pretty good

Garderobe *f* garderohb-uh
  cloakroom

  **für Garderobe wird nicht
  gehaftet** the management
  accepts no liability for items
  left here

Garten *m* garden

Gaspedal *n* gahss-pedahl
  accelerator

Gast *m* guest

Gastarbeiter *m* gast-arbyter,
  Gastarbeiterin *f* foreign
  worker

Gästebuch *n* gest-uh-booKH
  visitors' register

Gastfreundschaft *f* gastfroynt-
  shafft hospitality

Gastgeber *m* gast-gayber host

Gastgeberin *f* gast-gayberin
  hostess

Gasthaus *n* gast-howss inn

Gasthof *m* gast-hohf restaurant,
  inn

Gaststätte *f* gast-shtett-uh
  restaurant; pub; inn

Gastwirtschaft f gast-veert-shafft pub

geb. (geboren) born, née

Gebäude n geboyd-uh building

geben gayben to give

Gebiss n gebiss dentures

geblieben gebleeben stayed

geboren: geboren sein gebohren zine to be born

gebracht gebraKHt brought

Gebrauch m gebrowKH use; custom

 vor Gebrauch schütteln shake before using

gebrauchen gebrowKHen to use

Gebrauchsanleitung instructions for use

Gebrauchsanweisung beachten follow instructions for use

gebraucht gebrowKHt second-hand

gebrochen gebroKHen broken

gebt gaypt give

Gebühren fpl geb00ren charges

gebührenpflichtig liable to charge

Geburt f geb00rt birth

Geburtsort m geb00rts-ort place of birth

Geburtstag m geb00rts-tahk birthday

Gedächtnis n gedeshtnis memory

Gedanke m gedank-uh thought

Gefahr f gefahr danger

gefahren travelled; gone; driven

gefährlich gefairlish dangerous

Gefährliche Einmündung dangerous junction; danger: concealed exit

Gefährliche Kurve dangerous bend

gefallen: das gefällt mir dass gefellt meer I like it

Gefangene m/f gefangen-uh prisoner

Gefängnis n gefengniss prison

Gefriertruhe f gefreer-tr00-uh freezer

gefroren gefrohren frozen

Gefühl n gef00l feeling

gefunden gefoonden found

gegangen gegang-en gone

gegeben gegayben given

gegen gaygen against

Gegenanzeige contra-indications

Gegend *f* gaygent area

Gegenstand *m* gaygenshtant object

Gegenteil *n* gaygen-tile opposite

gegenüber gaygen-oober opposite

Gegenverkehr hat Vorfahrt oncoming traffic has right of way

gegessen eaten

Gegner *m* gaykner, **Gegnerin** *f* opponent

gehabt gehapt had

geheim gehime secret

Geheimnis *n* gehime-nis secret

Geheimzahl eingeben enter personal number

gehen gay-en to go; to walk

geht das? is that OK?

das geht nicht that's not on

Gehirn *n* geheern brain

Gehirnerschütterung *f* geheern-airshootteroong concussion

Gehör *n* gehur hearing

gehören ge-hur-ren to belong (to)

Geisel *f* gyzel hostage

Geistlicher *m* gystlisher priest

gekommen come

gekonnt been able to; masterly

gekühlt haltbar bis... if chilled will keep until...

gelassen relaxed; left

gelb gelp yellow

Gelbe Seiten gelb-uh zyten yellow pages

Geld *n* gelt money

Geldautomat *m* gelt-owtomaht cash dispenser, ATM

Geld einwerfen insert money

Geldeinwurf insert money

Geldrückgabe returned coins

Geldschein *m* geltshine banknote, (US) bill

Geldstrafe *f* geltshtrahf-uh fine

Geldwechsel *m* geltveksel bureau de change

Gelegenheitskauf *m* gelaygen-hites-kowf bargain

Gelenk *n* joint

Gemälde *n* gemayld-uh painting

gemocht gemoKHt liked

Gemüsehändler *m* gemooz-uh-hentler greengrocer

gemusst gemoosst had to

genau genow exact; exactly

Genf genf Geneva

genommen taken

genug genook enough

genug haben (von) to be fed up (with)

geöffnet guh-urfnet open; opened

geöffnet von... bis... open from... to...

Gepäck *n* gepeck luggage, baggage

Gepäckaufbewahrung *f* gepeck-owf-bevahroong left luggage, (US) baggage check

Gepäckausgabe *f* gepeck-owssgahb-uh baggage claim

Gepäckkontrolle *f* gepeck-kontroll-uh baggage check

Gepäckschließfach n gepeck-shleessfaKH luggage locker

Gepäckträger m gepeck-trayger porter

gepflegt gepflaykt well looked after; refined

gerade gerahd-uh just; straight

geradeaus gerahd-uh-owss straight on

Gerät n gerayt device

gerecht geresht fair

Gericht n gerisht court; dish

gern(e) gairn(uh) gladly
  etwas gern(e) tun to like doing something

Geruch m gerooKH smell

Gesamtpreis m gezamt-price total

Geschäft n gesheft shop; business

Geschäftsfrau f gesheftsfrow businesswoman

Geschäftsführer m geshefts-foorer manager

Geschäftsführerin f geshefts-foorerin manageress

Geschäftsmann m gesheftsmann businessman

Geschäftsreise f geshefts-rize-uh business trip

Geschäftszeiten hours of business

geschehen geshay-en to happen

Geschenk n geshenk present, gift

Geschenkartikel gifts

Geschichte f geshisht-uh story; history

geschieden gesheeden divorced

Geschirr n gesheer crockery

Geschirrtuch n gesheer-tooKH tea towel

Geschlecht n geshlesht sex

Geschlechtskrankheit f geshleshts-krank-hite VD

geschlossen closed

geschlossen von… bis… closed from… to…

Geschmack m geshmack taste; flavour

geschrieben geshreeben written

Geschwindigkeit f geshvindish-kite speed

Geschwindigkeitsbeschränkung f geshvindish-kites-beshrenkoong speed limit

Geschwindigkeitsbeschränkung beachten observe speed limit

geschwollen geshvollen swollen

gesehen gezay-en seen

Gesellschaft f gezellshafft society; company

Gesetz n gezets law

Gesicht n gezisht face

Gesichtscreme f gezishts-kraym face cream

gesperrt closed; no entry

Gesperrt für Fahrzeuge aller Art closed to all vehicles

Gespräch n geshpraysh call; conversation

Gestalt f geshtalt figure

gestattet geshtattet allowed

gestern gestern yesterday

gestorben geshtorben died

gesund gezoont healthy

Gesundheit f gezoont-hite health

Gesundheit! bless you!

getan getahn done

Getränkekarte f getrenk-uh-kart-uh drinks list

getrennt getrennt separate; separately

Getriebe n getreeb-uh gearbox

getrunken getroonken drunk

Gewehr n gevair gun

gewesen gevayzen been

Gewicht n gevisht weight

Gewichtsverlust durch Erhitzen weight loss through heating

Gewinn m gevinn prize; profit

gewinnen gevinnen to win

Gewitter n gevitter thunderstorm

Gewohnheit f gevohnhite habit

gewöhnlich gevurnlish usual; usually

geworden gevorden become

gewünschten Betrag wählen select required amount

gewünschte Rufnummer wählen dial number required

gewusst gevoosst known

Gezeiten getsyten tides

gibst geepst give

gibt geept gives

gibt es...? is/are there...?

es gibt... there is/are...

Gift n poison

giftig giftish poisonous

ging, gingen ging-en, **gingst** went

Gips m plaster (of Paris)

Gipsverband m gips-fairbant plastercast

Girokonto n Jeero-konto current account

Giroverkehr m Jeero-fairkair giro transactions

Gitarre f gitarr-uh guitar

Glas n glahss glass

glatt slippery; smooth

Glatteis n glatt-ice black ice

Glatteisgefahr black ice

Glatze f glats-uh bald head

glauben glowben to believe

gleich glysh equal; same; in a moment

Gleis n glice platform, **(US)** track

zu den Gleisen to the platforms/tracks

Glocke f glock-uh bell

Glück n glOOck luck; happiness

zum Glück tsoom fortunately

glücklich glOOcklish lucky; happy

Glücksbringer m glOOcks-bring-er lucky charm

Glühbirne f glOObeern-uh light bulb

GmbH (Gesellschaft mit beschränkter Haftung) gay-em-bay-hah Ltd, limited company

Gott n God

Gottesdienst m gottes-deenst church service; mass

Grab n grahp grave

Grammatik f grammar

Gras n grahss grass

gratis grahtiss free

grau grow grey

grausam growzahm cruel

Grenze f grents-uh border

Grenzkontrolle f grents-kontroll-uh border checkpoint

Griechenland n greeshenlant Greece

griechisch greeshish Greek

Griff m handle

grinsen grinzen to grin

Grippe f gripp-uh flu

Groschen m groshen old 10 pfennig piece

groß grohss big, large; tall

Großbritannien n grohss-britannee-en Great Britain

Größe f grurss-uh size

Großmutter f grohss-mootter grandmother

Großpackung f grohss-packoong large size

Großvater m grohss-fahter grandfather

grün grOOn green

der grüne Punkt suitable for recycling

Grund m groont cause

Grundierungscreme f groondeeroongs-kraym foundation cream

Grundschule f groont-shOOl-uh primary school

Gruppe f groopp-uh group; party

Gruppenreise f grooppen-rize-uh group excursion

Gruss m grOOss greeting

schöne Grüße an… shurn-uh grOOss-uh give my regards to…

grüßen grOOssen to greet; to say hello to

grüß Gott grOOss hello (South German)

gültig gOOltish valid

Gummi n goommee rubber

Gummiband n goommeebant rubber band

günstig gOOnstish favourable; convenient; inexpensive

Gürtel m gOOrtel belt

gut gOOt good; well

gutaussehend gOOt-owss-zay-ent handsome; good-looking

gute Besserung! gOOt-uh besseroong get well soon!

guten Abend gOOten ahbent good evening

gute Nacht gOOt-uh naKHt good night

guten Appetit! gOOten appeteet enjoy your meal!

guten Morgen gOOten good morning

guten Tag gOOten tahk hello

guten Tag, freut mich gOOten tahk froyt mish how do you do, nice to meet you

gute Reise gOOt-uh rize-uh have a good trip

Güterzug m gOOter-tsOOk goods train

gutmütig gOOtmOOtish good-natured

Gutschein m goot-shine voucher

Gymnasium n goom-nahzee-oom
  secondary school

H

H (Haltestelle) bus/tram stop

Haar n hahr hair

Haarfestiger m hahrfestiger
  conditioner

Haarschnitt m hahrshnitt haircut

Haarstudio n hahr-shtoodee-o
  hairdressing studio

haben hahben to have

Hafen m hahfen harbour, port

Hafenpolizei f hahfen-politsī
  harbour police

Hafenrundfahrt f hahfen-
  roontfahrt boat trip round
  the harbour

Haft f custody

Häftling m heftling prisoner

Hagel m hahgel hail

Haken m hahken hook

halb halp half

halbe Stunde f halb-uh shtoond-
  uh half an hour

Halbpension f halp-pangz-yohn
  half board

Hälfte f helft-uh half

Hallenbad n hallenbaht indoor
  swimming pool

Hals n halss neck

Halskette f halsskett-uh necklace

Hals-Nasen-Ohren-Arzt m
  halss-nahzen-ohrn-artst ear,
  nose and throat specialist

Halsschmerzen halss-shmairtsen
  sore throat

Halstabletten fpl halss-tabletten
  throat pastilles

halt! hallt stop!

Haltbar bis… best before…

Haltbarkeitsdatum
  best before date

Halte deine Stadt sauber
  keep your city clean

halten to hold; to stop

Haltestelle f hallt-uh-shtell-uh
  stop

Halteverbot no stopping;
  no waiting

hält nicht in… does not stop
  in…

Handarbeit f hant-arbite
  needlework

Handbremse f hantbremz-uh
  handbrake

Handel m deal; commerce

Handelsgesellschaft f (trading)
  company

Handelsbank f merchant bank

Handgelenk n hant-gelenk wrist

Handgepäck n hant-gepeck hand
  luggage/baggage

Handlung f hantloong shop;
  action

Handschuhe mpl hant-shoo-uh
  gloves

Handtasche f hant-tash-uh
  handbag, (US) purse

Handtuch n hant-tooKH towel

Handwerk n hantvairk crafts

Handy n hendi mobile, cell phone

Handy-Ladegerät n hendi-lahd-uh-gerayt phone charger

Handzettel m hant-tsettel leaflet

Hansaplast n hanzaplast Elastoplast, (US) Band-Aid

hart hard

Hase m hahz-uh hare; rabbit

Hass m hatred

hassen to hate

hässlich hesslish ugly

hast have

hat has

hatte hatt-uh had

hätte hett-uh would have; had

hatten, hattest had

Haupt- howpt main

Hauptbahnhof m howpt-bahnhohf central station

> Travel tip When you arrive in a city, check out the discount cards available at the tourist office or main train station. Usually known as Welcome Cards, these passes typically provide unlimited travel on public transport for 48 or 72 hours, and discounted entry to many city sights.

Hauptpost f howpt-posst main post office

Hauptprogramm n howpt-programm main feature

Hauptsaison f howpt-zaysong high season

Hauptstraße f howpt-shtrahss-uh main road; high street

Haus n howss house

zu Hause tsoo howz-uh at home

nach Hause gehen naKH-gay-en to go home

Haushaltsgeräte npl howss-hallts-gerayt-uh household equipment

Haushaltwaren howss-hallt-vahren household goods

Hausmeister m howss-myster caretaker, janitor

Hausnummer f howss-noommer street number

Hausordnung f howss-ordnoong house rules

Hausschuhe howss-shoo-uh slippers

Haustier n howsteer pet

Hauswirt m howssveert landlord

Hauswirtin f howss-veertin landlady

Haut f howt skin

Hautreiniger m howt-ryniger skin cleanser

Hbf (Hauptbahnhof) central station

Heft n exercise book

Heftzwecke f heft-tsveck-uh drawing pin

Heißlufttrockner m hice-looft-trockner hot-air hand-drier

heilen hylen to cure

Heiligabend m hylish-ahbent Christmas Eve

Heimwerkerbedarf DIY supplies

Heirat f hyraht marriage

heiraten hyrahten to get married

heiß hice hot

heißen hyssen to be called

wie heißen Sie? vee what's
your name?

Heißwachs *m* hice-vaks hot wax

Heizdecke *f* hites-deck-uh
electric blanket

Heizgerät *n* hites-gerayt heater

Heizung *f* hytsoong heating

helfen to help

hell light; bright

Hemd *n* hemt shirt

herabgesetzt reduced

**zu stark herabgesetzten
Preisen** prices slashed

Herbergsmutter *f* hairbairks-
mootter warden

Herbergsvater *m* hairbairks-
fahter warden

Herbst *m* hairpst autumn,
(US) fall

herein! hair-ine come in!

hergestellt in... made in...

Herr *m* hair Mr; gentleman

Herren gents' (toilet),
men's room

Herrenkleidung *f* hairen-
klydoong menswear

Herrenmoden men's fashions

Herrensalon *m* hairen-zalong
men's hairdresser

Herrentoilette *f* hairen-twalett-uh
gents' (toilet), men's room

herrlich hairlish lovely

Hersteller *m* manufacturer

herunterladen hairoonter-lahden
to download

Herz *n* hairts heart

Herzinfarkt *m* hairts-infarkt heart
attack

herzlich willkommen hairtslish
villkommen welcome

herzlichen Glückwunsch!
hairtslishen gl@ockvoonsh
congratulations!; happy
birthday!; happy anniversary!

Heufieber *n* hoyfeeber hay fever

heute hoyt-uh today

heute abend ahbent tonight

heute geschlossen
closed today

hier heer here

hier abreißen tear off here

hier abschneiden cut off here

hier einreißen tear off here

hier einsteigen enter here

hierher heerhair here

hierhin here

hier öffnen open here

hier Parkschein lösen buy
parking permit here

Hilfe *f* hilf-uh help

Himmel *m* sky; heaven

hinlegen: sich hinlegen zish
hinlaygen to lie down

hinsichtlich hinzishtlish
with regard to

hinten at the back

hinter behind

Hintergrund *m* hintergroont
background

Hinterhof *m* hinterhohf back yard

Hintern *m* bottom

Hinterrad *n* hinter-raht back wheel

Hirsch *m* heersh stag
Hitzewelle *f* hits-uh-vell-uh heat
  wave
hoch hohKH high
Hochschule *f* hohKH-shOOl-uh
  college; university
höchste hurkst-uh highest
Höchstgeschwindigkeit
  maximum speed
Hochzeit *f* hoKH-tsite wedding
Hochzeitstag *m* hoKH-tsites-tahk
  wedding anniversary
hoffen to hope
hoffentlich hoffentlish hopefully
Hoffnung *f* hoffnoong hope
höflich hurflish polite
Höhe *f* hur-uh height
höher hur-er higher
höhere Schule *f* hurer-uh
  shOOl-uh secondary school
Höhle *f* hurl-uh cave
holen hohlen to fetch, to get

holländisch hollendish Dutch
Holz *n* holts wood
hören hur-ren to hear
Hörer *m* hur-rer receiver; listener
Hörer abnehmen lift receiver
Hörer einhängen replace receiver
Hörerin *f* hur-rerin listener
Hörgerat *n* hur-gerayt
  hearing aid
Höschen *n* hurss-shen panties
Hose *f* hohz-uh trousers,
  (US) pants
Hr. (Herr) Mr
hübsch hOOpsh pretty
Hubschrauber *m* hOOp-shrowber
  helicopter
Hüfte *f* hOOft-uh hip
Hügel *m* hOOgel hill
Hund *m* hoont dog
Hunde bitte anleinen dogs
  must be kept on a lead

hundert hoondert hundred

Hunde sind an der Leine zu führen dogs must be kept on a lead

Hunger: Hunger haben hoong-er hahben to be hungry

Hupe f hoop-uh horn

Hupen verboten sounding horn forbidden

Husten m hoosten cough

Hut f hoot hat

Hypothek f hoopotayk mortgage

i.A. (im Auftrag) pp

ich ish I; me

Idee f eeday idea

i.d.T. (in der Trockenmasse) dry measure

ihm eem him; to him

ihn een him

ihnen them; to them

Ihnen eenen you; to you

ihr eer you; her; to her; their

Ihr eer your

ihre eer-uh her; their

Ihre eer-uh your

Illustrierte f illoostreert-uh magazine

im in (the)

immer always

Immobilienmakler m immobeel-yen-mahkler estate agent

Impfung f impfoong vaccination

indem indaym as; by

Industriegebiet n indoostree-gebeet industrial zone

infolge in-folg-uh as a result of

Infopostsendung f info-posst-zendoong printed matter

Informationsschalter m informats-yohns-shalter information desk

Inh. (Inhaber) proprietor

Inhalt contents

Initialen fpl inits-yahlen initials

Inland domestic

Inlandsflüge domestic flights

Inlandsgespräch n inlants-gespraysh inland call

Inlandsporto n inlants-porto inland postage

innen (im/in) inside

innerhalb inner-halp within

ins into the; to the

Insektenschutzmittel n inzekten-shoots-mittel insect repellent

Insel f inzel island

insgesamt altogether

Installateur m inshtalatur plumber

Intensivstation f intenzeef-shtats-yohn intensive care unit

interessant interesting

Interesse n interess-uh interest

irgend etwas eergent etvass something; anything

irgend jemand eergent yaymant somebody; anybody

irgendwo eergent-vo somewhere

irisch eerish Irish

isst eat; eats

ist is

Italien n itahlee-en Italy

italienisch ital-yaynish Italian

J

ja yah yes

Jacht f yaкнt yacht

Jachthafen m yaкнt-hahfen marina

Jacke f yack-uh jacket; cardigan

Jahr n yahr year

Jahreszeit f yahress-tsite season

Jahrhundert n yahr-hoondert century

Jahrmarkt m yahrmarkt fair

Jalousie f Jaloozee Venetian blind

Jausenstation f yowzen-shtats-yohn snack bar

je yay ever

jede yayd-uh each; every

jeden Tag yayden tahk every day

jeder yayder everyone; each

jedes yaydess each

jedesmal yaydessmahl every time

je... desto... yay desto the... the...

jemals yaymahlss ever

jemand yaymant somebody

jenseits yayn-zites on the other side (of); beyond

jetzt yetst now

JH (Jugendherberge) youth hostel

joggen: joggen gehen dJoggen gay-en to go jogging

Jucken n yoocken itch

jüdisch yOOdish Jewish

Jugendherberge f yOOgent-hairbairg-uh youth hostel

Jugendklub m yOOgent-kloop youth club

Jugendliche: für Jugendliche ab... Jahren for young people over the age of...

Juli m yOOlee July

jung yoong young

Junge m yoong-uh boy

junge Leute yoong-uh loyt-uh young people

Junge Mode fashions for the young

Junggeselle m yoong-gezell-uh bachelor

Juni m yOOnee June

Juwel m yoovayl jewel

Juwelier m yoov-uh-leer jeweller's

K

Kabel n kahbel cable

Kabine f kabeen-uh cabin

Kaffeefilter m kaffay-filter coffee filter

Kaffeehaus n kaffay-howss café

kahl bald

Kai m kī quay

Kalender m calendar; diary

kalt cold

kam kahm, **kamen** came

Kamin *m* kam**ee**n chimney;
fireplace

Kamm *m* comb

Kampf *m* fight

kämpfen k**e**mpfen to fight

kamst k**ah**mst came

Kanadier *m* kanah**dee**-er,
Kanadierin *f* Canadian

kanadisch kan**ah**dish Canadian

Kanal *m* kan**ah**l canal; Channel

Kaninchen *n* kan**ee**nshen rabbit

kann can

Kännchen *n* k**e**nnshen pot

Kanne *f* k**a**nn-uh (tea/coffee) pot

kannst can

Kanu *n* k**ah**n00 canoe

Kapitän *m* kapit**ay**n captain

Kappe *f* k**a**pp-uh cap

kaputt kap**oo**tt broken

Karfreitag *m* karfr**y**tahk
Good Friday

Karneval *m* k**a**rn-uh-val annual
carnival held in the pre-Lent
period with fancy-dress
processions and general
celebrating

Karte *f* k**a**rt-uh card; ticket

Karten tickets

Kartenleser *m* k**a**rten-layzer
card reader

Kartenspiel *n* k**a**rtenshpeel
card game

Kartentelefon *n* k**a**rten-telefohn
cardphone

Kasse *f* k**a**ss-uh cashdesk, till,
cashier; box office

Katalysator *m* katal00z**ah**tohr
catalytic converter

Kater *m* k**ah**ter hangover; tomcat

kath. (katholisch) Catholic

Katze *f* k**a**ts-uh cat

kaufen k**ow**fen to buy

Kaufhaus *n* k**ow**fhowss
department store

kaum kowm hardly

Kaution *f* k**ow**ts-yohn deposit

Kehle *f* k**ay**l-uh throat

Keilriemen *m* k**i**le-reemen
fan belt

kein(e)... k**i**ne(-uh) no...;
not...

　keine Ahnung k**i**ne-uh
　ahnoong no idea

　ich habe keine ish h**ah**b-uh
　k**i**ne-uh I don't have any

　keine... mehr k**i**ne-uh mair no
　more...

　kein... mehr k**i**ne mair no
　more...

kein Ausstieg no exit

keine heiße Asche einfüllen
do not put hot ashes in this
container

kein Einstieg no entry

keine Selbstbedienung no
self-service

keine Zufahrt no entry

kein Trinkwasser not drinking
water

**kein Verkauf an Jugendliche
unter... Jahren** sales
forbidden to minors under the
age of...

kein Zugang no entry

kein Zutritt no admittance; no entrance

kein Zutritt fur Jugendliche unter... Jahren no admission to minors under the age of...

Keller *m* cellar

Kellner *m* waiter

Kellnerin *f* waitress

kennen to know

Keramik *f* kairahmik china

Kerze *f* kairts-uh candle

Kette *f* kett-uh chain

Keuchhusten *m* koysh-hoosten whooping cough

Kiefer *m* keefer jaw; pine

Kind *n* kint child

Kinder *npl* children

Travel tip Wooden toys are excellent in Germany – beautifully crafted with superb attention to detail. Christmas markets are a great opportunity to pick these up; Nürnberg offers the best choice, but many towns have a Yule-themed shop open all year round.

---

für Kinder ab... Jahren for children from the age of...

Kinderarzt *m* kinder-artst, **Kinderärztin** *f* pediatrician

Kinderbett *n* cot

Kinderkleidung *f* kinder-klydoong children's clothing

Kindermoden children's fashions

Kindersitz *m* kinder-zits child seat

Kinderspielplatz *m* kinder-shpeelplats children's playground

Kindervorstellung *f* kinder-forshtelloong children's performance

Kinderwagen *m* kindervahgen pram

Kinn *n* chin

Kino *n* keeno cinema, movie theater

Kinocenter *n* keeno-senter multiplex cinema/movie theater

Kirche *f* keersh-uh church

Klammeraffe *f* klammer-aff-uh at sign

Klang *m* sound

klar clear; OK, sure

Klasse *f* klass-uh class

klebrig klaybrish sticky

Kleid *n* klite dress

Kleider klyder clothes

Kleiderbügel *m* klyder-boogel (coat)hanger

klein kline small

Kleinbus *m* kline-booss van

Kleingeld *n* kline-gelt change

Klempner *m* plumber

Klima *n* kleemah climate

Klimaanlage *f* kleemah-anlahg-uh air-conditioning

klimatisiert klimateezeert air-conditioned

Klingel *f* bell

klingeln to ring

Klippe *f* klipp-uh cliff

Klo *n* loo

Kloster *n* klohster convent; monastery

klug klook clever

Kneipe *f* k-nipe-uh pub, bar

Knie *n* k-nee knee

Knöchel *m* k-nurshel ankle

Knochen *m* k-noкНen bone

Knopf *m* k-nopf button

Knoten *m* k-nohten knot

Koch *m* koкН cook

Kochgeschirr *n* koкН-gesheerr cooking utensils

Köchin *f* kurshin cook

Kochnische *f* koкНneesh-uh kitchenette

Kochtopf *m* koкНtopf saucepan

Koffer *m* bag; suitcase

Kofferkuli *m* kofferkoolee luggage/baggage trolley

Kofferraum *m* koffer-rowm boot, (US) trunk

Kohle *f* kohl-uh coal

Kollege *m* kollayg-uh, **Kollegin** *f* colleague

Köln kurln Cologne

Kölnisch Wasser kurlnish vasser eau de Cologne

komisch kohmish funny

kommen to come

das kommt darauf an dahrowf it depends

Komödie *f* komurdee-uh comedy

kompliziert komplitseert complicated

Konditorei *f* kondeetori cake shop

Kondom *n* kondohm condom

König *m* kurnish king

Königin *f* kurnigin queen

Konkurrenz *f* konkoorents competition

können kurnen to be able to; can

können Sie…? zee can you…?

könnte kurnt-uh, **könnten**, **könntest** could

konnte konnt-uh, **konnten**, **konntest** could

Konservierungsstoffe preservatives

Konsulat *n* konzoolaht consulate

Kontaktlinsen *fpl* kontakt-linzen contact lenses

Konto *n* account

Kontrolle *f* kontroll-uh control

kontrollieren kontrolleeren to control

Konzert *n* kontsairt concert

Kopf *m* head

Kopfkissen *n* pillow

Kopfschmerzmittel *n* kopfshmairts-mittel aspirin

Kopfstütze *f* kopf-shtoots-uh headrest

Kopftuch *n* kopftooкН scarf

Kopfweh *n* kopf-vay headache

Kopie *f* kopee copy

kopieren kopeeren to copy

Korb *m* korp basket

Korkenzieher *m* korken-tsee-er corkscrew

Körper *m* kurper body

Körperpuder *m* kurper-p00der talcum powder

Kosmetika *npl* kosmaytikah cosmetics

kostbar kostbar precious

kosten to cost

kostenlos kosten-lohss free of charge

köstlich kurstlish delicious

Kostüm *n* kost00m ladies' suit

Kragen *m* krahgen collar

Krampf *m* cramp

krank ill, sick

Kranke *m/f* krank-uh sick person

Krankenhaus *n* kranken-howss hospital

Krankenkasse *f* krankenkass-uh medical insurance

Krankenpfleger *m* kranken-pflayger male nurse

Krankenschein *m* kranken-shine health insurance certificate

Krankenschein nicht vergessen don't forget your health insurance certificate

Krankenschwester *f* kranken-shvester nurse

Krankenwagen *m* krankenvahgen ambulance

Krankheit *f* krank-hite disease

Krawatte *f* kravatt-uh tie, necktie

Krebs *m* krayps cancer

Kreditabteilung accounts department

Kredite kraydeet-uh loans

Kreditkarte *f* kraydeetkart-uh credit card

Kreditkrise *f* kraydeet-kreez-uh credit crunch

Kreis *m* krice circle

Kreisverkehr *m* krice-fairkair roundabout, traffic circle

Kreuz *n* kroyts cross

Kreuzfahrt *f* kroytsfahrt cruise

Kreuzung *f* kroytsoong junction; crossroads, intersection

Kreuzworträtsel *n* kroytsvort-raytsel crossword puzzle

Kriechspur crawler lane

Krieg *m* kreek war

kriegen kreegen to get

Krücken *fpl* kr00cken crutches

Krug *m* kr00k jug

Küche *f* k00sh-uh cooking, cuisine; kitchen

Küchenbedarf for the kitchen

Kugel *f* k00gel ball

Kugelschreiber *m* k00gel-shryber biro

Kuh *f* k00 cow

kühl k00l cool

Kühler *m* k00ler radiator (on car)

kühl lagern keep in a cool place

Kühlschrank *m* k00l-shrank fridge

kühl servieren serve chilled

Kultur *f* koolt00r culture

Kulturbeutel *m* koolt00r-boytel toilet bag

Kumpel *m* koompel pal

Kunde *m* koond-uh, **Kundin** *f* customer

Der Kunde ist König
the customer is always right

Kundenparkplatz customer car park/parking lot

Kunst *f* koonst art

Kunstgalerie *f* koonst-galeree art gallery

Kunsthalle *f* koonst-hal-uh art gallery

Künstler *m* koonstler, **Künstlerin** *f* artist

künstlich koonstlish artificial

Kupplung *f* kooploong clutch

Kurbelwelle *f* koorbel-vell-uh crankshaft

Kurort *m* koor-ort spa

Kurs *m* koorss rate; exchange rate; course

Kurswagen *m* koors-vahgen through coach

Kurve *f* koorv-uh bend

Kurvenreiche Strecke bends

kurz koorts short

kurz nach naкн just after

kurz vor for just before

kurzsichtig koorts-zishtish shortsighted

Kurzstrecke *f* koorts-shtreck-uh short journey

Kurzwaren *fpl* koortsvahren haberdashery, (US) notions

Kusine *f* koozeen-uh cousin

Kuss *m* kooss kiss

küssen koossen to kiss

Küste *f* koost-uh coast

Küstenwacht *f* koosten-vaкнt coastguard

L

l (Liter) litre

Labor *n* labohr laboratory

lächeln lesheln to smile

Lächeln *n* smile

lachen laкнen to laugh

lächerlich lesherlish ridiculous

Laden *m* lahden shop

Ladenstraße *f* lahdenshtrahss-uh shopping street

Laken *n* lahken sheet

Lampe *f* lamp-uh lamp

Land *n* lant country

landen to land

Länder *npl* lender administrative districts of Germany, each with its own parliament

Landeskennzahl *f* landess-kenntsahl country dialling code

Landkarte *f* lantkart-uh map

Landschaft *f* lantshafft countryside; landscape; scenery

> **Travel tip** Farmstays are a great alternative to traditional hotel accommodation. Popular with city families interested in a rural escape, rooms on working farms make good bases for country pursuits such as walking or riding, and many offer local homemade produce for breakfast.

Landstraße *f* lant-shtrahss-uh country road

Landtag *m* lant-tahk regional
  parliament
**Land- und
  forstwirtschaftlicher
  Verkehr frei** agricultural and
  forestry vehicles only
lang long
lange lang-uh for a long time
Länge *f* leng-uh length
langsam langzahm slow; slowly
Langsam fahren drive slowly
langweilig langvile-ish boring
Lärm *m* lairm noise
lassen to let; to leave
lässig lessish relaxed
Laster *m* lorry, truck
Lastwagen *m* lasst-vahgen
  lorry, truck
Latzhose *f* lats-hohz-uh
  dungarees
laufen lowfen to run
Läufer *m* loyfer runner; rug
laut lowt loud; noisy
lauwarm low-varm lukewarm
Lawine *f* laveen-uh avalanche
Lawinengefahr danger of
  avalanches
Leben *n* layben life
leben to live
lebendig lebendish alive
Lebensgefahr *f* laybens-gefahr
  danger
Lebenshaltungskosten *pl*
  laybens-haltoongs-kosten
  cost of living
Lebenslauf *m* laybens-lowf
  CV, résumé

Lebensmittel *pl* laybens-mittel
  groceries
Lebensmittelhandlung *f*
  laybensmittel-hantloong grocer's
Lebensmittelvergiftung *f*
  laybensmittel-fairgiftoong
  food poisoning
Leber *f* layber liver
Leck *n* leak
lecker tasty
Leder *n* layder leather
Lederwaren leather goods
ledig laydish single
leer lair empty
Leerung *f* lairoong collection
  Nächste Leerung
  next collection
legen laygen to put
Lehrer *m* lairer, **Lehrerin** *f*
  teacher; instructor
leicht lysht easy; light
leicht verderblich will not keep,
  perishable
Leid: tut mir Leid toot meer lite
  I'm sorry
leiden lyden to suffer
leider lyder unfortunately
leihen ly-en to borrow; to lend
Leihgebühr *f* ly-geboor rental
Leim *m* lime glue
Leiter *f* lyter ladder
Leiter *m*, **Leiterin** *f* leader;
  manager
Lenkrad *n* lenkraht steering wheel
Lenkung *f* lenkoong steering
lernen lairnen to learn
lesen layzen to read

Leser *m* layzer, **Leserin** *f* reader
letzte(r,s) letst-uh,-er,-ess last
Leute *pl* loyt-uh people
Licht *n* lisht light
Licht einschalten turn on lights
Lichtspiele cinema, movie theater
Lidschatten *m* leet-shatten
  eye shadow
Liebe *f* leeb-uh love
lieben leeben to love
lieber leeber rather
Liebhaber *m* leep-hahber,
  Liebhaberin *f* lover
Lieblings- leeplings favourite

Lied *n* leet song
Lieferant *m* leeferant supplier
liefern to deliver
liegen leegen to lie; to be situated
Liegestuhl *f* leeg-uh-shtool
  deckchair
Liegewagen *f* leeg-uh-vahgen
  couchette
lila leelah purple
Limousine *f* limoozeen-uh
  saloon car
Linie *f* leen-yuh line; airline
Linienflug *m* leen-yen-flook
  scheduled flight

links left

links (von) fon on the left (of)

Linksabbieger left filter

Links halten keep left

linkshändig links-hendish
left-handed

Linse f linz-uh lens

Lippe f lipp-uh lip

Lippenstift m lippen-shtift lipstick

Liste f list-uh list

Lkw m el-kah-vay lorry, truck;
heavy goods vehicle, HGV

Loch n loKH hole

Locke f lock-uh curl

Lockenwickler m locken-vickler
curler

Löffel m lurfel spoon

los lohss loose

   los! come on!

   was ist los? what's up?

Löwe m lurv-uh lion

Lücke f loock-uh gap

Luft f looft air

luftdicht verpackt airtight
pack

Luftdruck m looft-droock air
pressure

Luftkissenboot n looftkissen-boht
hovercraft

Luftpost: per Luftpost pair
looftposst by airmail

Luftpostsendungen airmail

lügen loogen to lie

Lunge f loong-uh lung

Lungenentzündung f
loongen-ent-tsOOndoong
pneumonia

Lust haben auf loost hahben owf
to feel like

Luxus m looksoos luxury

M

machen maKHen to make;
to do

mach schon! maKH shohn get on
with it!

mach's gut gOOt take care

Mädchen n maytshen girl

Mädchenname m maytshen-
nahm-uh maiden name

mag mahk like; likes; may

Magen m mahgen stomach

Magenschmerzen mpl mahgen-
shmairtsen stomach ache

Magenverstimmung f mahgen-
fairshtimmoong indigestion

magst mahkst like

Mahlzeit f mahl-tsite meal

   nach den Mahlzeiten
   einzunehmen to be taken
   after meals

   vor den Mahlzeiten
   einzunehmen to be taken
   before meals

Mai m my May

mailen maylen to e-mail

Mal n mahl time

   zum ersten Mal tsoom airsten
   for the first time

malen mahlen to paint

man one; you

man spricht Englisch English
spoken

manchmal manshmahl
sometimes

Mandelentzündung f mandel-
ent-tsoondoong tonsillitis

Mandeln fpl tonsils

Mangel m shortage

Mann m man; husband

männlich mennlish male

Mannschaft f mannshafft
team; crew

Mantel m coat

Markt m market

Markthalle f markt-hal-uh
indoor market

März m mairts March

Masern mahzern measles

Massenmedien npl massen-
mayd-yen mass media

Matratze f matrats-uh mattress

Mauer f mower wall

Maus f mowss mouse

maximale Belastbarkeit
maximum load

Mechaniker m meshahneeker
mechanic

Medikament n medicine

Meer n mair sea

mehr mair more

mehrere mairer-uh several

Mehrfachstecker m mairfaKH-
shtecker adaptor

Mehrfahrtenkarte f mairfahrten-
kart-uh multi-journey ticket

Mehrheit f mairhite majority

Mehrwertsteuer f mairvairts-
shtoyer Value Added Tax, VAT

mein mine, **meine** mine-uh my

Meinung f mynoong opinion

meiste: das meiste (von)
myst-uh (fon) most (of)

Melone f melohn-uh melon;
bowler hat

Menge f meng-uh crowd

Mensch m mensh person

Mensch! wow!

Menschen people

menschlich menshlish human

Messe f mess-uh (trade) fair

Messer n knife

Meter m mayter metre

Metzger m metsger butcher

Metzgerei f metsgerī butcher's

mich mish me

Mietauto n meet-owto hire car,
rental car

Miete f meet-uh rent

mieten meeten to rent

Mietkauf m meetkowf lease
purchase

Militärisches Sperrgebiet
keep off: military zone

Milliardär m mill-yardair,
Milliardärin f billionaire

Millionär m mill-yonair,
Millionärin f millionaire

min. (Minute) minute

Minderheit f minderhite minority

mindestens at least

Mindestens haltbar bis... will
keep at least until...

Mineralölsteuer f minerahl-url-
shtoyer oil tax

Minirock m miniskirt

mir meer me; to me

mir geht's gut gayts goot
I'm OK

Mischung f mishoong mixture

Missbrauch strafbar penalty
for misuse

Missgeschick n miss-geshick
mishap

Missverständnis n miss-
fairshtentnis
misunderstanding

Mist! bugger!, shit!

Miststück n mist-shtoock bitch

mit with

**Mitbringen von Hunden nicht
gestattet** no dogs allowed

Mitfahrzentrale f mitfahr-
tsentrahl-uh agency for
arranging lifts

Mitleid n mit-lite pity

mitnehmen mit-naymen to take;
to give a lift to

   zum Mitnehmen to take away,
to go

Mittag m mittahk midday

Mittagessen n mittahk-essen
lunch

mittags mittahks at midday

mittags geschlossen closed at
lunchtime

Mitte f mitt-uh middle

Mitteilung f mit-tyloong message

Mittel n means

Mittelalter n mittel-alter
Middle Ages

mittelgroß mittel-grohss
medium-sized

Mittelmeer n mittel-mair
Mediterranean

Mitternacht f mitternakнt
midnight

Mittwoch m mittvoкн Wednesday

Möbel pl murbel furniture

möbliert mur-bleert furnished

möchte mursht-uh would like to

   ich möchte gern gairn
I would like

Mode f mohd-uh fashion

Modeartikel fashions

modisch mohdish fashionable

Mofa n mohfah small moped

mögen murgen to like

möglich murklish possible

Möglichkeit f murklishkite
possibility

Monat m mohnaht month

Monatskarte f mohnats-kart-uh
monthly ticket

Monatsraten mohnahts-rahten
monthly instalments

Mond m mohnt moon

Montag m mohntahk Monday

Mord m mort murder

Mörder m murder, **Mörderin** f
murderer

morgen tomorrow

Morgen m morning

morgens in the morning

Motor abstellen switch off
engine

Motorboot n mohtorboht
motorboat

Motorhaube f mohtohr-howb-uh
bonnet, hood (of a car)

Motorrad n motohr-raht
motorbike

Möwe *f* murv-uh seagull

müde mood-uh tired

Mühe *f* moo-uh trouble

Müll abladen verboten
no tipping (rubbish/garbage)

Mülltonne *f* mooll-tonn-uh
dustbin, trashcan

München moonshen Munich

Mund *m* moont mouth

Münzeinwurf insert coin here

Münzen moontsen coins

Münztank *m* moonts-tank
coin-operated pump

Muschel *f* mooshel shell; mussel

Muskel *m* mooskel muscle

muss mooss must

müssen moossen to have to

musst moosst, **müßt** moosst
must

musste moosst-uh, **mussten,
musstest** had to

Muster *n* mooster pattern;
specimen

mutig mootish brave

Mutter *f* mootter mother; nut

Mutti *f* moottee mum

Mütze *f* moots-uh cap

MWSt (Mehrwertsteuer) VAT

N

nach naKH after; to; according to

Nachbar *m* naKHbar, **Nachbarin**
f neighbour

nachdem naKHdaym after;
afterwards

nachher naKH-hair afterwards

Nachmittag *m* naKHmittahk
afternoon

Nachmittags geschlossen
closed in the afternoons

Nachname *m* naKHnahm-uh
surname

Nachricht *f* naKHrisht message

Nachrichten *pl* naKHrishten news

nachsenden naKHzenden
to forward

nächste naykst-uh next; nearest

  nächstes Jahr next year

Nacht *f* naKHt night

Nachtdienst *m* naKHt-deenst late
night chemist's/pharmacy

Nachteil *m* naKHtile disadvantage

Nachthemd *n* naKHt-hemt
nightdress

Nachtportier *m* naKHt-port-yay
night porter

Nachtruhe *f* naKHtroo-uh sleep

nachts naKHts at night

Nacken *m* nape of the neck

nackt naked

Nadel *f* nahdel needle; pin

Nagel *m* nahgel nail

Nagelfeile *f* nahgelfile-uh
nailfile

Nagellack *m* nahgel-lack
nail polish

Nagellackentferner *m* nahgel-
lack-entfairner nail polish
remover

Nagelschere *f* nahgel-shair-uh
nail clippers

nah(e) nah(-uh) near

Nähe: in der Nähe in dair nay-uh
near here

nähen nay-en to sew

nahm, nahmen, nahmst took

Nahschnellverkehrszug m nah-
shnell-fairkairs-tsook local train

Nahverkehrszug m local train

Narkose f narkohz-uh anaesthetic

Nase f nahz-uh nose

Nasenbluten n nahzenblooten
nosebleed

nass wet

natürlich natoorlish natural;
of course

Naturprodukt m natural
produce

Nebel m naybel fog

Nebelschlussleuchte f naybel-
shlooss-loysht-uh rear fog light

neben nayben next to

Nebenstraße f nayben-
shtrahss-uh minor road

nee nay nope

Neffe m neff-uh nephew

nehmen naymen to take

Neid m nite envy

neidisch nydish envious

nein nine no

Nerven pl nairfen nerves

Nervenzusammenbruch m
nairfen-tsoozammenbrookh
nervous breakdown

nervös nairvurss nervous

nett nice

Nettogewicht n net weight

Nettoinhalt m net contents

Netz n nets net; network

Netzkarte f netskart-uh
travelcard, runabout ticket

neu noy new

Neubau m noybow new building

Neujahr n noy-yar New Year

neulich noylish recently;
the other day

neun noyn nine

neunzehn noyn-tsayn nineteen

neunzig noyn-tsish ninety

nicht nisht not

nicht... do not...

nicht berühren do not touch

nicht betriebsbereit not ready

nicht bügeln do not iron

Nichte f nisht-uh niece

**Nichtgefallen: bei
Nichtgefallen Geld zurück**
money back if not satisfied

nicht hinauslehnen do not
lean out

nicht hupen sounding horn
forbidden

**nicht in der Maschine
waschen** do not machine wash

nicht rauchen no smoking

Nichtraucher non-smokers

Nichtraucherabteil n
nishtrowkher-aptile non-
smoking compartment

nichts nishts nothing

nicht schleudern do not
spin-dry

nicht stürzen fragile

**nicht zur innerlichen
Anwendung** not for
internal use

Nichtzutreffendes bitte streichen please delete as appropriate

nie nee never

Niederlage f neederlahg-uh defeat

Niederlande pl needer-land-uh Netherlands

niederländisch needer-lendish Dutch

niemals neemalss never

niemand neemant nobody

Niere f neer-uh kidney

niesen neezen to sneeze

nimmst take

nimmt takes

nirgends neergents nowhere

noch noKH still; even; more

   noch ein(e)... ine(-uh) another...

   noch nicht nisht not yet

nochmal noKHmahl again

Norden m north

Nordfriesische Inseln fpl nortfreezish-uh inzeln North Frisian Islands

nordirisch nort-eerish Northern Irish

Nordirland n nort-eerlant Northern Ireland

nördliche Stadtteile city north

nördlich von nurtlish fon north of

Nordsee f nortzay North Sea

Normal n normahl two-star petrol, regular gas

Norwegen n norvaygen Norway

norwegisch norvaygish Norwegian

Notarzt m noht-artst emergency doctor

Notaufnahme f noht-owfnahm-uh casualty department, A&E

Notausgang m noht-owssgang emergency exit

Notausstieg m noht-owss-shteek emergency exit

Notbremse f nohtbremz-uh emergency brake

Notfall m nohtfal emergency

   im Notfall Scheibe einschlagen smash glass in case of emergency

Notfälle noht-fell-uh emergencies

nötig nurtish necessary

Notizbuch n noteets-booKH notebook

Notruf m noht-roof emergency call

Notrufsäule f noht-roof-zoyl-uh emergency telephone

notwendig nohtvendish necessary

Nr. (Nummer) No., number

nüchtern einzunehmen to be taken on an empty stomach

null nooll zero

Nummer f noommer number

Nummernschild n noommern-shilt number plate

nun noon now

nur noor only; just

nur begrenzt haltbar will keep for a limited period only

nur für Anlieger access for residents only

nur für Bedienstete staff only

nur für Busse buses only

nur für Erwachsene adults only

nur für Gäste patrons only
(in hotel)

nur gegen Voranmeldung by
appointment only

nur im Notfall benutzen
emergency use only

nur mit der Hand waschen
hand wash only

nur solange der Vorrat reicht
only as long as stocks last

nur werktags weekdays only

**nur zur äußerlichen
Anwendung** for external
use only

Nutzer-ID *f* nootser-idee user ID

nützlich nootslish useful

O

ob op whether; if

oben ohben top; at the top;
upstairs

Obergeschoss *n* upper floor;
top floor

Oberweite *f* bust measurement,
chest measurement

Obst und Gemüse fruit and
vegetables

obwohl opvohl although

oder ohder or

oder? isn't it?; don't you?; aren't
I? etc; OK?

offen open

offensichtlich offenzishtlish
obvious

öffentlich urfentlish public

Öffentlichkeit *f* urfentlish-kite
public

öffnen urfnen to open

Öffnung *f* urfnoong opening

**Nach Öffnung nur
beschränkt haltbar** will keep
for a limited period only after
opening

Öffnungszeiten urfnoongs-tsyten
opening times

oft often

ohne ohn-uh without

ohne Konservierungsstoffe
no preservatives

ohne künstliche Aromastoffe
no artificial flavouring

**Ohnmacht: in Ohnmacht
fallen** ohn-maкHt to faint

Ohr *n* ohr ear

Oktoberfest *n* Munich beer
festival (held in September)

Ölstand *m* urlshtant oil level

Ölwechsel sofort oil change
while you wait

Oma *f* ohmah granny

Omnibus *m* omneebooss bus

Onkel *m* uncle

Opa *m* ohpah grandad

Oper *f* ohper opera

Operationssaal *m* opairats-
yohns-zahl operating theatre/
room

Opfer *n* victim

Optiker *m* optician

Ordner *m* ortner folder; steward

Ordnung *f* ordnoong order

in Ordnung all right

Ort *m* town; place

örtliche Betäubung *f* urtlish-uh betoyboong local anaesthetic

Ortsgespräch *n* orts-geshpraysh local call

Ortsnetz *n* ortsnets local network

Ortszeit *f* orts-tsite local time

Ossi *m* ossee East German

Osten *m* east

Ostern *n* ohstern Easter

Österreich *n* urster-rysh Austria

Österreicher *m* urster-rysher Austrian

Österreicherin *f* urster-rysherin Austrian (woman)

österreichisch urster-ryshish Austrian

Ostfriesische Inseln *fpl* ostfreezish-uh inzeln East Frisian Islands

östliche Stadtteile city east

östlich von urstlish fon east of

Ostsee *f* ostzay Baltic

P

Paar *n* pahr pair

paar: ein paar... a few...

Päckchen *n* (*pl*) peckshen small parcel(s)

packen to pack

Packung *f* packoong pack

Paket *n* pakayt parcel, package

Paketannahme *f* pakayt-an-nahm-uh parcels counter

Palast *m* palace

Panne *f* pann-uh breakdown

Pannendreieck *n* pannen-dry-eck emergency triangle

Pannenhilfe *f* pannen-hilf-uh breakdown services

Papier *n* papeer paper; litter

Papier(hand)tücher *pl* papeer-(hant)toosher paper handkerchiefs, tissues

Pappe *f* papp-uh cardboard

Parfüm *n* parfoom perfume

Parkausweis *m* park-owssvice parking permit

Parkbucht *f* parkbookHt parking space

Parkdauer parking allowed for...

parken to park

Parken nur mit Parkscheibe parking disc holders only

Parken nur mit Parkschein parking only with parking permit

Parken verboten no parking

Parkett *n* stalls

Parkhaus *n* parkhowss multistorey car park/parking garage

Parkplatz *m* parkplats car park, parking lot

Parkscheinautomat *m* parkshine-owtomaht car park/parking lot ticket vending machine

Parkschein entnehmen take a ticket

Parkuhr *f* park-oor parking meter

Parkverbot no parking

Pass *m* pas passport; pass

Passagier *m* passah-Jeer
passenger

Passkontrolle *f* pas-kontroll-uh
passport control

Passwort *n* pas-vort password

Pauschalreise *f* powshahl-rize-uh
package tour

Pause *f* powz-uh interval,
intermission; rest

Pech *n* pesh bad luck

peinlich pine-lish embarrassing

Pelz *m* pelts fur

Pelzmantel *m* peltsmantel
fur coat

Pension *f* pangz-yohn guesthouse

Personalausweis *m* pairzonahl-
owssvice identity card

Personaleingang *m* staff
entrance

Personenzug *m* pairzohnen-tsook
passenger train, stopping train

Perücke *f* perOOck-uh wig

Pfandleihe *f* pfant-ly-uh
pawnbroker

Pfanne *f* pfann-uh frying pan

Pfd. (Pfund) pound (German
pound = 500g)

Pfeife *f* pfife-uh pipe

Pferd *n* pfairt horse

Pferderennbahn *f* pfaird-uh-
rennbahn race course

Pferdeschwanz *m* pfaird-uh-
shvants ponytail

Pfingsten *n* Whitsun

Pflanze *f* pflants-uh plant

Pfund *n* pfoont pound (German
pound = 500g); pound (Sterling)

Phonoartikel hi-fi equipment

Pickel *m* spot

pikant savoury; spicy

Pille f pill-uh pill

Pinsel m pinzel paint brush

Pinzette f pintsett-uh
tweezers

Pistole f pistohl-uh gun

Pkw m pay-kah-vay private car

Plakat n plakaht poster

Plakate ankleben verboten
stick no bills

Plastik n plastic

Plastiktüte f plastik-toot-uh
plastic bag

platt flat

Plattenspieler m platten-shpeeler
record player

Platz m plats seat; square; place;
space

Platzanweiserin f plats-anvyzerin
usherette

Platzkarte f plats-kart-uh seat
reservation

pleite plite-uh broke

Plombe f plomb-uh filling

plötzlich plurtslish suddenly

PLZ (Postleitzahl) postcode,
zip code

Pokal m pohkahl cup

Polen n pohlen Poland

Politik f politeek politics

Politiker m poleeticker,
Politikerin f politician

politisch poleetish political

Polizei f politsi police

Polizeipräsidium n politsi-
prayzeedee-oom
police headquarters

Polizeiwache f politsi-vakH-uh
police station

Polizist m politsist policeman

Polizistin f politsistin
policewoman

polnisch polnish Polish

Pony m ponnee fringe

Portemonnaie n port-monnay
purse

Portier m port-yay porter

Porto n postage

portugiesisch portoo-geezish
Portuguese

Porzellan n portsellahn porcelain;
china

Post f posst mail; post office

Postamt n posst-amt post office

Postanweisung f posst-
anvyzoong postal/money order

Postanweisungen money orders

Postkarte f posstkart-uh postcard

postlagernd posst-lahgernt poste
restante, (US) general delivery

postlagernde Sendungen poste
restante, (US) general delivery

Postleitzahl f posst-lite-tsahl
postcode, zip code

Postscheckkonto n posst-sheck-
konto (post office) giro account

Postsparkasse f posst-shparkass-
uh post office savings bank

Postwertzeichen n(pl) posst-
vairt-tsyshen postage stamp(s)

**Postwertzeichen in kl.
Mengen** stamps in small
quantities

praktisch praktish practical

praktische Ärztin f praktish-uh airtstin GP

praktischer Arzt m praktisher artst GP

Präservativ n prezairvateef condom

Praxis f praksis doctor's surgery; practice

Preis m price price

zum halben Preis half price

preisgünstig price-g00nstish cheap; inexpensive

Preis reduziert price reduced

Preissenkung reduction

preiswert bargain price, inexpensive

prima! preemah good!

Prinz m prints prince

Prinzessin f printsessin princess

Privateigentum private property

Privatgrundstück private property

Privatparkplatz private car park/parking lot

pro: pro Woche voKH-uh per week

Probe f prohb-uh rehearsal; sample

probieren probeeren to taste; to try

Programmkino n programm-keeno arts cinema

Prospekt m brochure

prost! prohst cheers!

Prozent n prohtsent per cent

Prozess m proh-tsess trial; process

prüfen pr00fen to check

Publikum n p00blikoom audience

Puder m p00der powder

Pumpe f poomp-uh pump

Punkt m poonkt point; dot; full stop

pünktlich p00nktlish punctual

Puppe f poopp-uh doll

putzen pootsen to clean

Putzfrau f pootsfrow cleaning lady

Q

Qualität f kvalitayt quality

Qualitätsware quality goods

Qualle f kvall-uh jellyfish

Quatsch m kvatsh nonsense

Quelle f kvell-uh spring; source

Quittung f kvittoong receipt

R

Rabatt m reduction, discount

Rad n raht wheel

Radfahren n raht-fahren cycling

Radfahrer m raht-fahrer cyclist

Radfahrer frei cyclists only

Radfahrerin f raht-fahrerin cyclist

Radiergummi n radeer-goommee rubber, eraser

Radweg m raht-vayk cycle path

Radweg kreuzt cycle track crossing

Rand m rant edge; rim

Rang m row; stalls; grade

Rasen m rahzen lawn

Rasierapparat m razeer-apparaht razor

Rasiercreme *f* razeer-kraym
shaving cream

rasieren: sich rasieren zish
razeeren to shave

Rasierklinge *f* razeerkling-uh
razor blade

Rasierpinsel *m* razeer-pinzel
shaving brush

Rasierseife *f* razeerzife-uh
shaving foam

Rasierwasser *n* razeervasser
aftershave

Raststätte *f* rast-shtett-uh
services area

Rat *m* raht advice; council

Rate *f* raht-uh instalment; rate

raten rahten to guess; to advise

Ratenzahlung *f* rahten-tsahloong
hire purchase, installment plan

Ratenzahlung möglich credit
terms available

Rathaus *n* raht-howss town hall

Rätsel *n* raytsel puzzle

Ratskeller *m* rahtskeller
restaurant and bar close
to town hall

Ratte *f* ratt-uh rat

Rattengift *n* rattengift rat poison

Raub *m* rowp robbery

Raubüberfall *m* rowp-ꞷober-fal
armed robbery

Rauch *m* rowкн smoke

rauchen rowкнen to smoke

Rauchen einstellen
no smoking

**Rauchen und offenes Feuer
verboten** no smoking or
naked lights

Rauchen verboten no smoking

Raucher smokers

Raucherabteil *n* rowкнer-aptile
smoking compartment

rauh row rough

raus! rowss get out!

Rechner *m* reshner calculator;
computer

Rechnung *f* reshnoong bill, (US)
check

rechts reshts right

Rechtsabbieger right filter lane

Rechtsanwalt *m* reshts-anvalt
lawyer

Rechtsanwältin *f* reshts-anveltin
lawyer

rechts fahren keep to the right

rechts halten keep right

rechtshändig reshts-hendish
right-handed

rechts (von) reshts (fon)
on the right (of)

rechtzeitig resht-tsytish on time

reduziert reduced

Reformhaus *n* reform-howss
health food shop

Reformkost *f* health food

Regen *m* raygen rain

Regenmantel *m* raygen-mantel
raincoat

Regenschirm *m* raygen-sheerm
umbrella

Regierung *f* regeeroong
government

regnen rayknen to rain
  es regnet ess rayk-net
  it's raining

regnerisch raⁱknerish rainy

Reh n ray roe deer

Reibe f ribe-uh grater

reich rysh rich

reichen: das reicht rysht
that's enough

reif rife ripe

Reifen m ryfen tyre

Reifendruck m ryfendroock
tyre pressure

Reifenpanne f ryfenpann-uh
puncture

Reihe f ry-uh row; series

reine Baumwolle pure cotton

reine Schurwolle pure wool

reine Seide pure silk

reine Wolle pure wool

reinigen rynigen to clean

Reinigung f rynigoong laundry

Reinigungscreme f rynigoongs-
kraym cleansing cream

Reise f rize-uh journey

Reiseandenken souvenirs

Reiseapotheke f rize-uh-
apotayk-uh first aid kit

Reiseauskunft f rize-uh-
owsskoonft travel information

Reisebedarf m rize-uh-bedarf
travel requisites

Reisebüro n rize-uh-bOOro
travel agency

Reiseführer m rize-uh-fOOrer
guide; guidebook

reisen rize-en to travel

Reisende ryzend-uh passengers

Reisepass m rize-uh-pas
passport

Reiseproviant m rize-uh-prohvee-
ant food for the journey

Reisescheck m rize-uh-sheck
travellers' cheque

Reißverschluss m rice-
fairshlooss zip

Reitsport m rite-shport
horse riding

Reitweg m rite-vayk bridle path

Reklamationen complaints

Reklame f reklahm-uh
advertising; advertisement

Rennbahn f race track

Rentner m, **Rentnerin** f
old-age pensioner

Reparaturen repairs

Reparaturwerkstatt f
reparatOOr-vairkshtatt
garage, repairs

reparieren repareeren to mend,
to repair

Reportage f reportahJ-uh report

reservieren rezairveeren
to reserve

reserviert rezairveert reserved

Reservierung f rezairveeroong
reservation

Restgeld wird zurückgegeben
change will be given

Rettungsring m rettoongs-ring
lifebelt

Rezept n retsept recipe;
prescription

rezeptpflichtig sold on
prescription only

Rhein m rine Rhine

Rheuma n roymah rheumatism

Richter *m* rishter judge

Richterin *f* rishterin judge

richtig rishtish right; correct

Richtung *f* rishtoong direction

riechen reeshen to smell

Riegel *m* reegel bolt

Risiko *n* reezeeko risk

Rock *m* skirt; rock music

Rodelbahn *f* rohdelbahn
toboggan run

Rohr *n* rohr pipe

Rolle *f* rol-uh role; part

Rollsplitt loose chippings

Rollstuhl *m* rol-shtool
wheelchair

Rolltreppe *f* rol-trepp-uh escalator

Roman *m* romahn novel

Röntgenaufnahme *f* rurntgen-
owfnahm-uh X-ray

rosa rohza pink

Rosenmontagszug *m* rohzen-
mohntaks-tsook carnival
procession held on the Monday
before Ash Wednesday (public
holiday)

rot roht red

Röteln rurteln German measles

rothaarig roht-hahrish
red-headed

Rubin *m* roobeen ruby

Rücken *m* rOOcken back

Rückenschmerzen *pl*
rOOckenshmairtsen backache

Rückfahrkarte *f* rOOckfahrkart-uh
return/round trip ticket

Rücklichter *npl* rOOcklishter
rear lights

Rückseite *f* rOOckzite-uh
back; reverse

rücksichtslos rOOckzishts-lohss
reckless

Rücksitz *m* rOOckzits back seat

Rückspiegel *m* rOOck-shpeegel
rearview mirror

rückwärts rOOckvairts backwards

Rückwärtsgang *m* rOOckvairts-
gang reverse gear

Ruderboot *n* rOOderboht
rowing boat

Ruf *m* rOOf call

ruf doch mal an somebody
somewhere wants a phonecall
from you

rufen rOOfen to call; to shout

Rufnummer *f* rOOfnoommer
telephone number

Rufsäule *f* rOOfzoyl-uh emergency
telephone

Ruhe *f* rOO-uh quiet; rest

ruhestörender Lärm
disturbance of the peace

Ruhetag closed all day

ruhig rOO-ish quiet

ruhige Lage peaceful, secluded
spot

rund roont round

Rundfahrt *f* rOOntfahrt
guided tour

Rundgang *m* guided tour (on
foot)

Rundreise *f* rOOnt-rize-uh
guided tour

russisch rOOssish Russian

Russland *n* rOOsslant Russia

S

Sache *f* zaKH-uh thing; matter; affair

Sachsen *n* zakzen Saxony

Sackgasse *f* zack-gass-uh cul-de-sac, dead end

sagen zahgen to say

man sagt, dass... zahkt they say that...

sagenhaft zahgenhaft terrific

sah zah, **sahen, sahst** saw

Salbe *f* zalb-uh ointment

Salon *m* zalong lounge

salzig zaltsish salty

Sammelkarte *f* zammel-kart-uh multi-journey ticket

sammeln zammeln to collect

Sammlung *f* zamloong collection

Samstag *m* zamstahk Saturday

samstags zamstahks on Saturdays

Sandstrand *m* zant-shtrant sandy beach

Sanitäter *m* zanee-tayter ambulanceman

Sanitätsdienst *m* zanitayts-deenst ambulance service

Sanitätsstelle *f* zanitayts-shtell-uh first aid centre

Satz *m* zats sentence; rate

sauber zowber clean

säubern zoybern to clean

sauer zower sour; pissed off

Sauerstoff *m* zowershtoff oxygen

SB (Selbstbedienung) self service

S-Bahn *f* ess-bahn local urban railway

SB-Tankstelle *f* ess-bay-tankshtell-uh self-service petrol/gas station

Schachtel *f* shaKHtel box; packet

schade: das ist schade shahd-uh it's a pity

Schädel *m* shaydel skull

Schaden *m* shahden damage

Schaf *n* shahf sheep

Schaffner *m* shaffner conductor

schal shahl stale

Schal *m* scarf

Schallplatte *f* shallplatt-uh record

Schalter *m* shalter counter; switch

Schalterstunden hours of business

Schaltknüppel *m* shaltk-nOOppel gear lever

schämen: sich schämen zish shaymen to be ashamed

scharf sharf sharp; hot

Schatten *m* shatten shade

Schauer *m* shower shower

Schaufenster *n* show-fenster shop window

Scheck *m* sheck cheque, (US) check

Scheckheft *n* sheck-heft cheque book

Scheckkarte *f* sheck-kart-uh cheque card

Scheibe *f* shibe-uh slice

Scheibenwischer *m* shyben-visher windscreen wiper

Schein *m* shine note, bill;
appearance

Scheineingabe insert banknote

scheinen shynen to shine;
to seem

Scheinwerfer *mpl* shine-vairfer
headlights

Scheiße! shice-uh shit!

Scheißkerl *m* shice-kairl bastard

Schenkel *m* shenkel thigh

Schere *f* shair-uh scissors

scheu shoy shy

Schiedsrichter *m* sheets-rishter
referee

Schiff *n* shiff ship; boat

Schild *n* shilt sign

Schirm *m* sheerm umbrella;
screen

Schlafanzug *m* shlahf-ants00k
pyjamas

schlafen shlahfen to sleep

Schlaflosigkeit *f* shlahflohzish-
kite insomnia

Schlafmittel *n* shlahfmittel
sleeping drug

Schlafraum *m* shlahfrowm
dormitory

Schlafsaal *m* shlahfzahl
dormitory

Schlafsack *m* shlahfzack
sleeping bag

Schlaftablette *f* shlahf-tablett-uh
sleeping pill

Schlafwagen *m* shlahfvahgen
sleeper, sleeping car

Schlafzimmer *n* shlahf-tsimmer
bedroom

Schlafzimmerbedarf
for the bedroom

schlagen shlahgen to hit

Schläger *m* shlayger racket;
hooligan

Schlange *f* shlang-uh
snake; queue

Schlange stehen shtay-en
to queue

schlank shlank slim

Schlauch *m* shlowKH inner tube

schlecht shlesht bad; badly;
unwell

Schlechte Fahrbahn
bad road surface

schlechter shleshter worse

schlechteste shleshtest-uh
worst

Schleudergefahr danger of
skidding

schleudern shloydern to skid

Schleuderpreise prices slashed

schließen shleessen to close

Schließfach *n* shleessfakH
left luggage locker

Schließfächer luggage lockers

schloss shloss shut

Schloss *n* castle; lock

Schluckauf *m* shloock-owf
hiccups

schlucken shloocken to swallow

Schluss *m* shlooss end

Schlüssel *m* shlÜÜssel key;
spanner; wrench

schmackhaft shmack-haft tasty

schmecken shmecken to taste;
to taste good

Schmerz *m* shmairts pain

schmerzen shmairtsen to hurt

schmerzhaft shmairts-haft painful

Schmerzmittel *n* shmairts-mittel painkiller

schminken: sich schminken zish shminken to do one's make-up

Schmuck *m* shmoock jewellery

schmutzig shmootsish dirty

schnarchen shnarshen to snore

Schnauze! shnowts-uh shut your mouth!

Schnee *m* shnay snow

schneebedeckt snow-covered

Schneeketten *pl* snow chains

Schneeverhältnisse *pl* shnay-fair-heltniss-uh snow conditions

Schneeverwehung *f* shnay-fairvayoong snow drift

schneiden shnyden to cut
  sich schneiden to cut oneself

Schneiderei *f* shnyderī tailor's

schneien shny-en to snow

schnell shnell fast

Schnellimbiss *m* shnell-imbiss snackbar

Schnellzug *m* shnell-tsook express train

Schnupfen *m* shnoopfen cold

Schnurrbart *m* shnoorrbart moustache

schon shohn already

schön shurn beautiful; fine; nice

Schönheitspflege *f* shurnhites-pflayg-uh beauty care

Schönheitssalon *m* shurnhites-zalong beauty salon

Schornstein *m* shorn-shtine chimney

Schotte *m* shott-uh Scotsman

Schottin *f* shottin Scotswoman

Schrank *m* shrank cupboard

Schranke *f* shrank-uh barrier

Schraube *f* shrowb-uh screw

Schraubenschlüssel *m* shrowben-shloossel spanner, wrench

Schraubenzieher *m* shrowben-tsee-er screwdriver

schreiben shryben to write

Schreibmaschine *f* shripe-masheen-uh typewriter

Schreibpapier *n* shripe-papeer writing paper

Schreibtisch *m* shripe-tish desk

Schreibwaren *pl* shripe-vahren stationery

Schreibwarenladen *m* shripe-vahren-lahden stationer's

schreien shry-en to scream

schrieb shreep, **schriebst, schrieben** wrote

Schriftsteller *m* shrift-shteller, **Schriftstellerin** *f* writer

Schritt *m* shritt step

Schritt fahren drive at walking speed

schüchtern shooshtern shy

Schuhcreme *f* shoo-kraym shoe polish

Schuhe *mpl* shoo-uh shoes

Schuhmacher *m* sh00makHer
shoe repairer

Schuhreparaturen shoe repairs,
heelbar

Schulbedarf school items

Schulden *fpl* sh00lden debts

schuld: er ist schuld air ist
sh00lt it's his fault

schuldig sh00ldish guilty

Schule *f* sh00l-uh school

Schüler und Studenten school
children and students

Schulhof *m* sh00l-hohf
school playground

Schulter *f* sh00lter shoulder

Schüssel *f* sh00ssel bowl

Schutt abladen verboten no
tipping

schützen sh00tsen to protect

Schützenfest *n* sh00tsenfest
local carnival

Schwaben *n* shvahben Swabia

schwach shvaKH weak

Schwachkopf *m* shvaKH-kopf
idiot, wally

Schwachsinn *m* shvaKH-zin
rubbish

Schwager *m* shvahger
brother-in-law

Schwägerin *f* shvaygerin
sister-in-law

Schwamm *m* shvamm sponge

schwanger shvang-er pregnant

Schwanz *m* shvants tail

schwarz shvartz black

Schwarzes Brett *n* shvartsess
noticeboard

Schwarzwald *m* shvartsvalt
Black Forest

schwarz-weiß shvarts-vice
black and white

Schwein *n* shvine pig

Schweiz *f* shvites Switzerland

Schweizer *m* shvytser Swiss

Schweizerin *f* shvytserin
Swiss woman

schwer shvair heavy; difficult

Schwerlastverkehr heavy vehicles

Schwester f shvester sister

Schwiegermutter f shveeger-mootter mother-in-law

Schwiegersohn m shveegerzohn son-in-law

Schwiegertochter f shveeger-toKHter daughter-in-law

Schwiegervater m shveegerfahter father-in-law

schwierig shveerish difficult

Schwimmbad n shvimmbaht swimming pool

Schwimmen n shvimmen swimming

schwimmen to swim

schwimmen gehen gay-en to go swimming

Schwimmen verboten no swimming

Schwimmer m shvimmer, **Schwimmerin** f swimmer

Schwimmweste f shvimmvest-uh life jacket

schwindlig shvintlish dizzy

schwitzen shvitsen to sweat

schwul shvool gay

sechs zeks six

sechzehn zesh-tsayn sixteen

sechzig zesh-tsish sixty

See m zay lake

See f sea

seekrank zaykrank seasick

Segelboot n zaygelboht sailing boat

Segeln n zaygeln sailing

Segler m zaygler yachtsman

Seglerin f zayglerin yachtswoman

sehen zay-en to see

Sehenswürdigkeit f zay-ens-voordishkite sight

sehr zair very

sei zy be

seid zite are

seien Sie zy-en zee be

Seide f zide-uh silk

Seife f zife-uh soap

Seil n zile rope

sein zine to be; his; its

seine zine-uh his; its

seit zite since

seitdem zite-daym since

Seite f zite-uh side; page

Seitenstreifen nicht befahrbar soft verges, keep off

Sekunde f zekoond-uh second

selbe zelb-uh same

selbst zelpst even

  er/sie selbst himself/herself

Selbstbedienung f zelpst-bedeenoong self-service

selbstverständlich zelpst-fairshtentlish of course

Selbstwählferndienst direct long-distance dialling

seltsam zeltzahm strange

senden zenden to send

Sender m zender (radio/TV) station

Sendung f zendoong programme

sensibel zenzeebel sensitive

Serviervorschlag serving suggestion

Sessellift *m* zessel-lift chairlift

setzen zetsen to put

  sich setzen to sit down

sexistisch seksistish sexist

sicher zisher sure; safe

Sicherheitsgurt *m* zisherhites-goort seat belt

Sicherheitsnadel *f* zisherhites-nahdel safety pin

Sicherung *f* zisheroong fuse

Sicht *f* zisht visibility

sie zee she; her; they; them

Sie you

sieben zeeben seven

siebzehn zeep-tsayn seventeen

siebzig zeep-tsish seventy

Sieg *m* zeek victory

siehe... see...

siehst zeest see

sieht zeet sees

siezen zeetsen to use the more formal 'Sie' form

Silber *n* zilber silver

silbern zilbern silver

Silvester *n* zilvester New Year's Eve

simsen zimzen to text

sind zint are

singen zing-en to sing

sinken zinken to sink

Sitz *m* zits seat

Sitz für Schwerbehinderte seat for handicapped

Sitzplätze seats

skifahren sheefahren to ski

Skifahren *n* skiing

Skigebiet *n* shee-gebeet skiing area

Skihose *f* shee-hohzuh ski pants

Skilehrer *m* shee-lairer, **Skilehrerin** *f* ski instructor

Skipiste *f* sheepist-uh ski slope

Skistiefel *mpl* shee-shteefel ski boots

Skistock *m* shee-shtock ski pole

Smoking *m* dinner jacket

so zo so; this way

  so... wie vee as... as

sobald zohbalt as soon as

Socke *f* zock-uh sock

Sodbrennen *n* zohtbrennen heartburn

sofort zofort immediately

Sohn *m* zohn son

solange zohlang-uh as long as

Sommer *m* zommer summer

Sommerfahrplan *m* zommerfahrplahn summer timetable/schedule

Sommerferien *pl* zommer-fairee-en summer holidays/vacation

Sommerschlussverkauf summer sale

Sonderangebot *n* zonder-angeboht special offer

Sonderflug *m* zonderflook special flight

sondern zondern but

Sonderpreis *m* zonder-price special price

Sondervorstellung *f* zonderforshtelloong special performance

Sonnabend *m* zonnahbent Saturday

Sonne *f* zonn-uh sun

sonnenbaden zonnenbahden to sunbathe

Sonnenbrand *m* zonnenbrant sunburn

Sonnenbrille *f* zonnenbrill-uh sunglasses

Sonnenöl *n* zonnen-url suntan lotion; suntan oil

Sonnenschein *m* zonnen-shine sunshine

Sonnenstich *m* zonnen-shtish sunstroke

Sonnenuntergang *m* zonnen-oontergang sunset

sonnig zonnish sunny

Sonntag *m* zonntahk Sunday

Sonntagsfahrer *m* zonntahks-fahrer roadhog, Sunday driver

sonn- und feiertags on Sundays and public holidays

sonst zonst otherwise

Sorge *f* zorg-uh worry

sich Sorgen machen (um) zish zorgen maкhen (oom) to worry (about)

Sorte *f* zort-uh kind; sort

Souterrain *n* zootereng basement

soweit zovite as far as

sowieso zoveezoh anyway

sowohl... als auch... zovohl alss owкн both... and...

Spanien *n* shpahnee-en Spain

sparen shpahren to save

Sparguthaben *n* shpahrgoot-hahben savings account

Sparkasse *f* shpahrkass-uh savings bank

Spaß *m* shpahss fun; joke

spät shpayt late

wie spät ist es? vee what time is it?

Spaten *m* shpahten spade

Spätschalter *m* shpayt-shalter night counter

Spätvorstellung *f* shpaytforshtelloong late performance

spazieren gehen shpatseeren gay-en to go for a walk

Spaziergang *m* shpatseergang walk

Speiche *f* shpysh-uh spoke

Speisegaststätte *f* shpize-uh-gast-shtett-uh restaurant

Speiseraum *m* shpize-uh-rowm dining room

Speisesaal *m* shpize-uh-zahl restaurant, dining room

Speisewagen *m* shp**i**ze-uh-vahgen restaurant car

Speisezimmer *n* shp**i**ze-uh-tsimmer dining room

Sperrgebiet prohibited area

Spiegel *m* shp**ee**gel mirror

Spiel *n* shp**ee**l game; match

spielen shp**ee**len to play

Spielende Kinder children at play

Spieler *m* shp**ee**ler, **Spielerin** *f* player; gambler

Spielkasino *n* shp**ee**l-kazeeno casino

Spielplatz *m* shp**ee**lplats playground

Spielwaren *fpl* shp**ee**l-vahren toys

Spielzeug *n* shp**ee**ltsoyk toy

Spinne *f* shp**i**nn-uh spider

spinnen: du spinnst wohl! d**oo** shp**i**nnst vohl you've got to be joking!, you're out of your mind!

Spion *m* shpee-**oh**n spy

Spirale *f* shpeer**ah**l-uh spiral; IUD

Spitze shp**i**ts-uh fantastic, magic

Spitzenqualität top quality

Spitzname *m* shp**i**tsnahm-uh nickname

Sportartikel sports goods

Sportplatz *m* shp**o**rt-plats sports ground

Sporttauchen *n* shp**o**rt-towKHen skin-diving

Sportverein *m* shp**o**rt-fair-ine sports club

Sportwagen *m* shp**o**rt-vahgen sports car; buggy

Sportzentrum *n* shp**o**rt-tsentroom sports centre

Sprache *f* shprahKH-uh language

Sprachenschule *f* shprahKHen-sh**oo**l-uh language school

Sprachführer *m* shprahKH-f**oo**rer phrasebook

sprechen shpr**e**shen to speak; to talk

Sprechstunde *f* shpr**e**sh-shtoond-uh surgery

Sprechzimmer *n* shpr**e**sh-tsimmer surgery (room)

spricht shpr**i**sht speaks

    wer spricht, bitte? vair shpr**i**sht b**i**tt-uh who's calling please?

springen shpr**i**ngen to jump

Spritze *f* shpr**i**ts-uh injection

Sprungschanze *f* shpr**oo**ng-shants-uh ski jump

Spüle *f* shp**oo**l-uh sink

spülen shp**oo**len to do the dishes; to rinse

Spülmittel *n* shp**oo**l-mittel washing-up liquid

Staat *m* shtaht state

Staatsangehörigkeit *f* shtahts-an-gehur-rish-kite nationality

Staatsanwalt *m* shtahts-anvalt public prosecutor

Stadion *n* shtahdee-on stadium

Stadt *f* shtatt town; city

Stadthalle *f* shtatt-hal-uh city hall

Stadtmitte *f* shtatt-mitt-uh city centre

Stadtplan *m* shtatt-plahn map

Stadtzentrum *n* shtatt-tsentroom city centre

Stammgast *m* shtammgast regular customer

Stammtisch *m* shtammtish table for regulars

stand shtant, **standen** shtanden stood

Standesamt *n* shtandess-amt registry office

Standlicht *n* shtantlisht sidelights

starb shtarp, **starben** shtarben died

stark shtark strong; great

Starkes Gefälle steep gradient

Start *m* shtart start; take-off

Station *f* shtats-yohn (hospital) ward; stop

statt shtatt instead of

Stau *m* shtow tailback, traffic jam

Staub *m* shtowp dust

Staubsauger *m* shtowp-zowger vacuum cleaner

Std. (Stunde) hour

stechen shteshen to sting

Stechmücke *f* shtesh-m00ck-uh mosquito

Steckdose *f* shteck-dohz-uh socket

Stecker *m* shtecker plug

stehen shtay-en to stand

das steht mir shtayt meer it suits me

stehlen shtaylen to steal

Stehplätze *pl* shtayplets-uh standing room

steil shtile steep

Stein *m* shtine stone

Steinschlag falling rocks

Steinschlaggefahr danger of falling rocks

Stelle *f* shtell-uh place

stellen shtellen to put

Steppdecke *f* shteppdeck-uh continental quilt

sterben shtairben to die

Stereoanlage *f* shtayray-o-anlahg-uh stereo system

Stern *m* shtairn star

Steuer *f* shtoyer tax

Steuer *n* steering wheel

Stiefel *m* shteefel boot

Stift *m* shtift pen

Stil *m* shteel style

Stille *f* shtill-uh silence

stillen shtillen to breastfeed

Stimme *f* shtimm-uh voice; vote

stimmt shtimmt that's right

Stimmung *f* shtimmoong mood

Stirn *f* shteern forehead

Stock *m* shtock floor, storey; stick

Stockwerk *n* shtockvairk floor, storey

Stoff *m* shtoff material; fabric

stolz shtolts proud

Stöpsel *m* shturpsel plug

stören shtur-ren to disturb

stört es Sie, wenn ich…? shturt ess zee venn ish do you mind if I…?

Störungsstelle *f* shtur-roongs-shtell-uh faults service

Stoßdämpfer *m* shtohss-dempfer shock-absorber

Stoßstange f shtohss-shtang-uh bumper, fender

Str. (Straße) street

Straßenbauarbeiten roadworks

Straßenkilometer kilometres by road

Strafe f shtrahf-uh penalty; punishment

Strand m shtrant beach

Strandgut n shtrant-goot flotsam and jetsam

Strandkorb m shtrantkorp wicker beach chair

Strandpromenade f shtrant-promenahd-uh promenade

Straße f shtrahss-uh street; road

Straßenbahn f shtrahssenbahn tram

Straßenbauarbeiten pl shtrahssenbow-arbyten roadworks

Straßenschild n shtrahssen-shilt road sign

Straßenverkehrsordnung f shtrahssen-fairkairs-ordnoong highway code

Strecke f shtreck-uh route; stretch

streichen shtryshen to paint; to cancel

Streichholz n shtrysh-holts match

strengstens untersagt strictly prohibited

Streugut grit

stricken shtricken to knit

Strickwaren knitwear

Strom m shtrohm electricity; stream

Stromausfall m shtrohm-owss-fal power cut

Stromkosten shtrohm-kosten electricity costs

Strömung f shtrurmoong current

Strümpfe pl shtroompf-uh stockings

Strumpfhose f shtroompf-hohz-uh tights, pantyhose

Stück n shtoock piece; play

Student m shtoodent, **Studentin** f student

Stuhl m shtool chair

Stunde f shtoond-uh hour; lesson

Stundenplan m shtoonden-plahn timetable, (US) schedule

stündlich shtoontlish hourly

Sturm m shtoorm storm

stürmisch shtoormish stormy

Sturz m shtoorts fall

suchen zookHen to look for

Sucher m zookHer viewfinder

Süden m zooden south

südliche Stadtteile city south

südlich von zootlish fon south of

Summe f zoomm-uh sum

Super n zooper four-star petrol, premium (gas)

super zooper great

Suppenteller m zooppenteller soup plate

süß zooss sweet

T

Tabak m tahbak tobacco

Tabakwaren tobacconist's

Tabelle f tabell-uh (league) table

Tablett *n* tray

Tablette *f* tablett-uh pill, tablet

Tacho *m* taкно speedometer

Tafel *f* tahfel plate; blackboard

Tag *m* tahk day

Tag der Deutschen Einheit
Day of German Unity, 3rd
October, a public holiday

Tagebuch *n* tahg-uh-bOOKH diary

Tagesdecke *f* tahgess-deck-uh
bedspread

Tageskarte *f* tahgess-kart-uh day
ticket; menu of the day

Tageszeitung *f* tahgess-tsytoong
daily newspaper

Travel tip It's fairly easy to
find British and US newspa-
pers in German towns, and
larger newsagents in cities
carry many of the London-
printed editions at lunchtime
on the same day. The best
place to look for foreign
media is at newsagents in
the main train station, which
also carry a small stock of
international magazines.

---

täglich tayklish daily

täglich frisch fresh every day

Taille *f* tal-yuh waist

Taillenweite *f* tal-yen-vite-uh
waist measurement

Tal *n* tahl valley

Talsperre *f* tahlshpair-uh dam

Tankstelle *f* tankshtell-uh petrol/
gas station

Tankwart *m* tankvart petrol/
gas pump attendant

Tanne *f* tann-uh fir tree

Tante *f* tant-uh aunt

Tanz *m* tants dance

Tanzcafé *n* tants-kaffay café with
dancing

tanzen tantsen to dance

Tapete *f* tapayt-uh wallpaper

tapezieren tapetseeren
to wallpaper

tapfer brave

Tasche *f* tash-uh pocket; bag

Taschendieb *m* tashen-deep
pickpocket

Taschenlampe *f* tashen-lamp-uh
torch, flashlight

Taschenmesser *n* tashen-messer
penknife

Taschenrechner *m* tashen-
reshner calculator

Taschentuch *n* tashentOOKH
handkerchief

Tasse *f* tass-uh cup

tat taht, **tatst, taten** did

taub towp deaf

tauchen towкнen to dive

Tauchen verboten no diving

tauschen towshen to exchange

tausend towzent thousand

Tauwetter *n* tow-vetter thaw

Taxistand *m* taksi-shtant taxi rank

TEE *m* tay-ay-**ay** Trans-Europe
Express

Teekanne *f* taykann-uh teapot

Teelöffel *m* tay-lurfel teaspoon

Teestube *f* tayshtOOb-uh tea room

Teich *m* tysh pond

Teil *m* tysh part

teilen tylen to share

teils… teils… tiles partly…
partly…

Teilzahlung möglich credit
available

Telefax n fax

Telefonbuch n telefohn-booKH
phone book

Telefonieren ohne Münzen
cardphone

Telefonkarte f telefohnkart-uh
phonecard

Telefonnummer f telefohn-
noommer phone number

Telefonzelle f telefohn-tsell-uh
phone box

Teller m plate

Teppich m teppish carpet

Teppichboden fitted carpet

Termin m tairmeen appointment

Terrasse f tairass-uh patio

Tesafilm m tayzah-film Sellotape,
Scotch tape

teuer toyer dear; expensive

Theaterstück n tay-ahtershtoock
play

tief teef deep; low

Tiefe f teef-uh depth

Tiefgeschoss lower floor,
basement

Tiefkühlkost frozen food

Tier n teer animal

Tierarzt m teer-artst vet

Tiergarten m teergarten zoo

Tierpark m teerpark zoo

Tinte f tint-uh ink

Tisch m tish table

Tischdecke f tishdeck-uh
tablecloth

Tischtennis n tish-tennis
table tennis

Tochter f toKHter daughter

Tod m toht death

Todesgefahr! danger of death!

Toilettenpapier n twaletten-
papeer toilet paper

toll! tremendous!, brilliant!

Tollwutgefahr danger of rabies

Ton m tohn sound; clay

Topfpflanzen fpl topf-pflantsen
pot plants

Tor n goal; gate

tot toht dead

Tote m/f toht-uh dead man/
woman

töten turten to kill

Trage f trahg-uh stretcher

tragen trahgen to carry

Tragödie f tragurdee-uh tragedy

Trainingsanzug m traynings-
antsook tracksuit

trampen trempen to hitchhike

Trampen n trempen hitchhiking

trank, trankst, tranken drank

Trauer f trower sorrow

Traum m trowm dream

träumen troymen to dream

traurig trowrish sad

Trauring m trowring
wedding ring

treffen to meet

Treffen n meeting

Treffpunkt m treffpoonkt meeting
place

Treibstoff *m* tripe-shtoff fuel

Treppe *f* trepp-uh stairs

Treppenhaus *n* treppen-howss stairs; staircase; stairwell

treu troy faithful

Trikot *n* treekoh jersey

Trimm-dich-Pfad jogging track; keep-fit track

trinken to drink

Trinkgeld *n* trink-gelt tip

trocken dry

trocknen to dry

Tropfen *m* drop

trotz trots in spite of

trotzdem trots-daym in spite of that; all the same; nonetheless

tschüs chooss cheerio

Tuch *n* tookH cloth

tun toon to do; to put

Tür *f* toor door

Türkei *f* toor-ky Turkey

Turm *m* toorm tower

Turnschuhe *mpl* toornshoo-uh trainers

TÜV *m* tooff **(Technischer Überwachungs-Verein)** MOT

Typ *m* toop guy, bloke

U

U-Bahn *f* oo-bahn underground, (US) subway

U-Bahnhof *m* oo-bahnhohf underground/subway station

über oober over; above

überall oober-al everywhere

überfahren ooberfahren to run over

Überfall *m* oober-fal attack

übergeben oober-gayben to hand over

    sich übergeben to be sick

Übergewicht *n* ◌◌bergevisht
overweight; excess baggage

überholen ◌◌berhohlen
to overtake

Überholen verboten
no overtaking

Überholverbot no overtaking

Überlebende *m/f* ◌◌berlaybend-uh
survivor

übermorgen ◌◌bermorgen
the day after tomorrow

Übernachtung *f* ◌◌bernaKHtoong
night

Übernachtung mit Frühstück
f mit fr◌◌shtoock bed and
breakfast

überqueren ◌◌ber-kvairen
to cross

überraschend ◌◌ber-rashent
surprising

Überraschung *f* ◌◌ber-rashoong
surprise

überreden ◌◌ber-rayden
to persuade

Überschwemmung *f*
◌◌bershvemmoong flood

übersetzen ◌◌berzetsen
to translate

Übersetzer *m* ◌◌berzetser,
Übersetzerin *f* translator

übertreiben ◌◌bertryben
to exaggerate

Überweisung *f* ◌◌ber-vyzoong
transfer

überzeugen ◌◌ber-tsoygen
to convince

üblich ◌◌plish usual

Ufer *n* ◌◌fer shore

Uhr *f* ◌◌r clock; o'clock

Uhrmacher *m* ◌◌rmakHer
watchmaker

UKW (Ultrakurzwelle)
◌◌-kah-vay FM

um oom around; at

 um… Uhr at… o' clock

 um zu in order to

umbringen oombring-en to kill

Umgebung *f* oomgayboong
surroundings; environment

Umgehungsstraße *f* detour;
by-pass

Umkleidekabine *f* oomklide-uh-
kabeen-uh changing room

Umleitung *f* oom-lytoong diversion

Umschlag *m* oomshlahk envelope

Umstandskleid *n* oomshtants-
klite maternity dress

umsteigen oom-shtygen
to change (trains etc)

umstoßen oom-shtohssen
to knock over

umtauschen oom-towshen
to exchange

**Umtausch gegen bar ist nicht
möglich** goods cannot be
exchanged for cash

**Umtausch nur gegen
Quittung** goods may not be
exchanged without a receipt

umziehen: sich umziehen zish **oo**mtsee-en to change (clothes)

unabhängig **oo**nap-heng-ish independent

unangenehm **oo**n-angenaym unpleasant

unbedeutend **oo**n-bedoytent unimportant

unbefugt unauthorized

unbekannt **oo**n-bekannt unknown

und oont and

Unebenheiten uneven surface

Unentschieden *n* **oo**n-entsheeden draw

Unfall *m* **oo**nfal accident

Unfallgefahr accident black spot

Unfallrettung *f* **oo**nfal-rettoong ambulance, emergency service

Unfallstation *f* **oo**nfal-shtats-yohn casualty department

ungefähr **oo**n-gefair approximately

ungeschickt **oo**n-geshickt clumsy

unglaublich oon-gl**ow**plish incredible

Unglück *n* **oo**n-gl∞ck disaster; accident; unhappiness

unglücklich **oo**n-gl∞cklish unhappy; unfortunate

ungültig **oo**n-g∞ltish invalid

unhöflich **oo**n-hurflish impolite, rude

Unkosten *pl* **oo**n-kosten overheads

unmöbliert **oo**n-mur-bleert unfurnished

unmöglich **oo**n-m**ur**klish impossible

uns **oo**nss us

unschuldig **oo**n-shooldish innocent

unser **oo**nzer**, unsere** **oo**nzer-uh our

unsicher **oo**n-zisher unsafe; unsure

Unsinn *m* **oo**nzinn nonsense

unten **oo**nten down; at the bottom; downstairs

unter **oo**nter below, under; underneath; among

Unterbodenwäsche *f* oonterb**oh**den-vesh-uh underbody cleaning

unterbrechen **oo**nterbreshen to interrupt

Unterführung *f* oonterf**oo**roong underpass

Untergeschoss *n* **oo**nter-geshoss basement

Unterhaltung *f* oonterh**a**ltoong entertainment; conversation

Unterhemd *n* **oo**nter-hemt vest, (US) undershirt

Unterkunft *f* **oo**nterkoonft accommodation

Unternehmen *n* oontern**a**ymen company; undertaking

Unterricht *m* **oo**nter-risht lessons

untersagt prohibited

Unterschied *m* **oo**ntersheet difference

unterschreiben oontershr**y**ben to sign

Unterschrift *f* **oo**ntershrift signature

untersuchen oonter-z**oo**KHen to examine

Untersuchung f oonter-zooKHoong
examination; check-up

Untertasse f oonter-tass-uh
saucer

Untertitel m oonterteetel subtitle

Unterwäsche f oonter-vesh-uh
underwear

untreu oontroy unfaithful

unverbleit oonfairblite
unleaded

unverkäufliches Muster not
for sale, sample only

unverschämt oonfairshaymt
outrageous

Unverschämtheit f oon-
fairshaymt-hite cheek, nerve

unwichtig oonvishtish
unimportant

uralt oor-alt ancient

Urlaub m oorlowp holiday,
vacation

Urlauber m oor-lowber,
Urlauberin f holidaymaker

Urteil n oortile sentence;
judgement

usw. (und so weiter) etc

V

vakuumverpackt vacuum-
packed

Vater m fahter father

Vati m vahtee dad

Ventil n venteel valve

Ventilator m ventilahtor fan

Verabredung f fair-ap-raydoong
appointment

verantwortlich fair-antvortlish
responsible

verärgert fair-airgert angry

Verband m fairbant bandage;
association

verbergen fairbairgen to hide

verbessern fairbessern to
improve

Verbindung f fairbindoong
connection

verbleit fairblite leaded

verboten fairbohten forbidden,
prohibited

Verbrauch m fairbrowKH
use; consumption

   **zum baldigen Verbrauch
   bestimmt** will not keep

Verbraucher m fairbrowKHer,
Verbraucherin f consumer

Verbrecher m fairbresher,
Verbrecherin f criminal

verbrennen: sich verbrennen
zish fairbrennen to burn oneself

Verbrennung f fairbrennoong
burn

verdammt (noch mal)!
fairdammt (noKH mahl)
bloody hell!

verdienen fairdeenen to earn; to
deserve

Verein m fair-ine club

Vereinigte Staaten pl fair-ine-
isht-uh shtahten United States

Vereinigtes Königreich n fair-
ine-ishtess kurnish-rysh
United Kingdom

Verengte Fahrbahn
road narrows

Verengte Fahrstreifen
road narrows

Verfallsdatum *n* fairfals-dahtoom
best before date

Vergaser *m* fairgahzer carburettor

vergessen fairgessen to forget

Vergewaltigung *f* fairgevaltigoong rape

vergleichen fair-glyshen to compare

Vergnügen *n* fairg-noogen
pleasure

vergriffen unavailable,
out of stock

Vergrößerung *f* fair-grursseroong
enlargement

verhaften fairhaften to arrest

verheiratet fair-hyrahtet married

verhindern fairhindern to prevent

Verhütungsmittel *n* fairhootoongs-mittel contraceptive

Verkauf *m* fairkowf sale

verkaufen fairkowfen to sell
zu verkaufen tsoo for sale

Verkauf nur gegen bar
cash sales only

verkaufsoffener Samstag
open on Saturday; Saturday
opening

Verkehr *m* fairkair traffic

verkehren fairkairen to run

verkehrt alle… Minuten runs
every… minutes

Verkehrspolizei *f* fairkairs-politsī
traffic police

Verkehrspolizist *m* fairkairs-politsist traffic policeman

Verkehrsunfall *m* fairkairs-oonfal
traffic accident

Verkehrszeichen *n* fairkairs-tsyshen roadsign

verlangen fairlangen to ask for

Verlängerungsschnur *f*
fairlengeroongs-shnoor extension
lead

verlassen fairlassen to leave

verleihen: zu verleihen tsoo
fair-lī-en for hire, to rent

verletzt fairletst injured

verliebt fairleept in love

verlieren fairleeren to lose

verlobt fairlohpt engaged

Verlobte *m/f* fairlohpt-uh
fiancé; fiancée

Verlobung *f* fairlohboong
engagement

Verlust *m* fairloost loss

vermeiden fairmyden to avoid

vermieten: zu vermieten tsoo
fairmeeten for hire/to rent; to let

Vermieter *m* fairmeeter landlord

Vermieterin *f* fairmeeterin
landlady

vermissen fairmissen to miss

Vermittlung *f* fairmittloong
operator

vernünftig fairnoonftish sensible

verpassen fairpassen to miss

verriegeln fair-reegeln to bolt

verrückt fair-roockt mad

verschieden fairsheeden
different

verschlafen fairshlahfen to
oversleep

verschlucken fairshl**oo**cken to swallow

Verschluss *m* fairshl**oo**ss shutter

verschmutzt fairshm**oo**tst polluted

verschwinden fairshv**i**nden to disappear

verschwinden Sie! go away!

Versicherung *f* fairz**i**sheroong insurance

Versicherungspolice *f* fairz**i**sheroongs-pol**ee**ss-uh insurance policy

verspätet fairshp**ay**tet late, delayed

Verspätung *f* fairshp**ay**toong delay

versprechen fairshpr**e**shen to promise

verstauchen fairsht**ow**KHen to sprain

verstehen fairsht**ay**-en to understand

ich verstehe nicht fairsht**ay**-uh nisht I don't understand

verstopft fairsht**o**pft blocked; constipated

Versuch *m* fairz**oo**KH attempt

versuchen fairz**oo**KHen to try

Verteiler *m* fairt**y**ler distributor

Vertrag *m* fairtr**ah**k contract; treaty

Vertreter *m* fairtr**ay**ter, **Vertreterin** *f* representative; agent; sales rep

verwählen: sich verwählen zish fairv**ay**len to dial the wrong number

verwitwet fairv**i**tvet widowed

Verzeihung! fair-ts**ī**-oong I'm sorry; excuse me

Verzogen nach... moved to...

Verzögerung *f* fairts**u**rgeroong delay

verzollen fairts**o**llen to declare

Vetter *m* f**e**tter cousin

viel feel much, a lot (of)

viele f**ee**l-uh many

vielen Dank f**ee**len thanks a lot

viel Glück! feel gl**oo**ck good luck!

viel Glück zum Geburtstag! tsoom geb**oo**rtstahk happy birthday!

vielleicht feel**y**sht maybe

vier feer four

Viertel *n* f**ee**rtel quarter; district

Vierwaldstätter See *m* veervalt-shtetter zay Lake Lucerne

vierzehn feer-ts**ay**n fourteen

vierzig f**ee**rtsish forty

Visitenkarte *f* veez**ee**ten-kart-uh card; business card

Visum *n* v**ee**zoom visa

Vogel *m* f**oh**gel bird

Volk: das Volk follk the people

voll fol full; crowded

voll belegt full, no vacancies

vollklimatisiert fully air-conditioned

Vollnarkose *f* fol-narkohz-uh general anaesthetic

Vollpension *f* fol-pangz-yohn full board

volltanken f**o**ltanken to fill up

vom Umtausch ausgeschlossen cannot be exchanged

von fon of; by

von... bis... from… to…

von... nach... from… to…

vor for before; in front of

vor... Tagen… days ago

vor dem Frühstück
before breakfast

vor Kindern schützen keep
out of reach of children

vor dem Schlafengehen
before going to bed

**Vorausbuchung unbedingt
erforderlich** reserved seats
only

voraus: im voraus vorowss in
advance

vorbei forby over

vorbei an... past…

Vorderrad *n* forder-raht front
wheel

Vorderseite *f* forder-zite-uh front

Vorfahr *m* forfahr ancestor

Vorfahrt *f* forfahrt right of way

Vorfahrt beachten give way

Vorfahrt gewähren give way

Vorfahrtsstraße *f* forfahrts-
shtrahss-uh major road (vehicles
having right of way)

vorgestern forgestern the day
before yesterday

Vorhang *m* forhang curtain

vorher forhair before

Vorhersage *f* forhairzahg-uh
forecast

Vorliebe *f* forleeb-uh liking

Vormittag *m* formittahk (late)
morning

vorn forn at the front

Vorname *m* fornahm-uh Christian
name, first name

Vorprogramm *n* for-programm
supporting programme

Vorschlag *m* forshlahk
proposal, suggestion

vorschlagen forshlahgen to
propose

Vorsicht *f* forzisht caution; take
care

Vorsicht bissiger Hund
beware of the dog

vorsichtig forzishtish careful

vorsichtig fahren drive carefully

Vorsicht Stufe! mind the step!

Vorstadt *f* forshtatt suburbs

vorstellen forshtellen to
introduce

Vorstellung *f* forshtelloong
performance; idea

nächste Vorstellung um...
next performance at…

Vorteil *m* fortile advantage

Vorurteil *n* for-oortile prejudice

Vorwahl *f* forvahl dialling code

Vorwahlnummer *f* forvahl-
noommer dialling code

vorziehen fortsee-en to prefer

W

wach vaкн awake

wachsen vaksen to grow

wagen vahgen to dare

Wagen *m* car; coach; carriage

Wagenheber *m* vahgen-hayber
jack

Wagenstandanzeiger
order of carriages

Wahl *f* vahl choice; election

wählen vaylen to choose; to elect; to dial

Wahlkampf *m* vahlkampf election campaign

Wahnsinn *m* vahnzinn madness

Wahnsinn! fantastic!

wahr vahr true

während vairent during; while

Wahrheit *f* vahr-hite truth

wahrscheinlich varshinelish probable; probably

Währung *f* vairoong currency

Wald *m* valt forest

Waliser *m* valeezer Welshman

Waliserin *f* valeezerin Welshwoman

walisisch valeezish Welsh

Wand *f* vant wall

wandern vandern to hike, to walk

Wanderweg *m* vandervayk walk, route; trail

wann van when

war vahr was

waren vahren were

Waren *pl* goods

Warenaufzug *m* vahren-owftsook service lift

Warenhaus *n* vahren-howss department store

warm varm warm; hot

warst varst, **wart** vart were

warten varten to wait

Wartesaal *m* vart-uh-zahl waiting room

Wartezimmer *n* vart-uh-tsimmer waiting room

warum? varoom why?

was? vass what?

Waschbecken *n* vashbecken washbasin

Wäsche *f* vesh-uh washing; laundry

waschen vashen to wash

sich waschen to wash (oneself)

Wäscherei *f* vesherī laundry

Waschlappen *m* vashlappen flannel; coward

Waschmaschine *f* vashmasheen-uh washing mashine

Waschpulver *n* vashpoolver washing powder

Waschraum *m* vashrowm wash room

Waschsalon *m* vash-zalong launderette, laundromat

Waschstraße *f* vash-shtrahss-uh car wash

Waschzeit washing time

Wasser *n* vasser water

wasserdicht vasserdisht waterproof

Wasserfall *m* vasser-fal waterfall

Wasserhahn *m* vasser-hahn tap, faucet

Wasserkessel *m* vasser-kessel kettle

wasserlöslich soluble in water

Wasserski *n* vassershee waterskiing

Wassersport *m* vasser-shport water sports

Waterkant f **vah**terkant North German name for the North German coastal area

Watte f vatt-uh cotton wool, absorbent cotton

wechselhaft vekselhaft changeable

Wechselkurs m veksel-koors exchange rate

wechseln vekseln to change

Wechselstube f veksel-sht00b-uh bureau de change

wecken vecken to wake up

Wecker m vecker alarm clock

weder... noch vayder – noкн neither... nor...

Weg m vayk path

wegen vaygen because of

Wegen Krankheit vorübergehend geschlossen temporarily closed due to illness

Wegen Umbauarbeiten geschlossen closed for alterations

weggehen vek-gay-en to go away

wegnehmen vek-naymen to take away

Wegweiser m vayk-vyzer signpost

wegwerfen vek-vairfen to throw away

weh tun: es tut weh ess t00t vay it hurts

weiblich vipe-lish female

weich vysh soft

Weihnachten n vynaкнten Christmas

weil vile because

Weile f vile-uh while

weinen vynen to cry

Weinhandlung f vine-hantloong wine shop

Weinprobe f vine-prohb-uh wine-tasting

Weinstraße f vine-shtrahss-uh route through wine-growing areas

Weinstube f vine-sht00b-uh wine bar (traditional style)

weiß vice know; knows; white

weißt vysst know

weit vite far; wide

weit entfernt far away

weiter vyter further

welche? velsh-uh which?

Welle f vell-uh wave

Welt f velt world

wenden venden to turn

sich wenden an to contact

wenig vaynish little; few

weniger vayniger less

wenn venn if

wenn vom Arzt nicht anders verordnet unless otherwise prescribed by your doctor

wer? vair who?

Werbung f vairboong advertising; publicity

werde vaird-uh will; become

werden vairden to become; will

werdet vairdet will; become

werfen vairfen to throw

Werkstatt f vairkshtatt auto repairs

Werktag m vairktahk weekday

Werkzeug *n* vairk-tsoyk tool

wert vairt worth

Wert *m* vairt value

Wertmünzen tokens

Wertsachen *pl* vairtzaкнen
valuables

Wespe *f* vesp-uh wasp

Wessi *m* vessee West German

Weste *f* vest-uh waistcoat,
(US) vest

Westen *m* vesten west

westliche Stadtteile city west

westlich von vestlish fon west of

Wette *f* vett-uh bet

wetten vetten to bet

Wetter *n* vetter weather

Wetterbericht *m* vetter-berisht
weather forecast

Wettervorhersage *f* vetter-
forhair-zahg-uh weather forecast

wichtig vishtish important

wider veeder against

widerlich veederlish
disgusting

**Widerrechtlich abgestellte
Fahrzeuge werden
kostenpflichtig
abgeschleppt**
illegally parked vehicles will be
removed at the owner's expense

widersprechen veeder-shpreshen
to contradict

widerwärtig veeder-vairtish
obnoxious

wie? vee how?

wie vee like

wie bitte? pardon (me)?,
what did you say?

wie geht es Ihnen? gayt ess
eenen how are you?

wie geht's? how are things?

wieder veeder again

wiederholen veeder-hohlen
to repeat

**Wiederhören: auf
Wiederhören** owf veeder-hur-
ren goodbye (said on the phone)

wiegen veegen to weigh

Wien veen Vienna

wieviel? veefeel how much?

wie viele? vee feel-uh
how many?

Wildleder n viltlayder suede

will vill want to; wants to

willkommen! villkommen
welcome!

willst villst want to

Wimperntusche f vimpern-toosh-
uh mascara

Windel f vindel nappy, diaper

windig vindish windy

Windschutzscheibe f vintshoots-
shibe-uh windscreen

Winterfahrplan m vinterfahrplahn
winter timetable/schedule

Winterschlussverkauf m
winter sales

wir veer we

wir müssen draußen bleiben
sorry, no dogs

wir sind umgezogen we have
moved

wird veert will; becomes

wirklich veerklish really

wirst veerst will; become

Wirt m veert landlord; host

Wirtin f veertin landlady; hostess

Wirtschaft f veert-shafft pub;
economy

Wirtshaus n veerts-howss inn;
pub

wissen vissen to know

wisst vist know

Witwe f vitv-uh widow

Witwer m vitver widower

Witz m vits joke

WLAN-Zugang m vay-lahn-
tsoogang wifi

wo? vo where?

woanders vo-anderss elsewhere

Woche f voKH-uh week

Wochenende n voKHen-end-uh
weekend

Wochenkarte f voKHenkart-uh
weekly ticket

Woge f vohg-uh wave

woher? vo-hair where from?

wohin? vo-hin where to?

Wohnblock m vohnblock block of
flats, apartment block

wohnen vohnen to live; to stay

Wohnmobil n vohn-mobeel
caravan, (US) trailer

Wohnort m vohn-ort place of
residence

Wohnung f vohnoong flat,
apartment

Wohnwagen m vohnvahgen
caravan, (US) trailer

Wohnzimmer n vohn-tsimmer
living room

Wolke f volk-uh cloud

Wolle f voll-uh wool

wollen vollen to want

wollen Sie…? do you
want…?

womit vo-mit with which; with what

worauf vo-rowf (up) on which

worden vorden been

worin vo-rin in which

Wort *n* vort word

Wörterbuch *n* vurterbooKH dictionary

wovon vo-fon from which; from what

wozu? vo-tsoo what for?

Wunde *f* voond-uh wound

wunderbar voonderbar wonderful

Wunsch *m* voonsh wish

wünschen voonshen to wish

wurde voord-uh was; became

würde voord-uh would

wurden voorden, **wurdest, wurdet** were; became

würzen voortsen to season

würzig voortsish spicy

wusste voosst-uh, **wussten, wusstest** knew

Wut *f* voot fury

wütend vootent furious

Z

zäh tsay tough

Zahl *f* tsahl number

zahlbar tsahlbar payable

zahlen tsahlen to pay

Zahlung *f* tsahloong payment

Zahn *m* tsahn tooth

Zahnarzt *m* tsahn-artst,

Zahnärztin *f* tsahn-airtstin dentist

Zahnbelag *m* tsahn-belahk plaque

Zahnersatz *m* tsahn-airzats dentures

Zahnklinik *f* tsahn-kleenik dental clinic

Zahnpasta *f* tsahn-pastah toothpaste

Zahnschmerzen *pl* tsahn-shmairtsen toothache

Zange *f* tsang-uh pliers

Zapfsäule *f* tsapf-zoyl-uh petrol/gas pump

Zaun *m* tsown fence

z.B. (zum Beispiel) eg

ZDF (Zweites Deutsches Fernsehen) tset-day-eff Second German Television Channel

Zebrastreifen *m* tsaybrah-shtryfen zebra crossing

Zehe *f* tsay-uh toe

zehn tsayn ten

Zehneuroschein *m* tsayn-oyro-shine ten-euro note/bill

Zeichen *n* tsyshen sign

zeichnen tsyshnen to draw

zeigen tsygen to show; to point

Zeit *f* tsite time

Zeitansage *f* tsite-anzahg-uh speaking clock

Zeitschrift *f* tsite-shrift magazine

Zeitung *f* tsytoong newspaper

Zelt *n* tselt tent

Zelten verboten no camping

Zeltplatz *m* tseltplats campsite

Zentimeter *m* tsentimayter centimetre

Zentner *m* tsentner 50 kilos

Zentralheizung *f* tsentrahl-hytsoong central heating

Zentrum *n* tsentroom centre

zerbrechen tsairbreshen to break

zerstören tsairshtur-ren to destroy

Zettel *m* tsettel piece of paper

Zeuge *m* tsoyg-uh, **Zeugin** *f* witness

Ziege *f* tseeg-uh goat

ziehen tsee-en to pull

Ziel *n* tseel aim; destination

ziemlich tseemlish rather

Zigarre *f* tsigarr-uh cigar

Zimmer *n* tsimmer room

Zimmer frei room(s) to let/rent, vacancies

Zimmermädchen *n* tsimmer-maytshen chambermaid

Zimmernachweis *m* tsimmer-naĸĸvice accommodation service

Zimmerservice *m* tsimmer-service room service

Zimmer zu vermieten rooms to let/rent

Zinsen *pl* tsinzen interest

Zinssatz *m* tsinss-zats interest rate

Zoll *m* tsol Customs

Zollbeamte *m* tsoll-buh-amt-uh, **Zollbeamtin** *f* customs officer

zollfrei tsolfry duty-free

zollfreie Waren *pl* tsolfry-uh vahren duty-free goods

Zone 30 zone with 30 km/h speed limit

zu tsoo to; too; shut

zubereiten tsoo-beryten to prepare

Zuckergehalt sugar content

zufrieden tsoofreeden pleased

Zug *m* tsook train; draught

zu den Zügen to the trains

Zugabe *f* tsoogahb-uh encore

zugelassen für... Personen carries... persons

zuhören ts00-hur-ren to listen

Zukunft f ts00koonft future

zum tsoom to the

zum Ochsen The Ox (name of bar etc)

zunächst ts00naykst first, firstly

Zunahme f ts00nahm-uh increase

Zuname m ts00nahm-uh surname

Zündkerze f ts00nt-kairts-uh spark plug

Zündung f ts00ndoong ignition

zunehmen ts00naymen to increase; to put on weight

Zunge f ts00ng-uh tongue

zur ts00r to the

zurück ts00r00ck back

zurückgeben ts00r00ck-gayben to give back

zurückkehren ts00r00ck-kairen to go back, to return

zurückkommen ts00r00ck-kommen to come back

zusammen ts00zammen together

Zusammenstoß m ts00zammen-shtohss crash

Zuschauer m ts00shower, **Zuschauerin** f spectator

Zuschlag m ts00shlahk supplement

zuschlagpflichtig ts00shlahk-pflishtish supplement payable

zustimmen ts00shtimmen to agree

Zutaten pl ts00tahten ingredients

Zutreffendes ankreuzen cross where applicable

Zutritt für Unbefugte verboten no admission to unauthorized persons

zuviel ts00feel too much

Zuwiderhandlung wird strafrechtlich verfolgt we will prosecute

zwanzig tsvantsish twenty

Zwanzigeuroschein m tsvantsish-**oyro**-shine twenty-euro note/bill

Zweck m tsveck purpose

zwei tsvy two

Zweibettzimmer n tsvybett-tsimmer twin room

Zweig m tsvike branch

Zweigstelle f tsvike-shtell-uh branch

Zweimal täglich einzunehmen to be taken twice a day

zweite(r,s) tsvite-uh, -er, -ess second

zweite Klasse f tsvite-uh klass-uh second class

zweiter Stock m tsvyter shtock second floor, (US) third floor

zweite Wahl seconds

Zwillinge pl tsvilling-uh twins

zwischen tsvishen between

Zwischenlandung f tsvishen-landoong stopover

Zwischenmahlzeit f tsvishen-mahltsite snack between meals

zwölf tsvurlf twelve

z.Zt. (zur Zeit) at the moment

Food

Essential terms

bread das Brot broht
butter die Butter bootter
cup die Tasse tass-uh
dessert der Nachtisch naκHtish
fish der Fisch fish
fork die Gabel gahbel
glass: a glass of... ein Glas...
  ine glahss
knife das Messer
main course das Hauptgericht
  howpt-gerisht
meat das Fleisch flysh
menu die Speisekarte shpize-uh-
  kart-uh
pepper der Pfeffer

plate der Teller
salad der Salat zalaht
salt das Salz zalts
set menu die Tageskarte
  tahgess-kart-uh
soup die Suppe zoop-uh
spoon der Löffel lurfel
starter die Vorspeise for-shpize-uh
table der Tisch tish

another..., please noch ein...,
  bitte noκH ine bitt-uh
excuse me! Entschuldigung!
  ent-shooldigoong
could I have the bill, please?
  kann ich bitte bezahlen? kan ish
  bitt-uh betsahlen

A–Z

Aal ahl eel

Aalsuppe ahlzoop-uh eel soup

Ananas ananass pineapple

angemacht mit prepared with

Äpfel epfel apples

Äpfel im Schlafrock shlahfrock baked apples in puff pastry

Apfelkompott stewed apples

Apfelkuchen -kooKHen apple pie

Apfelmeerrettich -mayr-rettish horseradish with apple

Apfelmus -mooss apple purée

Apfelrotkohl red cabbage cooked with apples

Apfelsinen apfelzeenen oranges

Apfelstrudel apple strudel

Apfeltasche -tash-uh apple turnover

Aprikosen aprikohzen apricots

Arme Ritter arm-uh bread soaked in milk and egg then fried

aromatisiert aromatic

Artischocken artichokes

Artischockenherz -hairts artichoke heart

Aspik aspeek aspic

Auberginen ohbairJeenen aubergines, eggplants

Auflauf owf-lowf (baked) pudding or omelette

Aufschnitt owf-shnitt sliced cold meats, cold cuts

Austern owstern oysters

Bachforelle baKH-forell-uh river trout

backen to bake

Backobst backohpst dried fruit

Backofen oven

Backpflaumen -pflowmen prunes

Baiser bezzay meringue

Balkansalat balkahn-zalaht cabbage and pepper salad

Bananen banahnen bananas

Bandnudeln bantnoodeln ribbon noodles

Basilikum basil

Bauernauflauf bowern-owflowf bacon and potato omelette

Bauernfrühstück -frooshtook bacon and potato omelette

Bauernomelett -omlet bacon and potato omelette

Baumkuchen bowmkooKHen cylindrical, layered cake

Béchamelkartoffeln sliced potatoes in creamy sauce

Béchamelsoße -zohss-uh creamy sauce with onions and ham

Beilagen bylahgen side dishes; side salads, vegetables

belegtes Brot belayktess broht sandwich

Berliner (Ballen) bairleener (bal-en) jam doughnut with icing

bestreut mit sprinkled with

Bienenstich beenen-shtish honey and almond tart

Bierschinken beer-shinken ham sausage

Biersuppe beerzoop-uh beer soup

Birnen beernen pears
Biskuit biskweet sponge
Biskuitrolle biskweet-rol-uh
Swiss roll
Bismarckheringe -hairing-uh
filleted pickled herrings
Blätterteig blettertike puff pastry
Blattsalat -zalaht green salad
Blattspinat -shpinaht leaf spinach
blau blow boiled, au bleu
Blaufelchen blow-faylshen blue
Lake Constance trout
Blaukraut blowkrowt red cabbage
Blumenkohl bloomenkohl
cauliflower
Blumenkohlsuppe -zoop-uh
cauliflower soup
blutig blootish rare
Blutwurst bloot-voorst black
pudding, blood sausage

Bockwurst large frankfurter
Bohnen beans
Bohneneintopf -ine-topf
bean stew
Bohnensalat -zalaht bean salad
Bohnensuppe -zoop-uh
bean soup
Bonbon bongbong sweet
Bouillon boolyong clear soup
Bouletten meat balls
Braten brahten roast meat
braten to fry
Bratensoße -zohss-uh gravy
Brathähnchen braht-haynshen
roast chicken
Brateringe -hairing-uh (pickled)
fried herrings (served cold)
Bratkartoffeln fried potatoes
Bratwurst -voorst grilled pork
sausage
Brezel braytsel pretzel
Brombeeren brombairen
blackberries
Brot broht bread
Brötchen brurtshen roll
Brotsuppe brohtzoop-uh
bread soup
Brühwurst broovoorst
large frankfurter
Brunnenkresse broonnen-kress-
uh watercress
Bückling bookling smoked red
herring
bunte Platte boont-uh plat-uh
mixed platter
Burgundersoße boorgoonder-
zohss-uh Burgundy wine sauce

Butterbrezel bootter-braytsel
butter pretzel

Buttercremetorte bootterkraym-tort-uh cream cake

Champignoncremesuppe -kraym-zoop-uh cream of mushroom soup

Champignons shampinyongs mushrooms

Champignonsoße -zohss-uh mushroom sauce

Chicorée shikoray chicory

Chinakohl sheena-kohl Chinese leaf

Chips crisps, potato chips

Cordon bleu veal cordon bleu

Curryreis -rice curried rice

Currywurst -voorst curried pork sausage

Dampfnudeln -noodeln sweet yeast dumpling

dazu reichen wir... served with...

deutsches Beefsteak doytshess mince patty

dicke Bohnen dick-uh broad beans

Dillsoße -zohss-uh dill sauce

durchgebraten doorsh-gebrahten well-done

durchwachsen doorsh-vacksen with fat

durchwachsener Speck shpeck streaky bacon

Edelpilzkäse aydelpilts-kayz-uh blue cheese

Ei i egg

Eier Ī-er eggs

Eierauflauf -owf-lowf omelette

Eierkuchen -kookнen pancake

Eierpfannkuchen pancake

Eierspeise -shpize-uh egg dish

eingelegt ine-gelaykt pickled

eingelegte Brathering pickled herrings

eingemacht ine-gemaкнt preserved

ein paar... some...

Eintopf ine-topf stew

Eintopfgericht -gerisht stew

Eis ice ice; ice cream

Eis am Stiel shteel ice lolly

Eisbecher -besher sundae

Eisbein -bine knuckles of pork

Eisbergsalat -bairk-zalaнt iceberg lettuce

Eisschokolade -shokolaнd-uh iced chocolate

Eissplittertorte -shplitter-tort-uh ice chip cake

Endiviensalat endeev-yen-zalaнt endive salad

englisch eng-lish rare

Ente ent-uh duck

Entenbraten entenbrahten roast duck

entgrätet boned

Entrecote sirloin steak

Erbsen airpsen peas

Erbsensuppe -zoop-uh pea soup

Erdäpfel airt-epfel potatoes

Erdbeeren airtbairen strawberries

Erdbeertorte -tort-uh
strawberry gâteau

Erdnüsse airtnooss-uh peanuts

Essig vinegar

falscher Hase fal-sher hahz-uh
meat loaf

Fasan fazahn pheasant

Faschierte Laibchen
fasheert-uh lipe-shen rissoles

Faschiertes fasheertess minced
meat

Feldsalat feltzalaht lamb's lettuce

Fenchel fennel

Filet fillay fillet (steak)

Fisch fish fish

Fischfilet fish fillet

Fischfrikadellen fishcakes

Fischgerichte fish dishes

Fischstäbchen -shtaypshen
fish fingers

Flädlesuppe flaydl-uh-zoop-uh
soup with strips of pasta

flambiert flambé

Fleisch flysh meat

> **Travel tip** The first choice for
> honest traditional food should
> be a *Gaststätte* or *Brauhaus*.
> Traditional and convivial,
> these are roughly equivalent
> to the British pub, and the
> cuisine is almost always
> unpretentious home-cooking
> that's filling, tasty and good
> value. Don't be surprised
> if you're asked to share a
> table. Most small places only
> accept cash.

Fleischbrühe -broo-uh bouillon

Fleischkäse -kayz-uh meat loaf

Fleischklößchen -klurss-shen
meat ball(s)

Fleischpastete -pastayt-uh
meat vol-au-vent

Fleischsalat -zalaht diced meat
salad with mayonnaise

Fleischtomate -tomaht-uh
beef tomato

Fleisch- und Wurstwaren
meats and sausages

Fleischwurst -voorst pork sausage

Flugente flook-ent-uh wild duck

Folienkartoffel fohl-yen-
baked potato

Fond font meat juices

Forelle forell-uh trout

Forelle blau blow trout au bleu

Forelle Müllerin (Art) moollerin
trout coated with breadcrumbs
and served with butter and
lemon

Frikadelle frickadell-uh rissole

frisch gepresst freshly squeezed

Frischwurst -voorst fresh sausage

fritiert friteert (deep-)fried

Froschschenkel frosh-shenkel
frogs' legs

Frühlingsgemüse froolings-
gemooz-uh spring vegetables

Frühlingsrolle -rol-uh spring roll

Gabelrollmops gahbel- rolled
pickled herring, rollmops

Gans ganss goose

Gänsebraten genz-uh-brahten

roast goose

Gänseleber -layber goose liver

Gänseleberpastete -pastayt-uh
goose liver pâté

gar cooked

garniert garneert garnished

Gebäck gebeck pastries, cakes

gebacken fried

gebeizt gebytst marinaded

gebraten gebrahten roast

gebunden geboonden thickened

gedämpft gedempft steamed

Gedeck set meal

gedünstet gedoonstet steamed

Geflügel gefloogel poultry

Geflügelleber -layber
chicken liver

Geflügelleberragout -ragoo
chicken liver ragout

Geflügelsalat -zalaht chicken/
poultry salad

gefüllt gefoolt stuffed

gefüllte Kalbsbrust kalpsbroost
veal roll

gegart cooked

gegrillt grilled

gehackt minced; chopped

Gehacktes minced meat

gekocht gekoKHt boiled

gekochtes Ei ī boiled egg

Gelee Jellay jelly

gemischter Salat gemishter
zalaht mixed salad

gemischtes Eis ice
assorted ice creams

Gemüse gemooz-uh vegetable(s)

Gemüseplatte plat-uh
assorted vegetables

Gemüsereis -rice
rice with vegetables

Gemüsesalat -zalaht
vegetable salad

Gemüsesuppe -zoop-uh
vegetable soup

gepökelt gepurkelt salted, pickled

geräuchert geroyshert smoked

gerieben gereeben grated

Germknödel gairm-k-nurdel
yeast dumplings

geschlagen geshlahgen whipped

geschmort geshmohrt
braised, stewed

geschnetzelt geshnetselt chopped

Geschnetzeltes strips of meat
in thick sauce

Geselchtes gezelshtess salted
and smoked meat

gespickt mit... larded with...

geschwenkt geshvenkt sautéed

Gewürze gevoorts-uh spices

Gewürzgurken -goorken
gherkins

Goldbarsch goltbarsh
type of perch

Götterspeise gurttershpize-uh
jelly

gratiniert gratineert au gratin

Grießklößchen greessklurs-shen
semolina dumplings

Grießsuppe -zoop-uh
semolina soup

grüne Bohnen groon-uh
French beans

grüne Nudeln noodeln green pasta

grüner Aal ahl fresh eel

Grünkohl (curly) kale

Gugelhupf googel-hoopf
ring-shaped cake

Gulasch goulash

Gulaschsuppe -zoop-uh
goulash soup

Gurke goork-uh cucumber;
gherkin

Gurkensalat -zalaht
cucumber salad

Hackepeter hack-uh-payter
minced meat

Hackfleisch -flysh minced meat

Hähnchen haynshen chicken

Hähnchenkeule -koyl-uh
chicken leg

Haifischflossensuppe
hyfishflossen-zoop-uh
shark-fin soup

halbes Hähnchen haynshen
half chicken

Hammelbraten -brahten
roast mutton

Hammelfleisch -flysh mutton

Hammelkeule -koyl-uh
leg of mutton

Hammelrücken -rOOcken
saddle of mutton

Handkäse hant-kayz-uh
very strong-smelling cheese

hartgekochtes Ei hartgekoKHtess
I hard-boiled egg

Hartkäse -kayz-uh hard cheese

Haschee hashay hash

Haselnüsse hahzelnOOss-uh
hazelnuts

Hasenbraten hahzenbrahten
roast hare

Hasenkeule -koyl-uh
haunch of hare

Hasenpfeffer jugged hare

Hauptgerichte main dishes

Hauptspeisen main courses

Hausfrauenart howssfrowenart
home-made style

hausgemacht howss-gemaKHt
homemade

Hausmacher (Art) howssmakHer
home-made style

Hausmarke howss-mark-uh
own brand

Hecht hesht pike

Hechtsuppe -zoop-uh pike soup

Heidelbeeren hydelbairen
bilberries

Heilbutt hile-boott halibut

Heringssalat hairings-zalaht
herring salad

Heringsstipp -shtip herring salad

Heringstopf pickled herrings

Herz hairts heart

Himbeeren himbairen raspberries

Himmel und Erde oont aird-uh
potato and apple purée with
liver sausage

Hirn heern brains

Hirschbraten heershbrahten
roast venison

Hirschmedaillons -medah-yongs
small venison fillets

Holsteiner Schnitzel holshtyner

shnitsel breaded veal cutlet with vegetables, topped with a fried egg

Honig hohnish honey

Honigkuchen -kooKHen honeycake

Honigmelone -melohn-uh honeydew melon

Hoppelpoppel bacon and potato omelette

Hüfte hooft-uh haunch

Huhn hoon chicken

Hühnerbrühe hooner-broo-uh chicken broth

Hühnersuppe -zoop-uh chicken soup

Hülsenfrüchte hoolzenfroosht-uh peas and beans, pulses

Hummer hoommer lobster

Imbiss imbiss snack

inbegriffen included

Inklusivpreis all-inclusive price

Jagdwurst yahkt-voorst ham sausage with garlic

Jägerschnitzel yaygershnitsel pork with mushrooms

junge Erbsen yoong-uh airpzen spring peas

Kabeljau kahbelyow cod

Kaiserschmarren kyzershmarren sugared pancakes with raisins

Kalbfleisch kalpflysh veal

Kalbsbraten -brahten roast veal

Kalbsbries -breess sweetbread

Kalbsfrikassee veal fricassee

Kalbshaxe leg of veal

Kalbsmedaillons -medah-yongs small veal fillets

Kalbsnierenbraten -neeren- brahten roast veal with kidney

Kalbsschnitzel -shnitsel veal cutlet

kalte Platte cold meal

kalter Braten brahten cold meat

kaltes Bufett cold buffet

kalte Speisen cold dishes

Kaltschale kaltshahl-uh cold sweet fruit soup

kalt servieren serve cold

Kaninchen kaneenshen rabbit

Kaninchenbraten -brahten roast rabbit

Kapern kahpern capers

Karbonade karbonahd-uh carbonade, beef and onion stew cooked in beer

Karfiol karf-yohl cauliflower

Karotten carrots

Karpfen carp

Karpfen blau blow carp au bleu

Kartoffel potato

Kartoffelbrei -bry potato purée

Kartoffelklöße -klurss-uh potato dumplings

Kartoffelknödel -k-nurdel potato dumplings

Kartoffeln potatoes

Kartoffelpuffer -pooffer potato fritters

Kartoffelpüree -pooray potato purée

Kartoffelsalat -zalaht
potato salad

Kartoffelsuppe -zoop-uh
potato soup

Käse kayz-uh cheese

Käsebrötchen -brurtshen
cheese roll

Käsegebäck -gebeck
cheese savouries

Käsekuchen -kookhen
cheesecake

Käseplatte -plat-uh selection of
cheeses, cheeseboard

Käse-Sahne-Torte -zahn-uh-
tort-uh cream cheesecake

Käsesalat -zalaht cheese salad

Käseschnitzel -shnitsel
escalopes with cheese

Käsesoße -zohss-uh
cheese sauce

Käsespätzle -shpetz-luh home-
made noodles with cheese

Kasseler Rippenspeer rippen-
shpair salted ribs of pork

Kasserolle kasserol-uh casserole

Kassler smoked and braised
pork chops

Kastanien kastahn-yen chestnuts

Katenleberwurst kahtenlayber-
voorst smoked liver sausage

Katenrauchwurst -rowkh-voorst
smoked sausage

Keule koyl-uh leg, haunch

Kieler Sprotten keeler shprotten
smoked sprats

Kinderteller children's portion

Kirschen keershen cherries

klare Brühe klahr-uh broo-uh
clear soup

Klößchensuppe klurss-shen-
zoop-uh clear soup with
dumplings

Klöße klurss-uh dumplings

Knäckebrot k-neck-uh-broht
crispbread

Knacker frankfurter(s)

Knackwurst -voorst frankfurter

Knoblauch k-nohb-lowkh garlic

Knoblauchbrot -broht
garlic bread

Knochen k-nokhen bone

Knochenschinken -shinken
ham on the bone

Knödel k-nurdel dumplings

kochen kokhen to cook; to boil

Kohl cabbage

Kohlrabi -rahbee kohlrabi
(type of cabbage)

Kohlrouladen -roolahden
stuffed cabbage leaves

Kohl und Pinkel cabbage,
potatoes, sausage and smoked
meat

Kompott stewed fruit

Konfitüre konfitoor-uh jam

Königinpastete kurnigin-
pastayt-uh chicken vol-au-vent

Königsberger Klopse
kurniksbairger klops-uh
meatballs in caper sauce

Königskuchen kurniks-kookhen
type of fruit cake

Kopfsalat kopfzalaht lettuce

Kotelett kotlet chop

Krabben shrimps, prawns

Krabbencocktail

prawn cocktail

Kraftbrühe kraftbr00-uh
beef consommé, beef tea

Krapfen jam doughnut with
icing

Kräuter kroyter herbs

Kräuterbutter -bootter
herb butter

Kräuterkäse -kayz-uh cheese
flavoured with herbs

Kräutersoße -zohss-uh herb sauce

Krautsalat krowtzalaht coleslaw

Krautwickel -vickel
stuffed cabbage leaves

Krebs krayps crayfish

Kren krayn horseradish

Kresse kress-uh cress

Kroketten croquettes

Kruste crust

Küche k00sh-uh cooking; cuisine;
kitchen

Kuchen k00KHen cake; pie

> **Travel tip** A traditional late
> afternoon treat observed reli-
> giously by the older genera-
> tion, *Kaffee und Kuchen* (cof-
> fee and cakes) is best taken in
> an old-fashioned café. Most
> prepare fresh homemade
> gateaux piled with quantities
> of cream and chocolate to
> make dieters weep.

Kümmel k00mel caraway

Kümmelbraten -brahten roast
with caraway seeds

Kürbis k00rbiss pumpkin

Labskaus lapskowss meat, fish
and potato stew

Lachs lacks salmon

Lachsersatz -airzats sliced and
salted pollack

Lachsforelle -forell-uh
sea trout

Lachsschinken -shinken
smoked rolled fillet of ham

Lakritz liquorice

Lamm Lamb

Lammrücken -r00ken
saddle of lamb

Languste langoost-uh crayfish

Lauch lowKH leek

Lauchsuppe -zoop-uh leek soup

Leber layber liver

Leberkäse -kayz-uh baked pork
and beef loaf

Leberklöße -klurss-uh
liver dumplings

Leberknödel -k-nurdel
liver dumplings

Leberknödelsuppe -zoop-uh
liver dumpling soup

Leberpastete -pastayt-uh
liver pâté

Leberwurst -voorst liver sausage

Lebkuchen layp-k00KHen type of
gingerbread biscuit

legiert thickened

Leipziger Allerlei lipe-tsiger
al-er-ly mixed vegetables

Lendensteak loin steak

Linseneintopf linzen-inetopf
lentil stew

Linsensuppe -zoop-uh lentil soup

Lutscher lootsher lollipop

mager mahger lean
Majoran mahyo-rahn marjoram
Makrele makrayl-uh mackerel
Makronen makrohnen macaroons
Mandarine mandareen-uh
   tangerine
Mandeln almonds
Margarine margareen-uh
   margarine
Marille marill-uh apricot
Marinade mareenahd-uh marinade
mariniert marinaded, pickled
Markklößchen -klurss-shen
   marrow dumplings
Marmelade marmelahd-uh jam
Marmorkuchen marmor-kOOKHen
   marble cake
Maronen marohnen sweet
   chestnuts

Matjesfilet matyess-fillay fillet of
   herring
Matjes(hering) -hairing
   young herring
Maultaschen mowl-tashen
   pasta filled with meat,
   vegetables or cheese
Medaillons maydah-yongs
   small fillets
Meeresfische mairess-fish-uh
   seafish
Meeresfrüchte -frOOsht-uh seafood
Meerrettich mair-rettish
   horseradish
Meerrettichsoße -zohss-uh
   horseradish sauce
Mehl mayl flour
Mehlspeise -shpize-uh sweet
   dish, flummery
Melone melohn-uh melon
Menü set menu
Miesmuscheln meess-moosheln

mussels

Milch milsh milk

Milchreis -rice rice pudding

Mirabelle meerabell-uh small yellow plum

Mischbrot mishbroht rye and wheat bread

Mohnkuchen mohnkookнen poppyseed cake

Mohnstrudel poppy-seed strudel

Möhren mur-ren carrots

Mohrrüben mohr-rooben carrots

Mus mooss purée

Muscheln moosheln mussels

Muskat(nuss) mooskaht(nooss) nutmeg

nach Art des Hauses howzess à la maison

nach Hausfrauenart howss-frowenart home-made

nach Jahreszeit depending on season

Nachspeisen naкн-shpyzen desserts

Nachtisch naкнtish dessert

Napfkuchen napf-kookнen ring-shaped pound cake

natur natoor plain

nicht gar underdone

Nierenragout neeren-ragoo kidney ragout

Nudeln noodeln pasta

Nudelsalat -zalaнt noodle salad

Nudelsuppe -zoop-uh noodle soup

Nuss nooss nut

Nüsse nooss-uh nuts

Obst ohpst fruit

Obstsalat -zalaнt fruit salad

Ochsenschwanzsuppe oksen-shvants-zoop-uh oxtail soup

ohne Knochen filleted

Öl url oil

Oliven oleeven olives

Olivenöl olive oil

Omelett omlet omelette

Orangen oron-Jen oranges

Originalrezept original recipe

Palatschinken pallatshinken stuffed pancakes

Pampelmuse pampel-mooz-uh grapefruit

paniert paneert with breadcrumbs

Paprikarahmschnitzel papreekah-rahmshnitsel cutlet in creamy sauce with paprika

Paprikasalat -zalaнt pepper salad

Paprikaschote -shoht-uh pepper

Paradeiser paradyzer tomatoes

Parmesankäse parmezahnkayz-uh Parmesan cheese

Pastete pastayt-uh vol-au-vent; pâté

Pellkartoffeln potatoes boiled in their jackets

Petersilie payterzeel-yuh parsley

Petersilienkartoffeln potatoes with parsley

Pfannengerichte fried dishes

Pfannkuchen -kookHen pancake

Pfeffer pepper

Pfefferminz peppermint

Pfeffernüsse -nooss-uh gingerbread biscuits

Pfefferrahmsoße -rahmzohss-uh peppered creamy sauce

Pfifferlinge pfifferling-uh chanterelles

Pfirsiche pfeerzish-uh peaches

Pflaumen pflowmen plums

Pflaumenkuchen -kookHen plum tart

Pflaumenmus -mooss plum jam

Pichelsteiner Topf pishelshtyner vegetable stew with diced beef

Pilze pilts-uh mushrooms

Pilzsoße pilts-zohss-uh mushroom sauce

Pilzsuppe -zoop-uh mushroom soup

Platte plat-uh selection

Plätzchen plets-shen biscuit

pochiert posheert poached

Pökelfleisch purkelflysh salted meat

Pommes frites pom frit chips, French fries

Porree porray leek

Potthast pot-hast braised beef with sauce

Poularde poollard-uh young chicken

Preiselbeeren pryzel-bairen cranberries

Presskopf presskopf brawn

Prinzessbohnen printsess-unsliced runner beans

Pumpernickel black rye bread

Püree pooray (potato) purée

püriert pooreert puréed

Putenschenkel pootenshenkel turkey leg

Putenschnitzel -shnitsel turkey escalope

Puter pooter turkey

Quark kvark type of low-fat cream cheese, quark

Quarkspeise -shpize-uh dish made with low-fat cream cheese

Radieschen radeess-shen radishes

Rahm (sour) cream

Rahmschnitzel -shnitsel cutlet in creamy sauce

Räucheraal roysher-ahl smoked eel

Räucherhering -hairing kipper, smoked herring

Räucherlachs -lacks smoked salmon

Räucherspeck smoked bacon

Rauchfleisch rowKH-flysh smoked meat

Rehbraten ray-brahten roast venison

Rehkeule -koyl-uh haunch of venison

Rehrücken -rooken saddle of venison

Reibekuchen ribe-uh-kooKHen
potato waffles

Reis ryce rice

Reisauflauf -owf-lowf
rice pudding

Reisbrei rice-bry creamed rice

Reisfleisch -flysh meat with rice
and tomatoes

Reisrand -rant with rice

Reissalat -zalaht rice salad

Reissuppe -zoop-uh
rice soup

Remoulade remoolahd-uh
remoulade (mayonnaise and herb
dressing)

Renke renk-uh whitefish

Rettich rettish radish

Rhabarber rabarber rhubarb

rheinischer Sauerbraten
rynisher zowerbrahten
braised beef

Rinderbraten rinder-brahten
pot roast

Rinderfilet -fillay fillet steak

Rinderleber -layber ox liver

Rinderlende -lend-uh
beef tenderloin

Rinderrouladen -roolahden
stuffed beef rolls

Rinderschmorbraten -shmohr-
brahten pot roast

Rinderzunge -tsoong-uh
ox tongue

Rindfleisch rintflysh beef

Rindfleischsalat -zalaht
beef salad

Rindfleischsuppe -zoop-uh
beef broth

Rippchen ripshen spareribs

Rippe ripp-uh rib

Risi-Pisi reezee-peezee
rice and peas

roh raw

Rohkostplatte -plat-uh
selection of salads

Rollmops rolled-up pickled
herring, rollmops

rosa rare to medium

Rosenkohl Brussels sprouts

Rosinen rohzeenen raisins

Rostbraten -brahten roast

Rostbratwurst -braht-voorst
barbecued sausage

Rösti rurshtee fried potatoes and
onions

Röstkartoffeln rurst-
fried potatoes

Rotbarsch rohtbarsh
type of perch

rote Bete roht-uh bayt-uh
beetroot, red beet

rote Grütze roht-uh groots-uh
red fruit jelly

Rotkohl roht- red cabbage

Rotkraut -krowt red cabbage

Roulade roolahd-uh beef olive

Rühreier roor-i-er scrambled eggs

Russische Eier roossish-uh i-er
egg mayonnaise

Sachertorte zaKHertort-uh
rich chocolate cake

Sahne zahn-uh cream

Sahnesoße -zohss-uh cream sauce

Sahnetorte -tort-uh cream gateau

Salat zalaht salad; lettuce

Salate salads

Salatplatte -plat-uh salad

Salatsoße -zohss-uh salad dressing

Salatteller side salad; selection of salads

Salz zalts salt

Salzburger Nockerln zaltsboorger sweet soufflés

Salzheringe -hairing-uh salted herrings

Salzkartoffeln boiled potatoes

Sandkuchen zantkOOKHen type of Madeira cake

Sauerbraten zowerbrahten marinaded pot roast

Sauerkraut zowerkrowt white cabbage, finely chopped and pickled

Sauerrahm -rahm sour cream

Schafskäse shahfs-kayz-uh sheep's milk cheese

Schaschlik shashlik (shish-)kebab

Schattenmorellen morello cherries

Schellfisch haddock

Schildkrötensuppe shiltkrurten-zoop-uh real turtle soup

Schillerlocken shiller-smoked haddock rolls

Schinken shinken ham

Schinkenbrötchen -brurtshen ham roll

Schinkenröllchen -rurlshen rolled ham

Schinkenspeck -shpeck bacon

Schinkenwurst -voorst ham sausage

Schlachtplatte shlaKHtplat-uh selection of fresh sausages

Schlagobers shlahk-obers whipped cream

Schlagsahne -zahn-uh whipped cream

Schlei shly tench

Schmorbraten shmohrbrahten pot roast

Schnecken shnecken snails

Schnittlauch shnitt-lowKH chives

Schnitzel shnitsel cutlet

Schokolade shokolahd-uh chocolate

Scholle sholl-uh plaice

Schollenfilet -fillay fillet of plaice

Schulterstück shoolter-shtOOck slice of shoulder

Schwarzbrot shvartsbroht dark rye bread

Schwarzwälder Kirschtorte shvartsvelder keershtort-uh Black Forest gateau

Schwarzwurzeln -voortseln salsify

Schweinebauch shvine-uh-bowKH belly of pork

Schweinebraten -brahten roast pork

Schweinefilet -fillay fillet of pork

Schweinefleisch -flysh pork

Schweinekotelett -kotlet pork chop

Schweineleber -layber pig's liver

Schweinerippe -ripp-uh
cured pork chop

Schweinerollbraten -rolbrahten
rolled roast of pork

Schweineschmorbraten
-shmohr-brahten roast pork

Schweineschnitzel -shnitsel
pork fillet

Schweinshaxe shvine-ss-hacks-
uh knuckle of pork

Seelachs zaylacks pollack

Seezunge -tsoong-uh sole

Sellerie zelleree celery

Semmel zemmel bread roll

Semmelknödel -k-nurdel
bread dumplings

Senf zenf mustard

Senfsahnesoße -zahn-uh-zohss-
uh mustard and cream sauce

Senfsoße mustard sauce

serbisches Reisfleisch
zairbishess rice-flysh diced pork,
onions, tomatoes and rice

Sohle zohl-uh sole

Soleier zohl-i-er pickled eggs

Soße zohss-uh sauce; gravy

Spanferkel shpahn-fairkel
suckling pig

Spargel shpargel asparagus

Spargelcremesuppe -kraym-
zoop-uh cream of asparagus soup

Spätzle shpets-luh
home-made noodles

Speckkartoffeln shpeck-
potatoes with bacon

Speckknödel -k-nurdel
bacon dumplings

Speckstreifen -shrtyfen
strips of bacon

Speisekarte shpize-uh-kart-uh
menu

Spezialität des Hauses

our speciality

Spiegeleier shpeegel-ī-er
fried eggs

Spieß: am Spieß shpeess
on the spit

Spießbraten shpeess-brahten
joint roasted on a spit

Spinat shpinaht spinach

Spitzkohl shpits- white cabbage

Sprotten shprotten sprats

Stachelbeeren shtakнel-bairen
gooseberries

Stangenspargel shtangen-
shpargel asparagus spears

Stangen(weiß)brot shtangen-
(vice-)broht French bread

Steinbutt shtine-boott turbot

Steinpilze -pilts-uh
type of mushroom

Stollen shtollen fruit loaf

Strammer Max shtrammer
ham and fried egg on bread

Streuselkuchen shtroyzel-
kооkнen sponge cake with
crumble topping

Sülze zoolts-uh brawn

Suppe zoop-uh soup

Suppen soups

Suppengrün zoopengroon mixed
herbs and vegetables (in soup)

Süßigkeiten zoossish-kyten sweets

Süßspeisen zooss-shpyzen
sweet dishes

Süßwasserfische zooss-vasser-
fish-uh freshwater fish

Szegediner Gulasch
shegaydeener goulash with

pickled cabbage

Tafelspitz tahfel-shpits
soured boiled rump

Tagesgericht tahgess-gerisht
dish of the day

Tageskarte -kart-uh menu of the
day; set menu

Tagessuppe -zoop-uh soup of
the day

Tatar tatahr raw mince with
spices

Taube towb-uh pigeon

Teigmantel tike-mantel
pastry covering

Teigwaren -vahren pasta

Thunfisch toonfish tuna

Tintenfisch -fish squid

Tomate tomahtuh tomato

Tomatensalat -zalaht
tomato salad

Tomatensuppe -zoop-uh
tomato soup

Topfen quark

Törtchen turtshen tart(s)

Torte tort-uh gateau

Trauben trowben grapes

Truthahn troot- turkey

überbacken ооberbacken
au gratin

Ungarisches Gulasch
oongahrishess Hungarian
goulash

Vanilleeis vanill-uh-ice
vanilla ice cream

Vanillesoße -zohss-uh
vanilla sauce

vegetarisch vegaytahrish
vegetarian

> **Travel tip** Germany was
> once almost a no-go zone
> for vegetarians, but no more.
> Many large towns now have a
> vegetarian restaurant, salads
> are always meat-free unless
> stated, vegetarian pasta
> dishes abound and even
> traditional Schnitzel joints will
> list at least one vegetarian
> dish on the menu.

verlorene Eier fairlohren-uh ī-er
poached eggs

Vollkornbrot follkornbroht
dark rye bread

vom Grill grilled

vom Kalb veal

vom Lamm lamb

vom Rind beef

vom Rost grilled

vom Schwein pork

vorbereiten to prepare

Vorspeisen forshpyzen
hors d'œuvres, starters

Waffeln vaffeln waffles

Waldmeister valtmyster
woodruff

Waldorfsalat valdorf-zalaht salad
with celery, apples and walnuts

Wassermelone vasser-melohn-uh
water melon

Weichkäse vysh-kayz-uh
soft cheese

Weinbergschnecken vine-bairk-
shnecken snails

Weincreme vine-kraym
pudding with wine

Weinkraut -krowt sauerkraut

Weinschaumcreme -showm-
kraym creamed pudding with
wine

Weinsoße -zohss-uh wine sauce

Weintrauben -trowben grapes

Weißbrot vice-broht white bread

Weißkohl white cabbage

Weißkraut -krowt white cabbage

Weißwurst -voorst veal sausage

Wiener Schnitzel veener shnitsel
veal in breadcrumbs

Wiener Würstchen voorstshen
frankfurter(s)

Wild vilt game

Wildbret -brayt venison

Wildgerichte venison dishes

Wildschweinkeule viltshvine-
koyl-uh haunch of wild boar

Wildschweinsteak
wild boar steak

Windbeutel vintboytel cream puff

Wirsing veerzing savoy cabbage

Wurst voorst sausage

Wurstbrötchen -brurtshen
roll with sausage meat

Würstchen voorstshen
frankfurter(s)

Wurstplatte voorst-plat-uh
selection of sausages

Wurstsülze -zoolts-uh

sausage brawn

Würzfleisch -flysh spicy meat

Zander tsander pike-perch, zander

Zartbitterschokolade tsartbitter-shokolahd-uh plain chocolate

Ziegenkäse tseegen-kayz-uh goat's cheese

Zigeunerschnitzel tsigoyner-shnitsel veal or pork with peppers and relishes

Zitrone tsitrohn-uh lemon

Zucchini tsookeenee courgettes, zucchini

Zucker tsoocker sugar

Zuckererbsen -airpsen mangetout peas

Zunge tsoong-uh tongue

Zwiebel tsveebel onion

Zwiebelringe -ring-uh onion rings

Zwiebelrostbraten -rostbrahten steak with fried onions

Zwiebelsuppe -zoop-uh onion soup

Zwiebeltorte -tort-uh onion tart

Zwischengerichte entrées

Drink

Essential terms

beer das Bier

bottle die Flasche flash-uh

brandy der Weinbrand
vine-brant

coffee der Kaffee kaffay

cup: a cup of... eine Tasse...
ine-uh tass-uh

fruit juice der Fruchtsaft
frooKHtzaft

gin der Gin

a gin and tonic einen Gin
Tonic ine-en

glass: a glass of... ein Glas...
ine glahss

milk die Milch milsh

mineral water das
Mineralwasser
minerahlvasser

orange juice der Orangensaft
oronJen-zaft

red wine der Rotwein rohtvine

rosé der Roséwein rohzay-vine

soda (water) das Sodawasser
zohda-vasser

soft drink das alkoholfreie
Getränk alkohohlfry-uh getrenk,
der Soft drink

sugar der Zucker tsoocker

tea der Tee tay

tonic (water) das Tonic

vodka der Wodka vodka

water das Wasser vasser

whisky der Whisky

white wine der Weißwein
vice-vine

wine der Wein vine

wine list die Weinkarte vine-
kart-uh

another..., please noch ein...,
bitte noKH ine... bitt-uh

A–Z

alkoholfreies Bier alkohohlfry-ess beer alcohol-free beer

Alsterwasser -vasser shandy

Alt(bier) alt(beer) light brown beer, not sweet

Apfelsaft apfelzaft apple juice

Apfelschorle -shorl-uh sparkling apple juice

Apfelwein -vine cider

Äppelwoi eppelvoy cider

Auslese owsslayz-uh wine selected from ripest bunches of grapes in top wine category

Ausschankwein owss-shank-vine wine by the glass

Bananenmilch banahnen-milsh banana milkshake

Beerenauslese bairen-owsslayz-uh wine from specially selected single grapes in top wine category

> **Travel tip** *Bier* is not just the national drink but an integral part of German life. Düsseldorf brews a malty beer, served with fruit in summer as Altbierbowle; and Cologne is proud of its light, refreshing Kölsch beer. Bavaria produces all the usuals as well as a sweet Malzbier (malt beer). Munich's specials are Märzenbier and Hofbräu, and Bamberg's is the smoky Rauchbier.

Berliner Weiße bairleener vice-uh fizzy beer

Bier beer beer

Bockbier bockbeer strong beer

Bowle bohl-uh punch

Buttermilch boottermilsh buttermilk

Cidre seed-ruh cider

Doppelkorn grain schnapps

Eierlikör ier-likur advocaat

Eiswein ice-vine wine made from grapes picked after frost

entkoffeiniert entkoffay-eeneert decaffeinated

Erdbeermilch airtbair-milsh strawberry milkshake

Erzeugerabfüllung estate bottled

Federweißer fayder-vysser new wine

Feuerzangenbowle foyer-tsangen-bohl-uh red wine punch with rum which has been flamed off

Flasche flash-uh bottle

Flaschenwein flashen-vine bottled wine

fruchtig frooKHtish fruity

Fruchtsaft frooKHtzaft fruit juice

Gespritzter geshpritster wine and soda, spritzer

Getränke beverages

Glühwein gloo-vine mulled wine
Grog hot water with rum and sugar

halbsüß halp-zooss semi-sweet
halbtrocken halp- medium dry
Hefeweizen hayf-uh-vytsen fizzy beer made with yeast and wheat
Heidelbeergeist hydelbair-gyst blueberry brandy
heiße Milch hice-uh milsh hot milk
heiße Zitrone hice-uh tsitrohn-uh hot lemon
Helles helless lager
herb hairp very dry
Himbeergeist himbair-gyst raspberry brandy

Jahrgang yahrgang vintage

Kabinett light, usually dry, wine in top wine category
Kaffee kaffay coffee
Kaffee mit Milch milsh white coffee
Kakao kakow cocoa; hot chocolate
Kännchen (Kaffee) kennshen (kaffay) pot (of coffee)
Kellerei kellerī (wine) producers
Kir keer white wine with a dash of blackcurrant liqueur
Kir Royal royahl champagne with a dash of blackcurrant liqueur
koffeinfrei koffay-een-fry decaffeinated

Kognak konyak brandy
Korn type of schnapps
Kräuterlikör kroyterlikur herbal liqueur
Kräutertee -tay herbal tea
Krimsekt krimzekt Crimean champagne

Landwein lantvine country wine
Likör likur liqueur
Limo leemo lemonade
Limonade limonahd-uh lemonade
Liter leeter litre

Malzbier maltsbeer sweet stout
Maß mahss litre of beer (Bavaria)
Milchmixgetränk milshmix-getrenk milkshake
Mineralwasser minerahl-vasser sparkling mineral water
mischen mishen to mix
Mokka mocha
Most mosst fruit wine

Nektar fruit squash
neuer Wein noyer vine new wine

Obstler ohpstler fruit schnapps
offener Wein vine wine by the glass
Orangensaft oronJenzaft orange juice

Pikkolo quarter bottle of champagne

Portwein -vine port
Pulverkaffee poolver-kaffay instant coffee

Qualitätswein b.A. quality wine from a special wine-growing area
Qualitätswein m.P. top quality German wine

Radler(maß) rahtler-mahss shandy
Rosé(wein) rohzay(vine) rosé wine
Rotwein rohtvine red wine

Saft zaft juice
Schokolade shokolahd-uh chocolate
Schokomilch shoko-milsh chocolate milkshake
schwarzer Tee shvartser tay tea
Sekt zekt sparkling wine, champagne
Spezi shpaytsee Coke and lemonade
Spirituosen spirits
Sprudel(wasser) shproodel (-vasser) mineral water
Steinhäger shtine-hayger type of schnapps
Sturm shtoorm new wine

Tafelwasser tahfel-vasser still mineral water

Tafelwein tahfelvine table wine
Tee tay tea
Trinkwasser -vasser drinking water
trocken dry

vollmundig fol-moondish full-bodied
vom Fass fom draught

Wasser vasser water
Wein vine wine
Weinberg vinebairk vineyard
Weinbrand vine-brant brandy
Weingut -goot wine-growing estate
Weinkarte -kart-uh wine list
Weinkeller -keller wine cellar
Weinkellerei -kellerī wine producer's
weiß vice white
Weißbier vicebeer fizzy, light-coloured beer made with wheat
Weißherbst -hairpst type of rosé wine
Weißwein -vine white wine
Weizenbier vytsenbeer wheat beer

Zitronentee tsitrohnen-tay lemon tea
Zwetschenwasser tsvetshen-vasser plum brandy

Picture credits

Front cover © Caro /Alamy
Michelle Bhatia (pp.5, 6, 32, 66, 74, 83, 88, 97, 105, 115, 123, 130, 146, 197, 233, 236, 240)
Roger d'Olivere Mapp (pp.16, 36, 42, 44, 48, 58, 152, 162, 170, 180, 188, 215, 224, 238, 242, 250, 255, 259)
Diana Jarvis (back cover, pp. 21, 46, 206)
All maps and photos © Rough Guides, unless otherwise stated.